# MISSING FROM ME

**HEATHER SHTUKA**

Tellwell Talent
www.tellwell.ca

ISBN
978-0-2288-8030-1 (Hardcover)
978-0-2288-8029-5 (Paperback)
978-0-2288-8031-8 (eBook)

To Scott,

Perhaps the greatest success a person has can be measured by the legacy they leave behind. Loving unconditionally and being loved equally in return will be yours, my love.

To Jordyn, Julianna and Max

For all of eternity, both the moon and the sun have danced across the sky, casting light and chasing darkness away. My beautiful children, your love radiates and fills the dark spaces around me. You are my universe.

To Ryan

It was written in the stars, my destiny to love the little boy you were, to the man you would one day become. I wish I had held you tighter, my son, so that I could have filled the rest of my days with nothing but sweet memories of you.

# Table of Contents

# Coming Home

*Beaumont, Alberta*

*June 18, 2018–February 20, 2019*

# *Preface*

I want Ryan to be forever known.

More importantly, I want to do what he may have been able to accomplish in his life if he had the chance. If there had been enough time. If he could have taken the lessons life gives to us and learned from them.

To change the world in some small way.

Even if it is just for my husband Scott, myself or the girls.

But maybe a year later, he has changed other lives as well.

What if Ryan was the reason for joining? For volunteering? For putting themselves out there intentionally and with kindness? For taking moments and enjoying them with a little more sweetness? For embracing this beautifully tragic life.

I want Ryan to be remembered by each and every person who has felt a shift in the way they view the world and themselves because of his story.

Ryan will forever be their reason.

And forty years from now, people will ask themselves how they came to be who they are.

And they will say, "Let me tell you a story ... it all began with a boy named Ryan."

PART

# The Family Years
*Beaumont, AB*
*1997–February 17, 2018*

# Introduction

G rief comes in waves. Unexpected, fierce, uncontrollable and without exception. The waves batter and bruise me continuously until I think I can't fight them anymore. But like with all storms, eventually they subside, coming less often and perhaps not always as strongly. Then comes the days where the skies are clear, nary a cloud to cover the bright blueness. Grief gently laps at my toes as I feel its serene, unmistakable undercurrents reminding me that it will never really leave.

Grief is the acknowledgment of the loss of someone you love. But grief is an acceptance of the loss of self. Fractured pieces that no longer fit together perfectly.

I was at a loss when the nurse handed me my new baby. Looking down at this precious newborn, the fear of what to do next was paralyzing. The sense of responsibility to protect, love and nurture Ryan overwhelmed me. I had to get it right. So, I turned to those who had gone before me and relied heavily on the experience and wisdom of our mothers to see me through my uncertainty. I meekly handed my power of motherhood to others so I didn't feel alone. So I wouldn't screw it up. But giving up what was mine to claim did not necessarily provide relief. Respite, perhaps, but not relief. What I did not know could be learned. Where hesitancy existed, certainty could prevail if time allowed me to make mistakes and correct them. But that is another lesson.

It did not take long for Scott and me to grow more comfortable with parenting, and we felt like experts with our own children in short order. Our confidence seemed unshakable.

Until there was a loss.

Now I feel like that new mother all over again. I don't understand the grief I have been given. I'm awkward, plodding forward, fearful of how I am perceived. My gravest concern is balancing the love and pain I feel for one child with the love and joy I feel for my girls. Is there a right way? I look to others who are suffering similar burdens for cues that might offer insight, but, like my early days of motherhood, this journey is unique. To move forward, I can only honour the individual pain. My hope is to find peace in a journey that cannot be learned but only experienced. It is a reminder of a love that cannot be diminished by grief nor loss.

# Our Perfectly Imperfect Life

Ordinary.

That is how I would describe my life. Ordinary. Routine. I suppose that could sound boring and dull, but I often think about the simple pleasures that I used to enjoy: ice cream on a muggy day, the fresh smell of rain that brushes away the dusty coating of all things stationary, or the great passion that comes wrapped in the arms of someone who loves you. Simple, perhaps, but filled with such emotions that you could never confuse ordinary with a lack of. Ordinary. Not filled with dastardly deeds or epic heroism, but the sort of life that one craves. Normality and the very realness it represents. Life as flawed and imperfect as the people who inhabit it.

I was a daughter, a sister, a wife and then a mother. In between all these titles, I went to school, played sports, made friends, skinned knees, had a first kiss, experienced butterflies, broken hearts, adventures, a career, a wedding and three uneventful but deeply moving births. I stayed at home, volunteered, went to work, helped with homework and cheered from the sidelines with a frenzy that can only come from being a proud parent. There were mortgages, car payments, sick days, holidays, unending laundry and picking up toys. There were days I felt strong and pretty. There were days I felt grouchy and uncomfortable in my own skin. It was an ordinary that

I took for granted. It was an imperfectly perfect life that was of my own making, until it was not.

We never mark the moments when everything is the same until the terrifying realization that it all has changed irrevocably. How could we? And yet we will spend an extraordinary amount of time in the aftermath wondering where it all went wrong and what we could have done to change the tides of fortune.

Love is infinite. Life is not.

February 17, 2018, in Edmonton, Alberta, was as mercurial as my mood: icy and irritated with a daytime temperature of -19°C. How I detest winter at its coldest. The days seem dreary, night comes early, and the temperatures take your breath away. Even a holiday in late winter that is focused on love cannot diminish the long and bitterly cold days. It is only the expectation of an early spring that allows me hope that the season will come to a close soon.

Scott and I spent the day driving our oldest daughter, Jordyn, to and from her ringette games in a weekend tournament that is over an hour away. Despite the distance, I so enjoyed watching Jordyn play defence. I admired her skill, speed and an aggressiveness that is completely out of character in her everyday life. The team finished the day, and with back-to-back losses, it seemed the tournament was over as well. By eight o'clock, I was back at home settled in the living room with a glass of wine and cozy fire, intent on catching up my friend Nancy, whose daughter played with Jordyn but could not attend. It was in between our texts that I received one from Ryan's friend James.

There was no sense of looming disaster or impending doom.

His contact was in my phone as "Jimmy James," a nickname that had stuck after Scott had teasingly started using it. I could see him as none other. Ryan and James had been fast friends since the early days of high school. He was a constant in our house and at the lake in the summer. He had worked at the Edmonton International Airport with a company that supported below-the-wing operations for WestJet, the company I worked for, before leaving with Ryan to find a seasonal position in Sun Peaks as a lift operator for the winter. On the nights we found ourselves working a night shift together, James would bring me green tea from Tim Hortons before he left for home. He was part of our extended family, so a text from him on a Saturday night did not linger in my mind as remarkable, and I left it unread as I finished my text exchange with Nancy. One minute passed and then another. I was blissfully unaware that our lives would shatter the moment I opened that text.

"Hey Heather, hate to text you like this. Haven't seen Ryan since last night and starting to get worried about him. We ended up filing a police report so I wouldn't be surprised if the police give you a call as well. Just thought I should let you know."

Words. I have always loved them. Comforting, illuminating, expansive. A jumble of letters formed to create emotions. I've spent endless hours reading, and I wanted to infuse a love of the written word into the minds of my children. The words of this short communication shaped a moment that can never be taken back.

After countless interviews, social media entries and even a documentary, I have been asked every question imaginable. But of all those questions, the one I dread the most is, "Tell me about Ryan. Who was he? What was he like?" How do you summarize a person's life into a few short, descriptive adjectives?

Ryan John Marcus Shtuka. Born March 17, 1997, at 10:17 a.m. He weighed 5 lb., 15 oz. and 19½ inches long. He was our first child, and although I found myself sick for almost all of the pregnancy, his birth was effortless and quick. Scrawny, red faced with a shocking amount of black hair, I instantly fell in love when I looked into the eyes of this baby boy. It's cliché, but I completely own every Hallmark moment where the mother discovers this transformative love deep within herself and it changes her worldview, and it's all because of this one tiny human being. Those eyes rested on mine with a blind trust and a calming surety that I would care for and protect him. It is a heady feeling heavy with responsibility.

Ryan was curious and bright. With no experience to draw from, everything he did was either cause for concern or a celebration of his intellect and a by-product of our excellent parenting skills. As mothers and fathers, we put so much pressure on the milestones and the progress as a mark of who we are as parents. The birth of your first child brings nothing but "helpful" tips and sly suggestions your way. They're guaranteed to make you doubt yourself. We judge others who are participating in a play that does not come with a script. Honestly, it was exhausting. Learning to let go of judgement was an ongoing practice, but I enjoyed being a new mother. Perhaps not the early mornings, but there is a price to pay for everything.

We brought Ryan home and adjusted to our new reality of delights and worries as best we could. I remember his pitiful cries as I struggled with breastfeeding, resorting to feed him via a syringe in those first days home. One obstacle overcome only led to the overwhelming panic that he slept so far away from us, so we moved him into our room and slept restlessly with the lights on. Challenge presented, faced and then on to the next. We were all in this together, our little family of three.

Ryan was active and strong despite his initial weight. He loved bouncing in his ducky swing so much that Scott built headers for every doorway entry in our house. One would think that he was building strength in those tiny legs for early walking, but our son managed to always find an easier way to approach problems. Crawling was too slow and occupied the hands but walking exerted too much time and energy, so Ryan adopted a stance of one knee down and one foot on the ground to propel himself around, his hands holding on tightly to a dinosaur as he scooted around the house.

He grew plump and the dark hair was replaced by white blonde. His smiles came easy. Tiptoeing into his room each morning to his sweet cooing sounds always led to his eyes resting on mine and a tinkling of infectious giggles.

"Good morning, my handsome little man."

Ryan spoke early, often, endlessly. Questions. Play-by-plays. Interesting facts. His favourite word was "actually." It was unnerving to hear an eighteen-month-old matter-of-factly tell me, "Actually mommy, that is not correct." I quickly learned enough to be cautious with my words around this inquisitive boy. For someone that swears as often as I do, it was a challenge not easily won.

Healthy eating was problematic, and I admit I fostered some bad habits. Always eager to have this baby boy smile, it was easy to sway me away from the mushy peas to the tastier sweet potatoes. This led to a lifetime of encouraging Ryan to eat properly and expand his palate.

"I don't eat yuck food. I only like delicious food," he would say to relatives as he suspiciously eyed a plate filled with salads and fruits. I simply hung my head in embarrassment. I'm not even sure I can claim a victory when, at age twenty, Ryan enjoyed a beautiful steak and a fine wine at our dinner table. It was, after all, free food.

Ryan was stubborn and curious, always asking "Why?" He kept himself busy for hours playing with dinosaurs of every kind. He was fascinated with them and insisted that we watch *The Land Before Time* over and over. I will forever be impressed with the number of movies that were produced during this particular phase, if only to give us a moment's peace. Ryan then moved onto *Rescue Heroes*, with a small smattering of dinosaurs wreaking havoc on the lives of these courageous men and women. Almost every day, Ryan and his best friend Ryan Gingras (forever to be known as Ryan S. and Ryan G.) spent hours quietly playing in the playroom. Their friendship was unique in that I am not sure I ever saw them argue or fight. Whatever disagreements they had were sorted amongst themselves with no need for adult intervention. Given the two girls with the tattling and hurt feelings, the Ryans were the most peaceful playdates out of all the children, and their friendship continued for years to come. The two little blonde-haired boys played soccer together in the high summer sun, Ryan G. chasing the ball while Ryan S. chased butterflies (it took some time to nurture that competitive spirit before it expressed itself in my son). We summered at the lake together where the boys built forts, swam and played baseball in the fields. As the boys grew and moved apart, summer and the lake meant the boys came together again, year after year.

We settled in a routine that continued until the birth of Jordyn, our first daughter, three years later. Five years after that, our youngest, Julianna, was born. Being educated but having no rutter to steer me in any one direction, I was content to stay at home for the first twelve years before returning to the workforce. After that, the years were busy; filled with playdates, shuffling kids to practices and games, homework struggles and juggling shift work. We took trips to visit my parents in the winter when we could and spent summers at the lake.

Adolescence and the teen years were upon us before we could all take a breath.

I cannot brag and say life was easy or perfect, but I can say that, even with our youngest, there were small acts of warfare in our household, but Scott and I always won the battle. Victory remains ours. The proudest moments were comments about the politeness of our children. My motto was always, "I love my children, but it is important for people to like them." That did not mean we didn't face rebellion, but talking back is a trait I can handle. I much preferred Ryan to experiment with his independence in the safety of his home than to fail miserably in public. And he did experiment. Eye rolls, rude comments and constant teasing become his uniform of choice. "A monkey" is how his Grade 1 teacher described him. The "monkey see, monkey do" kind of kid. Sitting outside his classroom, cutting laminated teaching aids as Jordyn played with her toys, I could hear a teacher's reprimand and then the childish giggles.

"Keenan, please stop tapping on the desk."

Pause.

"Ryan, when I tell Keenan to stop, that does not mean for you to start."

I caught his eye as he sheepishly walked by me and out to recess, shrugging his shoulders slightly as if to say, "What can I do?"

But one look from me could stop that boy in his tracks, even at age twenty. Lowering my voice and the unwavering look in my eye gave him pause to determine pushing me further would be done at his own peril. I remember overhearing him tell a friend in high school, "My dad is mad all the time, but when my mom gets mad, she is meaner than my dad will ever be."

Ouch. Although a small smile did form on my tight-lipped mouth that was pursed in displeasure I suppose. If you ever have the chance to meet Scott, you might be surprised to find that horns do not grow out of his head. The lines around his eyes show a man that smiles often, and the gentleness in the way he treats his girls is so evident. Take the words of a teenage boy about the restrictions his dad placed on him in the form of cleaning his room and refraining from teasing his sisters with a grain of salt. As for me, well, he might have been right. We were not spankers, for the most part. We disciplined in a certain way until we learned there were different, better ways. As the kids grew, that type of discipline, although infrequent, became obsolete. It wasn't a method that worked in our family because it didn't foster a behaviour we could all live with. It was through my words that my ingenious punishments would spill forth. I had the uncanny knack of discovering their worst fears around social embarrassment, and that became my promise. Are you afraid I will show up at school looking and acting inappropriately? Perfect, I can do that. Displays of affectionate in public? Of course, my specialty. If there were to be a contest of wills, you can be sure I would emerge victorious. Luckily, only Ryan felt the need to challenge me at times, but even he would admit that it was half-hearted. I hoped my lectures would be the most successful. I wanted to have frank, honest discussions with my children that allowed my experiences to pave a way for them to understand that each action has a reaction. There are always consequences to every act we perform, and it is for us to discover whether the outcome is a positive or negative one.

Once we moved to Beaumont, Alberta, at the end of Ryan's kindergarten year, there was a small group of kids that became fixtures in our home. Ryan was placed in French Immersion, which meant small classrooms with a limited number of children. The kids—girls and boys together—knew each other well, stuck together and grew as they moved year to year with the same group. It was the norm for them. In most cases, they were like brothers and sisters who saw each other warts and all. This meant we were free from the boy-girl drama until Grade 9, when Ryan entered high school.

New faces and the thrill of being somewhat unknown can be heady. Boys saw girls in a different way and vice versa, so it was hardly surprising that Ryan came home one day with a new status: boyfriend. Of course, it was not announced, but you don't live in a smaller town with your ear to the ground and a chatty nature to match and not find things out. Looking at his day-to-day interactions gave no indication that he was "dating," and I came to understand why. I suppose he felt pressured in some ways to be like his friends and ask someone out, so he chose a long-time friend. I think he understood the purpose of getting a girlfriend, but he struggled to know what to do next. As someone who wanted to hang out with his friends and play video games and sports, having a girlfriend was a bit draining, and he "broke up" with her soon after. While not cruel, I would characterize his attitude as indifferent. I was aware that he had no experience with break-ups, which meant he couldn't see himself in her shoes.

"Ryan, this is what I want you to know," I said when he told me. "I think you are an attractive kid who is just beginning to navigate adult relationships. You are not ready right now, and that is OK. That shows maturity to understand what works and what doesn't. How you behave with the knowledge that someone likes you and you don't share the same feelings is important. You will go through life with, perhaps, lots of girls liking you. Please don't be cruel. There may be a time that will come that someone you care for won't see the same future with you. You will wish for the same compassion."

"I know, I know. God, mom," he mumbled, his face flamed with embarrassment at having such a conversation with his mother. He made a hasty retreat.

The problem with instilling pearls of wisdom is that you never know if or how the message will grow. A pearl changes as a result of disturbance or irritation. Either we stay stagnant or we embrace necessity and curiosity.

High school was uneventful. There were no punishments for broken curfews, bad grades or unsavoury friends. No late-night phone calls or sneaking out. Scott and I pinched ourselves because raising this young man was so easy. We continued to go to soccer games, and then football and rugby. There were new friends that stopped by and an increase in social media. Ryan started working at the local grocery store in town. He was growing up.

He appeared ready to share some of his time with another person, and he dated a girl for about a year. As much as we liked here, it was probably more consuming than what Scott and I would have liked. Over time, Ryan felt the same. There was less time to spend with friends and more circumstances outside of his control that taxed him. I knew this, but having confidence in your child's independence means that, unless it is dangerous, sometimes you just have to stand by with a safety net, if need be. So, I checked in often and waited.

One night in November, Ryan came to our bedroom door as Scott and I lay in bed reading.

"Mom, can I talk to you? About something important?"

I confess, in that first moment I had this overwhelming fear that the next words would be ones every parent of a teenager dreads: "She's pregnant." Thankfully, what he actually wanted to know was how to tell someone you cared about that you no longer saw yourself with them. He laid out his problem and concerns and seemed desperate for my advice. He was on the verge of tears and trying very hard to be an adult. My heart broke at his dilemma, but I was so proud of the care and concern he had for another person. They remained friends long after.

The lesson had indeed grown. My father always told me that there are three things that are required of you to be a successful and independent adult.

"You need to be able to get a job on your own, leave a job having not burned bridges, and have a relationship that is respectful."

Ryan was well on his way.

Days blended in months and into years. It seemed that in a blink of an eye, Ryan became a young man. He graduated high school. He fell in love one last time. I saw him become everything I could only imagine and more, and the world upon which he would make his mark was before him.

Motherhood over. Parenthood just beginning.

Looking back, some days seemed endless, but I always knew that these moments would not last. The unfailing trust, unconditional love, and knowledge that we gave our children grew and shifted imperceptibly with each tiny step they took, each glance into world beyond the one we showed them. I wanted to breathe it all in, take measure of it and be present.

Easier said than done, I suppose. Parenting is thankless, exhausting and all-consuming. Hindsight has granted me the ability to look back and regret so much. The harsh words, half-hearted responses, cursory listening and disengagement are like heavy chains that threaten to weigh me down on days when grief washes over me. It is not my only regret in life, but it is one I cannot possibly put to right.

Trying to portray our life is like describing the perfect sunrise. No amount of words can convey the golden hues of red and orange as they wake in the sleepy sky. It is like the promises of something glorious that have been beckoned to and answered in splendour—a new dawn and a new day where miracles can and do happen. A written account can never truly speak to the soul the way the eyes can. We weren't perfect. Our lives were normal and conventional. Until the day they weren't.

I stared at the text on my screen. Entirely innocuous and yet devastatingly ominous. Letters that created words. Words that formed sentences. Sentences that completed a paragraph that shattered our lives. So absolute.

"Scott," I called softly as I began to read the message out loud.

The panic in my voice alerted him right away. The words spun in my head as I tried to formulate the sentences that would break my husband's heart. They stuck in my throat. I couldn't get them out. I didn't know what I was saying, but I knew that once spoken, those words could never be taken back.

His face paled as he registered what I said. But like in all things, he steadied me with his eyes and asked me to repeat myself. I could not. Instead, I showed him the text. His knuckles whitened as he gripped the phone. A small sigh escaped. Over our twenty-five years of marriage, I have hurt him in countless ways. Perhaps all relationships bear this burden. But in this one span of time, the pain in my telling him can never be undone.

"Call James," he rasped. "Call him and find out what the hell is going on."

He turned his back to me as he looked up the number of the Kamloops RCMP.

They say that time slows down during traumatic experiences. Untrue. I couldn't do things fast enough. My fingers were stiff as I struggled with my phone. My mind raced with questions, but my mouth had trouble finding the right words.

"What is going on James? Tell me what happened," I managed to ask him.

It would be weeks before we got a clearer picture of the events that led to Ryan's disappearance. Even as I write this, there are still gaps that are hazy and out of focus. It's like trying to piece together a puzzle without a box top and all of the pieces. But in those first moments it was absolute confusion and chaos.

"We were out at the silent disco at Bottoms," James said quickly. "We left and went to a house party down on Burfield. I left early to come home, and Ryan stayed with our roommates, Chris and Kirstin. When they left, they thought Ryan was coming with them, but I guess he didn't. Tonight, his boss texted us and said Ryan hadn't shown up to work at all today. We have called everyone we know to see if he crashed at someone's house, but no one has seen him. So, we called the police."

Nothing about this made sense to me. Not the sequence, the locations or the reasoning. *This is utter madness* was my first thought. Then I bombarded him with questions.

"What is a silent disco?"

"It is held at the local bar."

"Bottoms?"

"Yes. Everyone is given headphones that have two different channels that play DJ music. Only you can hear the music."

"Where is Burfield?"

"It is down at the bottom of the hill right near our house."

"Where would he go?"

"It's like a five-minute walk to our house, but there are two paths he could have taken."

"Why didn't you notice that Ryan didn't come last night or today?"

"I was pretty drunk last night and passed out when I got home. I didn't work today, so I slept in and then went skiing. I just thought he was at work."

"Okay. What have you done since you got the text?"

"We called our friends and went to the house to see if maybe Ryan had just crashed there. We posted in the local Facebook group in case anyone saw him. We have walked the paths. We called the hospital and just talked to the police."

I could hear the panic in his voice, and I heard Scott speaking low and insistently on his phone as he talked to the RCMP. I could hear, but I couldn't think.

"Please go out and keep looking, James. I will call you back."

Scott looked at me with tears in his eyes as he asked the RCMP officer one last question.

"Should we come up there?"

His head hung and his breath released as he listened to the response. He looked older suddenly and said, "Thank you. We are leaving right now."

For one brief moment, we were still. There was so much to say but not a word passed our lips. We were a foot apart and yet miles away as we tried to understand the ramifications of one text message.

"Mom, what is happening? Where is Ryan?" Julianna said, moving into view from the doorway where she stood.

I looked at my twelve-year-old daughter numbly. There were no answers I could give that would soothe her worried heart. I saw confusion and fear as she crumpled in my arms. Jordyn stood at the bottom of the stairs. The knowing look in her eyes as she waited silently left me completely undone.

"Come on, Jubie, let's go help Mom pack."

*Pack? How is it that this seventeen-year girl can process in one minute the events that have unfolded and logically set about doing the things that need to be done?* Her words broke the spell and sent Scott out to the garage to get the truck ready. I heard rummaging as he looked for his winter clothes. Even my husband focused on creating a mental list of tasks.

I stood alone. I could neither cry nor move. Whirling strands of emotions whipped through my head, battering me as I wrapped my arms around my waist, hoping to contain the damage to just me. It was like sand slipping through my fingers—solid but too small to grasp. *If I can just stay still, stand motionless, will it hurt less?* I wonder. *Will it delay what is to come? Or if I cannot turn back time, can I at least keep it from moving forward?*

A hand gently touched my shoulder.

"Babe, the girls need you to help them pack. I called my mom. She is on her way."

*No. No. No. Telling others makes this real. Please let us have one more minute of peace. One more minute of pretense.* This is what I wanted to plead for, to beg of my husband. Instead, I looked into his eyes and saw he was barely hanging on, so I nodded and walked upstairs.

Julianna was curled around Oscar, our puppy, on my bed, her face wet with tears. If ever a puppy had a more important job than to comfort a frightened child, I don't know what it would be. With every lick, every nuzzle, Julianna poured her fears and he absorbed them. Jordyn was packing my clothes.

"I don't know what I need," I murmured absently. "What do I need?"

She put the suitcase on the bed and arranged sweaters and leggings.

"I have packed enough for a week. Will that be okay?" she asked.

I didn't know. But in the brief span of time that my world was shattered, I had learned one important lesson: I am the anchor. I am the matriarch of this family. There has never been another time that my husband and children need me more than in this moment. Resolve weaved through my spine, forcing me to stand tall, and I unclenched my hands.

"A week will be more than enough, baby girl," I said in a steady voice.

I gathered both girls together, and they collapsed in my arms. I kissed the tops of their heads and held their faces in hands.

"It is going to be OK," I said. "Ryan is probably crashing at someone's house. We will be back before you know it."

The lie stuck in my throat. If they realized the mistruth, they seemed desperate to hold on to it for as long as they could.

Moments later, Scott and I were saying goodbye. In the months to come, I will recognize the night for what it truly was: the unravelling of everything.

The drive to Sun Peaks, British Columbia, from Beaumont is about nine hours. It was the longest and shortest drive I have ever taken. There was no music to soothe our souls, and the cold, black night enveloped the truck and obscured our view. We were left with our fears and despair. For the first couple of hours, we forced ourselves to think rationally: What did we need to address immediately?

"Nancy," my voice trembled on the phone. "Scott and I are on our way up to Sun Peaks. Ryan didn't come home from a party last night. No one has seen him since. James and his roommates have called the police."

To her credit, this strong capable woman that I have been blessed to call my friend didn't ask me to repeat my words and didn't give way to the panic that was bubbling inside her.

"Where are the girls?" she asked calmly. "Do you need me to go to the house?"

*No, I need you to tell me this is crazy. I want you to say that everything will be fine*, I say in the silent recesses of my mind.

"No, Judy is coming to stay with them."

Slight pause.

"Put up a picture of him on Facebook asking if anyone has seen him or been in contact with him."

The instant she said it, I shook my head. I couldn't do that. God, he would be so embarrassed to have his picture plastered across social media. What would people think? Isn't that extreme? She interpreted my silence and understood all my unsaid thoughts and fears.

"Heather, you need to get the word out quickly," she said. "Once we know where he is, we can delete the post, but you have to reach his friends."

"I can't," I whisper. "I don't think I can do it."

To type the words, to find a picture, to actually put it to paper would make this real. Fear froze me.

"I can do it, love," she says. "I will take care of it."

Those are words that she uttered to me almost daily for the next several months. In my moments of inaction, Nancy become a beacon of stubborn energy. There was no task set before her that she would not do, no mountain that she could not climb or obstacle she would not overcome for the people she loved. Extraordinary? Perhaps, but not singular. In the days and months ahead, I felt the full weight of love that would come through the actions of not only friends and family but through complete strangers. Humanity at its finest.

Within minutes, my phone lit up with notifications. I looked at the post with pictures of my first born, the smiling face at odds with the words written beside them.

> Public Help Needed!!!!!!!!
> Have you seen Ryan Shtuka?
> Ryan was last seen in Sun Peaks, British Columbia @2:10 a.m. on Saturday 17/18. He did not show up at home nor to work there on Sunday, which is very uncharacteristic of him. Friends, housemates and co-workers cannot locate him. Authorities are aware and currently searching. His parents are on route to BC.
> Please share and share again.

All the cocoon of lies that I wrapped myself in were exposed in that one late-night post.

The busyness that followed helped me focus on getting through each kilometre. I called my friend Tianna next. Our families had been intertwined since the day Jordyn met her youngest daughter, Katie, at the age of three. Tianna's oldest daughter, Lexie, has been one of Ryan's best friends since the first grade, and we would often tease them about their upcoming nuptials that would tie our friendship into family. If Nancy is the unfiltered go-getter, then Tianna is the steady force that anchors me. I gravitate towards Nancy because she inspires me to embrace this world largely and wholly. I align myself with Tianna because she is of the same breath, encouraging me to live my most authentic self. I need both equally.

She answered immediately.

"What is going on? Lexie showed me this post on Facebook. Where is Ryan?"

Her voice breaking was almost my undoing. I tried to steady the beating of my heart. Explaining was so difficult because I had no answers, and she knew this intuitively.

"Where are you staying?" she asked.

Ah, the practical tasks. That I can handle. Like putting one foot in front of the other. Head down and fully concentrated.

"I don't know," was my weak reply.

"I will take care of it, Heather. I will look right now and text you the details."

Accommodations in a ski resort in winter. I winced at the thought. I let out a sigh. It would stretch a budget that was carefully maintained since the operation on my ruptured Achilles tendon and subsequent leave from work. How awful to think of the monetary burden in a time of crisis, but these thoughts occupied my mind.

"Don't worry about the cost, Heather. Just drive safe and let me know if you need anything else. Love you."

There is nothing else that Scott and I could do but drive on. Staring into the dark abyss of an endless road, I suddenly looked to my husband.

"Would I not know?"

Scott turned to face me.

"Would I, as his mother, not be able to feel it if he was gone?"

The question lingered in the air. Silence filled the cab of the truck. It was as if we were waiting for an "aha!" moment—a point of clarity that would show us the way forward. Scott sighed deeply and reached for my hand, his eyes fixed on the dark road ahead.

"I don't know, babe. I don't know."

It is human nature to plead for what we want or to beg to change the fates before us. We look to the skies and make bargains that rival olden day kings praying to ancient gods. I was no different.

*Please. I will be a better person. I will live a better life. I will do whatever you want, just don't take my son. I beg you; let him be safe.*

I whisper this in my mind over and over, but despite my desperate pleas there was no divine presence nor reassuring light that answered back. The hours went by. Ryan's poster was shared far and wide. It generated lots of exposure but nothing from our son.

Around 2 a.m., an incoming call from an unknown number showed on the truck display. For one terrifying moment, I thought, *This is it. The RCMP are calling to inform us that they found him. I'm not ready. My mother was right: nothing good comes after midnight.* No call at this hour will be good news, so we let it ring as if to stave off the inevitable. One ring, two, three. Finally, Scott couldn't stand it any longer, so he answered.

A grainy voice with a slight French accent filled the silence.

"Madam?"

I recognized the caller. It was Dany, one of Ryan's best friends from the time he was eight and Ryan ten. Every waking moment since meeting at club soccer, these boys had been inseparable. Such typical noisy boys that raided my pantry, ran throughout the house chasing the dog and yelled as they versed each other in online games. Two peas in a pod. I can still see the toe marks and chips in the basement drywall from when Dany, his older brother Manny and Ryan played tag and jumped through bedroom windows. They wore goofy smiles and were repentant about their destruction until the next time. And there was always a next time. Even the move to Saskatchewan when Dany was in his teens did nothing to diminish their friendship.

"Madam? Scott?" his voice came across again, interrupting my thoughts.

"Yes, Dany, we are here."

"What's happening? I just saw the post from Lexie about Ryan. Have you found him?"

Scott quickly explained what we knew. There was a slight hesitation before Dany responded, his voice seemed so incredibly young and so far away.

"You have to find him, Scott. Something is wrong. Ryan would never stay out all night and day without letting someone know where he was. He just wouldn't!"

The fear as he rushed to get his words out cut through my soul. He was right and I knew it, but I was willing to suspend all belief because the alternative was so much worse. If Ryan was not normally irresponsible then him being lost in the cold was quickly becoming a reality.

I looked at the temperature gauge in the truck and noted that it was getting colder with each kilometre we travelled. How long can someone survive in this temperature? Scott must have been thinking the same thing because he stepped on the gas slightly and sped up. But we were still a painful four hours away.

I knew we must be getting closer. Scott was restless. He was stopping more often. Stepping out in the cold air to clear his mind or to say a prayer, I didn't know. I was anxious to continue to our destination as soon as possible. Scott was dreading it. My face must have shown some signs of impatience because he took my hand before starting the car for the last time. Sun Peaks was forty-five minutes away.

"Heather," he said gently, "I'm afraid. I'm afraid that the RCMP have found him and just haven't called us because we are driving. That they are waiting up at the top of the hill to tell us."

The implications froze me more than the cold air creeping into the truck cab. Practical and forward thinking, my husband summed up what I wasn't able to process since the beginning of this journey. What would happen when we got to the top of the mountain? What was waiting there for us? We could only delay the inevitable for so long.

I have only been to Sun Peaks once before—in December of 2015 for a ski holiday. We rented a condo with Tianna and her family for New Year's and spent five wonderful days skiing, playing games, enjoying each other's company and wandering through the village. In truth, I don't remember the area much as we didn't stray far from the condo except to trudge in our ski equipment to the chairlifts and back again. Because there were so many of us, we didn't eat out or hit the local watering spots, so my memories of Sun Peaks were pleasant but vague. So when James was describing what happened that night, I couldn't really wrap my mind around the logistics. I had no idea where Ryan lived based on the street name. I didn't know where the house he left from was located, nor the distance between the two. I felt helpless.

The turn off to Sun Peaks came into view. The dove grey sky, devoid of warmth or comfort as dawn approached, illuminated the glitter of freshly fallen snow in the headlights of the truck. A cold winter morning made for late lie-ins snuggled in bed under heavy blankets waiting for the buds of spring to show their sleepy heads. I should have been content in my bed at home, not bracing against this bitter cold, driving into uncertainty and terror.

From the bottom of the turn off is the tiny hamlet of Heffley Creek. A post office, gas station, local convenience store, church and smattering of homes all lie at the base of the hill. From there it is thirty-two kilometres up a winding single lane road to reach Sun Peaks. As you navigate its twists and turns, the vast expanse of the area shows itself in all its majesty. Trees extend as far as they eye can see, rolling hills and mountains pave the way. Changes in the elevation caused my ears to pop, and the windiness of the road unsettles my stomach. It was breathtaking to behold despite our purpose, and it still catches my breath to this day.

The drive from Heffley Creek should take twenty-five to thirty minutes, but the roads were treacherous and we found ourselves trudging along slowly behind a snowplough. Hurry up and wait. What felt cold at the bottom steadily dropped the higher we climbed. Each kilometre drained us of our hope. High berms of snow lined the road on both sides. Everything seemed impassable.

The community of Whitecroft is at the halfway point. Calling it a community may be generous, for it is just a large roundabout nestled in the valley and surrounded with log cabin homes and a creek running along the backside of it. On the opposite side of Whitecroft is a path that leads visitors on a trail to a tucked away waterfall. It is a quiet community that is a refuge from the busyness of the ski resort and where neighbours know one another.

We finally reached the top of the mountain to see the municipality Sun Peaks before us. We were to meet the RCMP at the firehall at 7:00 a.m. In our last conversation with the constable hours before, he said the canine unit was out in full force until the late hours and would return at first light. Kamloops Search and Rescue (KSAR) would be taking command Sunday morning.

I am not sure what I expected when we arrived—a bustling of urgent, frenzied activity with throngs of people scurrying about calling Ryan's name? Foreboding music and an ominous scene where the hero is in undeniable peril like in every blockbuster movie? I was surprised that the town was still, quiet. Snow gently dusted the roads as the sky began to brighten. It was 6:30 a.m., and if Ryan was lost, it seemed like no one noticed.

In the winter months, there is only one way into and out of Sun Peaks by car. The main road, Sun Peaks Road, bisects the town from one end to the other, and houses create a quaint ski village with some shops in the centre of it all. At the entrance of the resort, just past the Burfield Hostel, is the house Ryan found himself living in. It was the only house on this road. Originally, it was the office of the property manager for the corporation before becoming a private residence. It was an odd choice, I suppose, to have a rental, but its proximity to staff accommodations right across the street and the ski out of the Back in Time run must have seemed attractive to Ryan and his roommates.

As we turned the corner, Ryan's car, covered in metres of snow, sat in the driveway. Reality came in increments; the hours travelling, Dany's frantic voice, the slow drive up the hill, and then seeing his car. I recall Ryan's look of excitement and satisfaction as he drove his brand new (to him) car up our driveway. He had done the research himself, committed to buying a Volkswagen Jetta and had asked Scott to go with him to test drive and possibly purchase it. It was the perfect car for him: heated leather seats, sporty with an upgraded stereo system and room to put his snowboard in. The smile on Ryan's face that day is one memory I carry with me on all the bad days. He was so incredibly proud. The Jetta sat lonely, abandoned in the lot, as we pulled in beside it that day.

After sitting for so long, my Achilles felt stiff and sore. I limped from the truck to the house, turning slightly as I waited for Scott to follow. He walked past the car and paused before brushing off the snow. I was at a loss as to what he is doing for a brief moment, but when he peered intently through the darkened windows, he looked to me and shook his head.

"He is not in there."

Startled, I hadn't thought of the possibility of our son stumbling home after being out all night and seeking refuge in his car.

"All of his snowboard equipment is in there, though."

James, looking haggard, opened the door and hugged me. Ryan's roommates, Chris and Kristen, were behind him. James introduced them, and I could see the exhaustion and sorrow in their faces. Although the small, dark, dingy house oozed sadness, frequent conversations with Ryan indicated nothing but happiness at his living arrangements. He had five other roommates. James, his friend from Beaumont, shared a room with him. Chris and Kristen, a boyfriend and girlfriend, shared the master bedroom, and Ellie and Jasmine shared a loft space over the living room. Ellie's boyfriend from New Zealand, Ben, had travelled to see her and had been there for almost a month as well. It seemed crowded but manageable. Looking past the tight space, I turned to the three of them.

"Walk me through what happened."

The details were much the same, but Chris and Kristen were much better at explaining. Ryan, an operator at the Tube Park, had worked that day. His job was to help guests get on and off tubes and push them down the lanes—nothing too strenuous—and he worked from 11:30 to 7:00 p.m. five days a week with Sundays and Mondays off. Not a bad gig for someone who wanted to snowboard each day. One of the perks was a ski pass for the season. After work, he texted James to let him know he was on his way home. That would be the last time Ryan sent or received a text. Arriving home, he quickly changed, grabbed something to eat and shotgunned a beer. Everyone was waiting on him. The plans were to head back up to the village to the silent disco at Bottoms. Normally the walk between the village and the house would take anywhere from twenty to thirty minutes—a brutal walk with temperatures dipping to around -24°C—so they arranged a ride with another employee. The municipality had a shuttle service that ran intermittently but no taxi service. Ryan was an anomaly because he had a car. Most of the workers arrived on work visas with only suitcases and ski equipment in hand. The local Facebook page is filled with ride requests down to Kamloops to make weekly grocery runs, so a smart entrepreneur decided to offer rides to and from the village for donations. The roommates and Ryan took advantage of this offer to get around that night.

By the time they arrived at Bottoms there was line-up to get in. Not wanting to wait outside, they headed to the bar next door, Masa's. A couple of drinks later there was an opening, so they all went to Bottoms. Each person was required to give their driver's license to the lady running the coat check before they were supplied with headphones. Having never been to a silent disco, I can only imagine the eerie silence as people danced to music no one else could hear. Photographers walked around capturing the moment, and it is from them that we have the last known picture of our son. He has his arm around Ben, a beer in his other hand and the biggest smile on his face. Imagine all the gaps that cannot be filled in around the disappearance of your only son and being given a memento of him looking happy and carefree.

Last call was announced around one o'clock in the morning, and there was a line-up to return the headphones. The weather had not improved, but with no other option a group of fourteen or so people headed out for the cold walk home. Ryan's house, the staff accommodations and rentals were all at the bottom of the hill on Burfield Crescent near Sun Peaks Road. The only thing dividing them was a creek running through the middle and brush on both sides. It's an easy pass in the summer months, but completely covered in snow during the winter. The amount of snow that had fallen at this point made it almost impassable without snowshoes.

As they began the long trek home, a shuttle bus that had finished its last guest drop off from the Kamloops Airport was heading back down, and a moment of generosity led the driver to pick up the entire group and drop them off just before the firehall. Some of the partygoers went home, but Ryan and his friends decided to head over to Burfield to carry on with the night at Wolves Den, Bluebird or Sunday Funday, the three houses that were being rented by lift operators or hotel staff. The party seemed to rotate days of the week, so the houses were gathering places for staff to hang out at. Ryan ended up at Sunday Funday. It had always been referred to as the party house, and perhaps there was a certain amount of truth to that, but any of those houses were open to employees or locals to gather at. Like many hangouts for young adults, there was a mix of people that frequented it. Some would have arrived sober having just finished a shift at one of the hotels, restaurants or bars. Some would have been drinking, doing recreational drugs or both. But a party might be a misnomer. There was around thirty people coming and going from the house until around 2:30 a.m. when the only ones left were known to the renters.

Ryan and his friends and roommates were among the thirty, and nine of them hung out on the couch in the living room. Not long after arriving, James was tired and bored, so he said his goodbyes and left. It was a relatively short walk home. Normally, they would walk out of the house, turn left, walk down the street to the end and head left. Right after the bridge, there is a dimly-lit path that was built below Sun Peaks Road for the safety of the residents and employees of the surrounding area after a hit and run occurred three years prior. The snow berms made it easier for people to walk on the actual road, but it was dangerous, so the path was created. To walk to their rental, James followed that path until the end and then popped up just beside the house. It is a relatively easy walk that most employees who didn't have transportation took.

However, having had drinks that night, a disoriented James walked out of the house and turned right, which is another way to get to the rental but slightly more difficult. He would again walk until the end of the road—a street that is not lit except for sensor lights on some houses. The high snow berms and cars lining the street no matter which way you left the house also presented challenges. The ski out was at the end of the crescent, and it was compacted and regularly groomed by the snow cats each night, but the path was less clear there, especially in the winter. Normally, you would walk to the end and turn right onto a bridge that goes over the creek. The Burfield Hostel is on the right, and Ryan's house was on the right side of that. In front is a crosswalk that leads to the chairlift on the opposite side. In the winter, the snow piled up and made the path indistinguishable, so if you didn't find the path and continued forward, you found yourself on an obscure path that eventually meets up with the old service road from Whitecroft to Sun Peaks. Turning left takes you up Back in Time, a ski run, which was a way home one could take if they were familiar with it. But both James and Ryan, having only been there for a couple of months, hadn't taken that route often. James, having realized his error, turned himself around and went home the way he was most familiar with. He said hi to his roommates at home and went to bed.

Soon after, Chris, Kristen and another partygoer, Jordan, indicated they were also ready to go home. As they began to leave, Ryan stood up and looked like he was putting on his coat. The three of them walked out the front door and turned left. A few minutes later, they looked behind them to see if Ryan was with them, but the street was empty. With the bitter cold, they assumed that either Ryan was slowly following behind or decided to stay with the others, so they continued on to the house. Jasmine had finished her shift at Masa's and had a couple of girlfriends over, so Chris and Kristen chatted with them for a bit before heading to bed as well.

That is the last known sighting of Ryan. No one remembers him leaving. People arriving at the house a short time later have no recollection of seeing him there.

My son vanished in the early morning of February 17, 2018.

# The Endless Wait

The next morning, one of the roommates—I can't recall who—received a text from Ryan's supervisor saying that Ryan wasn't at the Tube Park and she really needed him there. She wondered if they could check to see if he had slept in. From all accounts, Ryan was notoriously late almost every day. Only by a few minutes, but it was a pattern. He woke up early each day to hit the slopes and would always cut it close by taking the last run down before starting work. Arriving on time for work must be different in these environments because instead of reprimanding him, they offered him a supervisor position. Cheeky thing turned it down because he didn't think the additional seventy-five cents an hour was worth the added responsibility. Despite his tardiness, he was liked by staff and his supervisors.

When the roommates got the text, they didn't think much of it and assumed he was either stuck in a chairlift line or late getting down the runs because he wasn't in his room. His messy bed gave no indication that it was slept in or not. They responded, saying he wasn't there, and when there were no further messages, they thought Ryan had eventually showed up and all was well.

It wasn't until around seven o'clock in the evening that the supervisor texted them back and said Ryan had not shown up to work. That's when the panic began. They saw his employee pass and work boots in the corner and immediately started calling all the friends they were with the night before to see if Ryan had crashed with them. They also went to the Sunday Funday house to see if he had stayed the night and day there. Despite knowing Ryan for only two and a half months, their gut told them this was not normal. Ryan's pattern was to hang with them, and if they didn't go out, he would also stay home and game. He was most comfortable with them and wasn't the type to miss work and not contact anyone. They took to the Facebook page to ask if anyone in the community had seen Ryan or heard something. No answer. Full-blown panic set in as they dialed the number to the hospitals down in Kamloops. The negative response came with a suggestion to call the RCMP, which was when I received the text from James. I look at the timeline of events and still have difficulty processing how a seemingly innocent night could lead to this indescribable tragedy.

As I glanced around the house, I could see Ryan in the shadows. It hurt to breathe, and silence filled in the gap where there was no more story to tell.

"Thank you," I said simply.

It was time for us to meet the RCMP, but all I wanted to do was curl up in Ryan's bed and wrap myself in one of his blankets where I could inhale his scent. I wanted so desperately to feel my baby; to stop and rewind. As I closed my eyes to the tiredness that I felt, Ryan gently touched my shoulder and whispered, "It's okay, Mom. I'm here."

A foolish dream. A hopeful wish. An unspoken prayer.

It was a short drive to the firehall where the canine officers and their dogs were gathered. I knew they were out searching for Ryan until the wee hours in the morning and had just arrived back to start all over again, but they showed no signs of being exhausted as they shook our hands. The look of sympathy in their eyes as they detailed their progress thus far unsettled me. It is a look that Scott and I see now (and will forever) as people learn our story. But this was the early days. Having such raw emotion continuously shown to you takes a steel spine and a resolve in your heart not to fall to your knees and weep. It is a gaze I must hold. They were solicitous and considerate as they asked about Ryan and for any information that might help in the search. There were so many things I wanted to say about my son but none that would have assisted in the task ahead except that he wouldn't be out of contact with friends and family for so long.

As we stood there watching them pack up and move out, we saw the trucks of KSAR go by. A makeshift command centre was being established at the Ski Patrol situated beside the ski hill, and we would follow and wait there. Walking into that command centre was slow and measured. No one knew who we were. There wasn't a sign that marked us as tragic. Everyone was bustling as they set up communication, arranged rooms and readied themselves for the day ahead. One member looked at us in question; perhaps it was the defeat in our eyes that set us apart, but we were quickly acknowledged and ushered into a trauma room that had been made into a separated waiting room. This was to be my refuge and my prison for the day. Constables from the RCMP were there as well as the two case managers for KSAR. Behind them were two victim service advocates. All for us. All for Ryan.

We began telling the story of Ryan's life again, which is the hardest part. How do you describe your child? How do you even ascribe the qualities that make up all the pieces and parts of another human being in a way that allows even a glimpse of their sacredness and value? As we laid bare our lives, our child's life, I somehow felt like others were assessing my comments, looking for cracks, passing judgement. It was nonsense, but it was something I couldn't quite shake over the next few weeks.

There were nods, pens scratching in notebooks and an occasional question as we briefed them. They outlined the tasks for this search day and had their entire contingent of Search and Rescue on standby and ready to begin. There were numerous volunteers from the community, among them James, Chris and Kristen, who were signed in and anxious to help.

Having come to the end of the questions, the senior case manager looked at us before sombrely pronouncing, "Based on the amount of alcohol that he may have consumed, the time that has passed and the freezing temperatures, the likelihood of finding your son alive is slim to none." Shocking? Maybe. However, Scott and I appreciated his honest assessment. It was not the time for lies or false hope.

We sat in that stuffy little room processing the facts known to us as the search continued. Reliance on facts became our mantra as we commenced this journey and navigated through the lonely and uncertain days and months and years to come.

The day moved slowly. Each creak of the floor outside the door filled me with expectation. Every knock and every check from the outside world filled me with trepidation. I sat waiting for my world to officially come crashing down. For the confirmation of my worst fears. For my grieving to begin in earnest.

But I did not wait alone. My strong and stoic husband sat beside me. I know he wanted so much to be outside, to be alongside everyone out there searching and digging, looking for Ryan. But Scott stayed, holding my hand and absently rubbing my back. He would never leave me alone, and my injury meant I could barely walk, let alone take part. To not be by my side was unconscionable to him, so there we sat with the victim services advocates. They were terribly kind, but I didn't want them there. It felt like an awkward date where I was supposed to entertain. I wanted to break down, to rage at my cruel fate, to find comfort in the arms of my husband. Instead, I sat stiffly and held my emotions in check.

There were brief moments of breathing room. Halfway through the day, we were advised to check into our room at the Sun Peaks Grand Hotel and sleep for a bit. Unthinkable of course, but having a shower gave us the normalcy we craved. Since our arrival and this new knowledge, Scott and I had not had any time alone to evaluate what we'd been told and to process what the day would bring. But we couldn't hide in our room for long, and we were anxious to return.

In the hour we had been gone, we felt out of the loop, and the pit in our stomachs returned.

Feeling slightly refreshed, we braced ourselves back at the command centre for the news that would be coming anytime. The hours passed and no news comes. Why? Shouldn't this be a simple search? Ryan left the house late at night, intoxicated with alcohol and perhaps some recreational party drugs in freezing temperatures. He made a wrong turn or fell down an embankment or passed out in a snowbank. He succumbed to the weather. Open and shut case based on everyone's theories. So where was the pronouncement?

The day waned. The bright sunlight dimmed and darkness slowly crept in. The sounds of busyness outside the closed door subsided, and the command centre grew quieter and more sombre. Finally, Scott and I were persuaded to go back to our hotel room with the promise that once the search had ended, KSAR and the RCMP would come by and see us. With night approaching, staying at the command centre seemed cruel and unnecessary, but the hotel room provided no additional comfort. The Ski Patrol employees and advocates offered this buffer of busyness and noise that the two of us alone could not, so we were alone at the hotel with our fears and each other.

There was a knock on our door shortly after we arrived back. On the other side was our salvation. Although I am not overly religious, I swear the light shining on the faces before us was divinely sent. We looked upon five of our friends from Beaumont with shock. Nathalie, Tianna, Nancy, Jeff and Terri stood there with tears in their eyes but resolve in their souls.

"I told you not to come," I whispered.

"Yes, you did," Nancy replied.

"I told you I didn't need you."

"Yes, you did."

As the tears streamed down my face for perhaps the first time since that text, all I could do was hug each of them tightly and say "Thank you. Thank you. Thank you," over and over. These angels stood by us in a crowded hotel room as we talked about our day and remained with us as an RCMP officer and KSAR manager came for the last briefing of the day. They carefully outlined the tasks performed throughout the day, the measures that were taken to locate Ryan—dogs, drones, volunteers and grid searches. The words provided clarity but not comfort. The most common practice when hearing someone speak is listening with the intent to respond rather than listening to understand, but I could not comprehend the words that either of them were saying to us except that Ryan was not found. What was said next is a blur to me, but given the shock on our friends' faces I could tell it was important. I believed I thanked them and said I would see them the next day. If that seemed odd to them, they never let on.

For the first time in over thirty-six hours, we were surrounded by people that I did not have to explain, justify or defend my son to. I finally felt a sense of muted relief. If we were to unravel it would be in the safe comfort of our friends. It had been an exhausting day. We were emotionally drained, and to our everlasting horror it was just the beginning of long uphill battle. But despite a general feeling of foreboding, we remained unaware of just how difficult the next days, weeks and months would be.

It was a restless night. We tossed and turned, never quite finding a deep sleep. Our minds kept going over the events of the last day and a half. We would wake and find the other staring off into the dark. We would tell each other our fears. We clung to a hope that tomorrow a mistake would be corrected, Ryan would be found safe and our lives would go back to the way they were. We wanted to wake up to our mundane, routine life and celebrate how extraordinary it was.

Dawn erupted in brilliant sunshine. *A promise of a new day*, I thought. I couldn't have been more wrong.

We all gathered in the lobby before making our way to the command centre. Walking into Ski Patrol, it became startlingly clear exactly what the words that were spoken to us the night before were. It was an empty space with only a few employees going about their daily routine. The hustle and bustle of the day before had turned to an ordinary day, quiet and removed. Where was everyone? The RCMP? Kamloops Search and Rescue? The volunteers? If there was no one there, then who was looking for Ryan? *They told you last night*, my mind stubbornly reminded me. Turns out they said they had finished their tasks and would not be back until called by the RCMP. *Yes, but how will Ryan be found if they don't come back?* I asked myself. *By you,* was the simple response. *You will have to do it. Scott will have to do it. These five people standing beside you will have to do it. He came from you, and if he is to be found, you will have to find a way to do it.*

The mind is able to process so many things all at once. Humans are meant to multitask—not all complex motions and thought processes but simple necessities. The most successful individuals learn to compartmentalize so that they can tackle what needs to be done in efficient, productive ways. That morning, Scott and I stood in an empty command centre and put aside our grief and fear. We threw off the mantle of mourning, heartbroken parents and picked up the responsibility of Search and Rescue co-ordinators. The days ahead would require focus and logic. In a short period of time, we would be asked to learn a new skill and to lead others in the search for a missing child. We would become the cornerstones of this knowledge and tested through weather and the environment.

What would you have done?

Scott and Ryan
at Pembina

Ryan as a baby

Ryan selfie

Ryan's birthday at Montana's

Ryan's graduation

Ryan and graudation

Friends at football

Christmas 2017 at The Festival of Trees

Ryan, Jordyn and Julianna
at Festival of Trees 2017

Ryan at the Silent Disco
Feb 16, 2018

PART

# The Search
*Sun Peaks*
*February 19, 2018–June 18, 2018*

# The Search for Answers

I often wonder what I would have done if I had known Ryan was missing, lost in the swirling drifts of snow and bitter cold, sooner? Even though I couldn't get to him, I could have been with him in those final moments. I would have used whatever supernatural traits they give to parents to be by his side, whispering how much he is loved, how I am moving heaven and earth to find him, that he was so precious to me and his father and how I wished that I could change places. Maybe if there was to be any miracle, it would be from the warmth of a mother's love that would hold her son so he wouldn't feel scared or alone. Instead, I was tucked safely and warmly in my bed so unaware that my own life's blood was fading from my grasp. This thought and many others will continue to haunt me, I suspect, for the rest of my life.

Still, every journey begins with a single step. It doesn't matter if the journey is anticipated, planned for or the result of unimaginable circumstances. Staying static will not accomplish what needs to be done. We will not find a lost boy by curling up in our memories, grief, terror and heartbreak. But oh, how I wanted to.

I felt so helpless as I watched friends and community members set up a new command centre in the conference room of the Sun Peaks Grand Hotel. It was thoughtfully organized by my friend Lyette who travelled from Beaumont to help, one of the many logistical arrangements she would organize in the upcoming months along with Nathalie (Nat). Meal trains, volunteer lists, hotel accommodations and equipment checks will be some of the items they will organize and ensure completion of. I watched these two amazing women greet every volunteer with grace, charming them over and over again. Both French, the chattering between them was fast paced and sprinkled equally with laughter and sorrowful sighs. They finished each other's sentences, which, given the years of knowing each other, was hardly surprising. Nat has a steely resolve underneath such kindness that makes people underestimate her. She may smile as she directs you but won't move an inch when challenged if she believes the task is right or necessary. Lyette was our command go-to. She has this way of making you agree to her requests, believe it was your idea in the first place and scramble to get it done. I suppose they're both stubborn in their own ways, but they were exactly the people we needed to get the search off the ground. I would have been lost without them. Even to this day, they are amongst angels that fill my life with joy and love. Through Lyette's and Nat's organization, the command centre became a well-oiled machine where we planned the day, sent volunteers out with maps to search areas and ate our meals. It was a community connection of love and companionship in those early dark days.

With such efficiency, there was little for me to do. Scott woke early, put on his heavy winter clothing and set out to search for Ryan. He planned to go to the refuse centre to dig through garbage for clues, locate equipment to use for digging, and shovel and search through mounds of snow. Every night he came back exhausted and defeated but still got up the next morning to do it all over again. A painful routine that would seem never-ending.

I cursed my injury that forced such inactivity. *How can I possibly find peace in the outcome if I play no part?* I wondered. *Would I ever be able to reconcile the guilt that was plaguing me?*

They say that time slows down during traumatic experiences, but I think that all the extraneous thoughts we process throughout the day are burnt away and we are left with only the immediate problem. Whirling sands of emotions whipped through my head. I was at war with my emotions of grief and heartache and the logic of what needed to be done.

Paralyzed.

Inaction.

I foolishly wanted to believe that if I stood still long enough—even if I couldn't turn back time—I could keep it from moving forward. I just needed time to breathe. But time can only slow, it can never stop. I needed to find a way to overcome my weakness and fears so that I could stand tall, resolute. Guilt would have to come later; Ryan needed me now.

An opportunity to play a role besides grieving mother came in the form of social media. A Facebook group for Ryan was created in the hopes that showcasing his story would bring awareness, volunteers and resources. Even now, I am amazed at how much interest this page generated. At the very least, I felt I could man the page and ensure that his missing posters and information would be accurate as well as rally a call to action. I could also update friends, family and new members on our search status. It was very ambitious as the notifications were filling my phone at a rate that was hard to keep up with. The same question came over and over with such frequency: Is there any news? Has Ryan been found? To reply individually became time consuming, but I was determined to keep everyone informed. In the end, I felt that doing one post to address the questions was the most prudent way to stay ahead.

In a strange twist of fate about three weeks before Ryan disappeared, I was scrolling through Facebook and came across a news article about a young man who had gone missing from a house party after a night of drinking. The weather and the circumstances paralleled Ryan's story almost identically, and this young man had been found having succumbed to the frigid temperatures. A sad and terrible ending. The story filled me with such a sense of sorrow that I tried to find out more details, but there was nothing further.

I couldn't tell you the city, state or name of this young man now. It was a sad tale but, like most things in life, without reminders, it generally fades from your mind. I scrolled past and didn't think of it again until I was writing my post. Until I was trying to put in words everything that was swirling around me. I didn't want Ryan's story to be read and then forgotten. In that moment it was so important for Ryan's rescue or recovery that everyone remember and that they become involved.

So, I tried to make him real. Undeniable. As important to others as he was to us. I wrote about this beautiful boy that needed to be found. And then it seemed, I wrote some more.

February 19, 2018

Day 3 of searching has come to a close and nothing new to report. And yet so much happened. The police with their dogs came along with the helicopter. Our most precious friends spent the day searching everywhere. Ryan's friends did the same. There is still no sign of him. You must know hope remains, but my heart feels heavier each moment that passes. Night falls and it gets colder and my son is alone. Sometimes I think I can't bear it.

So, I want to tell you one thing about my firstborn. I want him to be real for you. Oh, I know you know he is loved by his friends and his family. He is smart and funny. Those are things anyone can say.

I want to tell you how much Ryan loved dinosaurs when he was young. Every day he would ask us to play the dinosaur game. We would take turns describing a dinosaur and the other would guess the type. Scott and I started to study paleontology to keep up with Ry. Time passes and what was once a passion faded. But it is these precious moments that I am trying so hard to hold onto.

So Ryan if you are out there ... "Let's talk about ... dinosaurs."

Thank you to everyone that has hope and prayers for Ryan. We are so overwhelmed by everyone who have gone above and beyond. You make this uncertainty more bearable. You will never know the depth of our gratitude.

February 20, 2018

What is a community except for a fellowship of people that share similar goals? Day 4 descended upon us with more and more people coming to volunteer. They volunteered their time, their knowledge, their expertise and their kindness. People that we have known forever and strangers that we have never met. The waves of love and compassion came over us. Never have I felt less alone. There is such a fierce determination to find Ryan.

I sit here with my candle burning, looking at Ryan's friends who spent the day searching for him. Is it possible at their age to know how valued they are by their peers? I am comforted by their presence. Ryan is valued and loved by his friends. He has always been surrounded by his community. If he could feel just a fraction of the love that everyone has for him, then he will forever know he is blessed.

I hate the thought of another day ending without answers. I miss him and it hurts but I know that him not being found is not because our community isn't trying. Our Alberta community or our BC community. You have our gratitude.

February 21, 2018

How is it possible to have 5 days pass with no sign of Ryan?

Not because of a lack of effort and determination from all these precious volunteers. Not because of the prayers and love from all of you. And not because I don't wish for it desperately each second of every moment.

And yet ... that is our reality.

Today, volunteers combed snowbanks with snowshoes and poles. They went deep in ravines and up and down roads. They came back dejected and cold, and bless them, they will come back tomorrow to do it all again. And the day after and the day after that.

How is it even possible to get through each day when you are sure that a piece of your being shatters as night draws near?

So, I try to remember moments spent together. When we were happy.

And I can breathe again.

\* \* \*

Lyette came to me in the early afternoon of February 22 to tell me that a candlelight vigil had been organized at the high school in Beaumont for that evening. The girls, Scott's family and my brother and sister-in-law would be attending. Friends had arranged the vigil as way to honour Ryan and to show love and support as a community to our family. It was but another reminder of the totality of devastation we were experiencing. Lyette and Nat gently asked if I wanted to hold a vigil in Sun Peaks simultaneously. If hope was the offering, then a unified lighting of candles would be a powerful expression of both love and grief. Within two hours, they had arranged the music, the venue and the equipment. All I had to do was to write the words.

It was another bitter night with the temperatures hovering around -20°C. The cold burned with every ragged breath I took. Heat leached from my body as I imagined my son alone in the cold. It was almost a relief to stand outside, bundled in winter clothing, to speak at the candlelight vigil because it seemed that the dreadful chill in my heart had found its rightful place among the artic temperatures.

February 22, 2018

Our candlelight vigil:

On behalf of Scott, myself, Ryan and daughters Jordyn and Julianna, we thank you for coming.

Saturday February 17 at 9:30 p.m. came the phone call that is every parent's nightmare.

"Your son is missing."

Shock, disbelief and this incredible sense of fear washed over us.

"Why?" and "How?" has now been replaced by "Where?"

Where is Ryan?

Each dawn starts a new day of searching, and as night falls and we don't find him we feel waves and waves of despair.

But tonight is about light, gratitude and hope.

Through these many terrible days has been the love and strength given to us by our friends and family.

We have been embraced by this wonderful community.

To each and every one of our volunteers here and in Alberta:

Your generosity of spirit and your determination to find Ryan has been a blessing.

I am not sure there will ever be enough words to express how thankful we are.

It is an honour to see that our son has made such a huge impact in his 20 years on this earth.

We find comfort knowing that Ryan has spent his last three months being surrounded by such amazing people. It is a continuation of what he has experienced his entire life.

We draw strength in knowing that with everyone's help and love, Ryan will be found.

Thank you again.

February 23, 2018

I suppose everyone wishes they could go back in time to a certain place ... a favourite holiday, a first love kiss. I loved this day. Ryan had taken a year off after school to work with Dad. He thought he might figure out what he wanted to do. He enjoyed the people he worked with but wasn't sure construction was his thing. I took a picture the day he went off to university. This was to be his year of school. He studied general sciences and enjoyed his classes and his experiences but didn't know what he would do with this degree. Fast forward to this year where he wanted to experience a year of adventure. To him that was his home at Sun Peaks to work and snowboard. Each year offered growth and shaped who he was. I think he was wonderful, and I was proud of him at every stage.

Oh, I wish I could go back in time, but I would never want to deny him the opportunity to be the man he is.

Today was tough, lots of ups and downs, but we persevere because we can do nothing else.

Tomorrow Search and Rescue will begin at the firehall. Pray that this nightmare comes to an end.

February 24, 2018

I won't lie. Every day has been tough since last Saturday, but yesterday was perhaps my lowest point. At 1:10 in the afternoon, I received a call that came up on my phone that said "Incoming: Ryan Shtuka." It showed the picture I attached to his name and the emojis I had given him. On the line came a creepy old lady's voice. At the end of what seemed like eternity came the voice: "You have been pranked by pranksters."

You see, I didn't know you could use an app on your phone and input someone's number to make it appear as if it came from them.

The cruelty that someone would do this is beyond anything I could comprehend. Did I break down? Of course, I did with great sobs. Of course, this came on the heels of someone messaging me to tell me that my family "was being punished but sleep well."

I don't tell you this to get you angry or upset. Believe me, at first, I was enough for all of us.

I tell you this because I realize that I would rather focus on the beautiful messages and kind words from loved ones than be stuck on the cruelty of others. I also tell you this because I believe Ryan was given to Scott and me because we are stubborn and determined. We will never give up searching for him. And because he would be for as long as he lives in this world and our hearts, loved beyond measure.

Today, a massive Search and Rescue force will be on hand at the firehall. I ask that you put all your best thoughts and wishes and pray today is the day we find him.

Be kind and full of love to yourself and one another.

*   *   *

What a horrific day. While I will never say that we, as the parents or loved ones of the missing, are victims, families often experience violations. The microscope under which we found ourselves was intense and unrelenting at times. Not everyone supported our efforts, decisions or how we conducted ourselves. We were prone to receive criticisms—outright and accusatory—from complete strangers, but also assessments presented in thinly veiled questions. We bore the brunt of wild speculations and terrifying theories that broke us down and tore us apart. We were forced to navigate through community services for financial support, addressing companies or banks on our loved one's behalf. The resources we may have needed were sometimes unclear and time consuming. It was a time of loss and grief on so many levels that sometimes just keeping our heads above water took more effort than we were able to give. However, we were still there. We were the casualties left from carnage.

It was startling to be sitting alone in an alcove outside the command centre and receive that text. I stared at the phone screen as my son's name appeared followed by the emojis I had given him: a monkey, a purple devil and a heart. Ice pumped through my veins as I answered the call. In that moment, two potential outcomes were evident. Either it was someone who found the phone and was looking for the owner or it was in fact my son. This many days into the search, I was not optimistic that it was Ryan. It would shatter all preconceived notions I had about him if he were alive and well and had allowed us to suffer so. Of course, now I know there can be several scenarios that may have contributed to him getting in touch four days later, but at the time, it seemed impossible.

Even if I had been privy to those scenarios, the phone call I received would never have made that list. A tinny and robotic voice with static in the background came across the line. It sounded like a Southern grandmother who had just gotten up from her wraparound porch to get you a glass of sweet tea. She (although the voice was distorted, so it could have been made by a man or a woman) kept asking for me to bring her something. She needed toilet paper. Could I stop by and bring her some? Why wasn't I going to help her.

Truthfully, the nature of the call took some time for me to process. I was preparing for Ryan or something about Ryan, so whoever was speaking to me made absolutely no sense.

"Why are you calling me? Why do you have my son's phone?" I kept repeating.

My voice and the panic in it caught the attention of a work colleague, Derryn, who was in the alcove across from me. His experience with the military police force attuned him to extraordinary circumstances. He must have seen the whiteness in my face because he immediately got up and came beside me. I showed him the name and put the call on speakerphone. He listened in for a moment before an announcer came on and said, "You've just been pranked by the ..."

The phone call ended, and I collapsed in tears. The very cruelty of it all brought me to my knees. Questions swirled around my head. How did this company get Ryan's phone? Was it set up by someone that did my son harm and wanted to terrorize us? Derryn's face showed such controlled rage, and I felt comforted that someone should be so outraged on our behalf. If the person responsible for that phone call were to be identified, they would regret being on the opposite side of this man and his anger. Despite the fury, he was familiar enough with these circumstances to ask to look at the phone. We noticed that the incoming call was not through the phone company but had "iPhone" underneath it. Someone just needed my phone number, which was on every missing poster, and an app that allowed them to punch in Ryan's number. All the information was turned over to the RCMP to be investigated, but we are still unsure who would have done this or why. Although Scott and I had numerous technical issues with our phones while in Sun Peaks, there was never another call like this one again.

It shook me to my core and left me in the most vulnerable state. All the fears I had managed to push away came back in such force. Where was my son? What had happened to him? Why can't we find him? What if someone harmed him in some way? Trauma like this makes any thoughtful reasoning difficult.

So many people in this community were eager to help, from donating to the meal trains, bringing snacks, water and hand warmers, to actively searching as part of our volunteers or taking purposeful walks. The offers of help were continuous. Employees pooled tips to help pay for dinners, businesses offered discounts and free services, and hotels gave reduced rates to those searching. One of those generous souls was Danielle, a therapist who offered her services not only at the command centre but continued to make house calls. She was available to Ryan's friends that had come up en masse to help, to our family and friends, to the girls and to us. She was the soft gentle voice that encouraged us to talk about our grief, our anger, our loss.

Oh, how I needed her that day. As I poured my fears and frustrations out with great sobs, she held my hand. I kept asking, "What if?" She listened without interruption until I was done.

"Heather, you are creating alternative realities," she said. "When you do that, all your reactions and actions are based on untruths and maybes. Focus on the facts—what you do know. Operate from that standpoint until you know more."

She didn't mean that those theories or scenarios wouldn't make an appearance in the deep recesses of my mind; it would be foolish to suggest that one wouldn't think about every and all possibilities. It is better to be prepared but not panicked, and I felt that allowing myself to process these speculations may make it easier if they were, in fact, to come true. But to live in this world each day adhering to a set of false realities would intrinsically change the way in which I viewed the world and those in it.

I won't say it was easy, but her wisdom was my saving grace. I won't lie and say that some days I don't give in to self-pity and resounding fear. But focusing on the facts I know has become a mantra that I try to live by, and it has helped me to push aside the negativity to focus on humanity and the generous outpouring of love and support.

That phone call didn't break me. It gave me strength.

February 25, 2018

So much guilt today. It is an insidious feeling that creeps up, plagues me when I least expect it and won't let go. I am told not to feel it, but it manifests itself when I am at my lowest.

We didn't find Ryan today.

As a parent, of course I am racked with guilt. I am fairly sure that is part of what you sign up for giving birth. Please ... I know that we are doing everything humanly possible to find him. I am at peace with the search. The volunteers number in the low hundred. People are not giving up. I admire their spirit.

The guilt comes in the small laughs we have during the day. The moments of normalcy that are rare. I feel guilty for eating and sleeping. After all, Ryan is out there waiting to be found.

That sort of guilt is to be expected. Part of the parent package I signed up for. I willingly accept it.

What I struggle most with is the guilt of our friends and family. They try so hard each day. I see their faces as they come back at day's end with no trace. I see their eyes and feel this sense of helplessness. My precious friends feel guilty for not being able to find him. They want to do this for me. What a terrible choice each day going out and hoping to find Ryan but hoping not to at the same time.

They feel guilty having to return to their life like I am not externally grateful for them being here in the first place. I see their emotions as they have to tell me bye.

No, I feel guilty that these wonderful, beautiful people suffer so greatly.

I know they must go just as I know we must stay. I can't leave until I find my son.

February 25, 2018

They tell you to cherish every moment with your children because this time, too, shall pass. I knew it logically, but I never thought the years would pass so quickly. I thought I would have all the time in the world. I was anxious for them to roll over, sit up, walk and so on. I couldn't wait for the next stage. It wasn't like I hated the one we were at, I just wanted to see what they would do next.

No one would be surprised that Ryan's a mama's boy. Oh, he adores his father. They hunt and fish and do sports together. They are so close, but Ryan and I had this ease between us.

Every Sunday night we had this ritual where we would lie in my bed and read. Him with his Captain Underpants books and me with my many series. In between chapters he would catch me up or tell me something random.

Around age 10 or 11, I remember one night. Perhaps I was feeling grateful about having this wonderful funny boy still wanting to carry on our Sunday nights together, but I turned to him and said "Ry, I am kinda sad." He immediately looked up and said, "Why, Mommy?" I replied, "Cause I know in a couple of years, you won't want to do this anymore. And that's okay, but I will miss it." He thought about it quite seriously and said, "I know, Mommy, I will miss it too."

Years pass, and although the teenage years weren't bad, his life outside the family became more important. It is a rite of passage. And although he still showed his love, it wasn't in the same open way.

I wasn't worried because I always thought we would come full circle again. That our relationship would transition from parent/child to that of adults.

I miss him tremendously.

February 26, 2018

We are more than this tragedy.

Scott and I married 23 years ago. Two years later came Ryan weighing in at 5 lbs 15 oz. So tiny, he fit in our hands. Truth be told, I thought our cat looked cuter. We were the first of friends to have children so Ryan was carted along everywhere we went. We waited 3 years before we decided to have another child. I couldn't imagine being able to love someone as much as I loved him. Of course, now I know that love is infinite and the more you share the more you have to give. And so, into our lives came the most beautiful girl, Jordyn. Precious and perfect. We thought life was complete.

And we were happy. And we grew.

Little did we know that our family was supposed to include our youngest. Sweet and funny, wild and lovely. Those are what words describe Julianna who came 8 years after our first.

I tell you this because the focus is on Ryan, as it should be. He is forever in the forefront of our minds. For this small while, we will pour all of our love and blessings into him to carry him through.

But I never forget my other babies. The smiles and look of love in their eyes shine exactly like their older brother's.

And I remember.

Once we were all together.

February 27, 2018

We are going on 10 days of searching, and the number of my angels looking over us continue to grow. From searchers on the ground to angels delivering food to everyone else who feeds our spirits. I am not sure we will ever be able to express even a fraction of our gratitude.

I want to tell you some of my thoughts:

I love the volunteers that show up every day. And when people ask if they can come up ... I want to hug you all and say yes. The reality of what we could be in for probably hit us Saturday night. The amazing Search and Rescue team again saturated this area with over 100 registered volunteers that included their specialized searchers. With no sign of Ryan, we were told that they would not be engaged until one of two things happened: a tip that may change the location, or an environmental change. I can't control the weather (believe me, working at the airport has convinced me of that), but I can try to influence the tips. Hence the reason why we created the Crime Stoppers page. We wanted somewhere for people to be able to anonymously leave tips if there were any.

However, that brought the point home ... if Search and Rescue have spent two days up here blitzing the area and found nothing, where do we go to from here? And then the thought loomed largely in our heads ... this might take longer than we imagined.

We do need volunteers, but now we need to be strategic. How awful is that?

Our friends are creating a list to spread their time out here as they must go home at some point as well. They want to ensure we have people here looking for Ryan as long as we are.

Does that mean you can't come now? No. If you have planned it or taken the time to arrange it, please know we are grateful that you want to help. We won't turn you away.

And if you were thinking of coming and another week works better, then we welcome you then if we are still here.

The last thing I want to mention is kinda hard to write. You have been so generous sending me information regarding mediums and psychics. Do I believe? Yes, I absolutely do. I have two amazing women that are helping and have been reaching out to Ryan since the beginning. And several more that are keeping in touch. And I am grateful.

I want him found. I am desperate for it. But you must know it is hard to go through that every day. The hardest part is that this is not an exact science. Interpretation plays a huge part. The information that streams in tends to come in generalities. If someone feels they have more concrete impressions, then please feel free to pass that on. But as hard as it is to feel Ryan is in your reach, I cannot in my present state continue to contact everyone you send me.

That is hard to say. I never want to sound ungrateful, so I hope you will understand a little of what we have to cope with day by day.

I thank you all.

February 28, 2018

I don't know how I got here.

When did I become the mother of a missing child.? How does that even happen?

There are no guarantees in life. I know that. You know that. I just never thought something like this would happen to me.

Oh, I was never naïve in thinking that tragedies couldn't occur. But I thought it would happen to someone else.

I thought I was exempt.

Now I find myself in this in between place where fear takes hold and never-ending grief is my constant companion.

"You are so strong," say the others.

I am because I am a mother forged of steel and fire. I need to be to withstand these winds that threaten to blow me over.

I won't break because my son needs to be found and brought home to me.

Only then can I fall to my knees and weep.

February 28, 2018

So, I am the mother of this one. Imagine a six-foot-tall young man dressed in tiny black bike shorts, a black crop top, whiskers adorning his face and cat ears perched on his head.

And then, I want you to imagine me coming down the stairs on Halloween morning to this pretty picture.

"So, do you think you can drive me to school?"

My blank face must have prompted the need for more explanation.

"'Cause I can't walk in this."

"No, I don't suppose you can. Nice outfit. Makes you look lean."

"Yah, I got this from Gaby. Can't believe it fits."

So that morning I dropped a sexy kitty and a cute teenage mutant ninja turtle off to school and waited for the phone call that would propel me to pick up my son for inappropriate attire.

To this day, I am utterly shocked I didn't receive one.

I want to say that this was an anomaly. But he does have a skewed sense of humour. Quick witted with a wee bit of sarcasm. Perhaps the apple doesn't fall too far from the tree.

Today, as worried and as sad as I am, I spent much of the day remembering this funny, irreverent kid. And I smile. Even if it is for a little while.

Sleep, my friends, for tomorrow brings renewed hope that we will find Ryan.

March 1, 2018

The snow is falling. Beautiful and pristine. I have never hated anything more. The snow is not my friend.

It falls and falls, making it difficult to search. Places we have been look like no one has been there. Footprints are covered.

Why can't we find him? The snow ensures success is based on luck and prayers.

I want sun and warmth. I want to remember the holidays we took as a family. The trips to places like Disney World, Hawaii and the Caribbean. Our yearly family vacations to Nana and Papa in Florida or summertime in the Okanagan.

I want to remember the weekends at our lake. Boat trips, campfires and building forts.

Every time I remember, I feel the warmth on my skin.

After this cold, will I ever get warm again?

\*     \*     \*

There are a lot of logistics and organization that go into circumstances such as ours. Command centres, supplies, equipment and mustering volunteers. Our search was made more difficult with the distance from our hometown and the community where Ryan went missing. It wasn't practical to regularly travel the nine and a half hours to regroup, recharge and reorganize, so a GoFundMe account allowed people—friends and complete strangers—to donate and keep us in Sun Peaks. How humbling. Every day that we stayed for those four and a half months was a blessing and a comfort.

Still, staying in a hotel room was becoming impractical. Our family and friends were continuing to come and stay with us. Our daughters were desperate to see us. We needed space to unwind after the long, tiring days and be able to do the simple tasks of cooking a meal, but it was impossible in a one-bedroom hotel room.

Some days, I was amazed at how the municipality of Sun Peaks came together for us and for Ryan. In our lowest moments, Sun Peaks looked for ways to alleviate our pain and reached out with amazing generosity. There were offers of beds, rooms, hotels and condos. In the height of ski season, if there was a bed free, it was ours to house search volunteers. One of the houses offered became ours on March 1 for the duration of our stay. A couple that managed it in off seasons reached out to the owners in Australia with the suggestion to allow us to rent. It was so incredibly generous and, having met both couples, unsurprising. The house itself was beautiful, with stunning views of the ski hill and floor-to-ceiling windows. It was an easy walk to the village each morning and could accommodate twelve people in the four bedrooms plus loft. It felt like home the moment we walked in. In this house we learned to breathe again, surrounded by friends and family. And while tears flowed often, there were joyful moments too. We were never alone, and that, I believe, was the reason we got through each day. The house was healing, filled with people who loved us and Ryan.

In the weeks and months to come, there would be a spotlight shone upon this community by a small but vocal group of overzealous people and with it negativity about who they were as a community and the type of people that made up their neighbourhood. I am fiercely protective of this community. They continued to open their arms wide to embrace us as a family and remained supportive in our efforts. I felt safe and loved there, and we have made everlasting friendships.

It was easy to settle into a routine. Each morning while Scott showered and readied himself for the long day ahead, I would sit in my bed and watch the snow fall as the flakes swirled and landed on the enormous trees that rose up from the ground to meet the grey sky. I was always greeted by birds that flapped their wings as if to say good morning. The steady sounds of activity in the bedrooms and kitchen below could be heard with a tinkling of laughter every once in a while. It was peaceful. A beautiful respite before another busy day. Downstairs, the aroma of coffee permeated the air as everyone staying with us gathered for breakfast.

Scott would take the truck and head to the areas he designated for searching, and I would walk the snowy paths to the command centre. That was my quiet time with Ryan. Conversations filled with regret and apologies that, if the chattering of woodland creatures that would startle me were any indication, was my son saying I shouldn't feel guilty. I reminisced about the best memories of our lives and spoke about an unconditional love that would see us through. In those early morning walks, I felt the energy of my son infuse the most tired parts of my soul and prepare me for the day ahead.

The command centre was a bustling, busy place. We would have three of them through our stay in Sun Peaks. The first was the Sun Peaks Grand Hotel and Conference Centre. Then we moved to The Hearthstone Lodge, where the delicious aromas of pizza from Mountain High Pizza or fries from Chez Joe Poutine filled the air, making it near impossible to concentrate. Our last command centre was perfect for the longest stay. We were situated at the old Ski Patrol in the parking lot of P2, right next to the high school portable. It was easy to store the big equipment, like bobcats and diggers and searching poles. Being right in the heart of the village, it was convenient to find and allowed for parking and signage, all generously donated by the hotels or the municipality. The command centres opened at 8 a.m., and people would stop in to ask questions, get maps and posters and meet up with searching groups throughout the day. It was well-organized chaos that continued on until the day grew long and the sun began to set.

I would wait until Scott finished his search for the day, and then we headed home. And it was home to me, a place to cast off our perceived failings, gather with those we loved and fill the empty space with laughter. A fireplace stood in the living room and centred the area with warmth and a beauteous glow. I would cozy up on the couch, my favourite spot that overlooked a backyard filled with spruce trees and snowy hills. A blanket to cover my legs and a glass of amaretto by my side, I would take the passions and thoughts of the day to write a post on Ryan's page. Staring at the darkening sky as the snow fell gently down, memories would dance in my head and words would magically find their way onto paper.

The season would soon begin to change, the day staying longer, the snow slowly starting to give way to gentle buds of green shoots, the white mountains casting off their winter coats with the warmer weather. It was so gradual that one might not notice that spring was on her way, despite the continual changes. I held an expectant breath in the hopes that soon we would find our son and leave this home behind.

March 2, 2018

I am not the same person I was 2 weeks ago.

I suppose that shouldn't come as a surprise to anyone.

I read the comments about my ability as a mom. "You are great. "You are amazing."

Wow that means so much. But to be honest, I am just like everyone else. Some good days and some bad.

I mean, I remember Ryan as a baby. I was not an early riser. Scott would bring Ryan downstairs and let him play while he got ready to work. He would bring him back up and put him beside me in bed. While I slept, Ryan watched the BBC version of Teletubbies. I realized it was a problem when he started speaking with an English accent.

"Mommy, where is Po's Scootaah?"

Fast forward a couple of years ...

Scott and I watched with amusement as Ryan unknowingly ate the penne pasta off Jordyn's plate that she had sucked the sauce off. Oh, I suppose we could have stopped it, but it was really funny.

Then came the high school years. My discipline strategy of counting 1-2-3 to get my son's attention seemed startlingly ineffective, so I had to be clever. *Hmmmmm ... okay my son.*

"So, Ryan, I won't speak to you again," I would say.

His eyebrow raised like, "And what will you do?"

"Love bug, I want you to imagine me coming to the high school. I'm thinking short shorts, bra optional. I am going to come up to you while you are surrounded by friends and I am going to say in my best mom voice, 'Honey, I thought about what you said and I promise you it will grow.'

His face paled. "You wouldn't dare."

"Try me."

My life was peaceful once we established my alpha female role.

I tell you this because, who is perfect? I try my best, I make mistakes. Some days I feel like Mother of the Year. Others I wish I was more present.

But what I know with absolute certainty is the ferocity with which I love. You are mine. I bore you.

I will never give up on you.

March 3, 2018

I am seeing angels everywhere.

No that doesn't mean I have lost hope. It just means that during the lowest moment in my life, I am still able to appreciate the blessings that surround me.

I see all of you. You have lifted me up and made me strong. The steps I take now are because of you.

I see my son. I see his heart, and I see his ability to bring so many people together.

He is my angel.

I look for Ryan everywhere.

March 4, 2018

It is day 16 since Ryan was last seen. Some of you have been here from the beginning, and some will join day by day. I am surprised each and every day by the threads posted and the willingness people have to want to help.

I write each day for two reasons:

1) I want Ryan to be real to you. He is more than the sum of the events that have led us to where we are now. He is loved and has value.
2) I need you to believe.

I recognize that as the days pass, it is natural—and it is even practical—for people to wonder why we can't find him. Maybe he isn't there.

I am a mother, fierce and strong as they come. I will fight and claw and protect.

Do you think I want the end result to be Ryan out in the elements waiting to be found? You have to know that if that is the case, then there is very little hope.

Do you realize how torturous it is each night to watch the faces of the searchers come back and have had found nothing? Or knowing that another night is passing and your baby is out there?

And yet every night is the same; like a nightmarish Groundhog Day.

And today I will do it again.

Because I believe Ryan is here in this community.

The terrain is treacherous and steep. The snow is deep. There are massive snowbanks and ravines. There are tree wells and snowdrifts. We have touched every inch but without the necessary skills or training, how effective can we be?

Scott gets up early every morning, puts on his snow gear and heads out to dig and walk and now excavate. He is so hard on himself because he is the father—How could he not find him? He takes few breaks.

But he believes Ryan is here.

We are realists. We have talked and discussed and hoped and prayed.

We want different results.

But we believe Ryan is here.

I need you to believe it as well. Because your belief and the determination of our friends and volunteers will help us find Ryan.

March 5, 2018

Ryan has always been a sport enthusiast. From soccer to football to rugby to snowboarding, he loved and excelled at them all.

Except skating.

I tried. Scott loved skating and played hockey. It seemed a natural thing.

But that is not my son's way.

When he was 3, my friend Sherry and I put Ryan S. and Ryan G. in CanSkate. Perhaps the worst 45 mins of my life as a young mother. He cried and moaned and laid on the ice. He was so embarrassing.

*Fine*, I thought. *We just need to find something our baby boy wants to try.* (Yes, I know. Sometimes I look back and roll my eyes at my own self.) He loved soccer, and so that is the path we took. Not that I was opposed to it. Soccer is my sport, and I loved watching him play. Scott, despite never playing lots, learned and coached him. I knew Ryan loved it because the very first game he played, during warm up, a ball hit his face and he experienced the worse nose bleed. He cried but played with blood-stained cheeks.

There I sat on the sidelines cheering him on and screaming, "Oh you are so cute Ryan!"

Eventually he expanded his sport repertoire.

High school was good. He played his soccer but he also tried football. Despite broken wrists and an ankle, he played with his heart and won. I became the football mom yelling in the stands as he scored his touchdowns, "Ryan, you are so cute!"

I may suggest that he couldn't really hear me with the helmet on because I was allowed to come to the games.

His latest adventure was his love of rugby. He made great friends, played the game and was fast. I asked if I was allowed to come, and he responded with "Sure. You know, like not a lot of moms come to the games."

"Oh, that's too bad for them," I naïvely said.

"Well, like it's over 21 you know. So, like some of these guys are like Dad's age."

You would think that would be a deterrent. But nope. On the sidelines, I came when I could. I bit my tongue and silently cheered, "You are so cute, Ryan!"

Well, mostly silent.

I enjoyed being part of all these moments.

Until recently when my beautiful, darling baby boy approached me with his biggest parental complaint: "I really wish you put me in hockey."

March 6, 2018

Christmas has always been my most favourite holiday. I love the coming together of family and friends. I love the busyness of shopping, baking and wrapping. I love the way the snow blankets the world as we sit by the fire watching our favourite movies.

But most of all, I love the traditions we have created.

Each year, we headed to Edmonton's Festival of Trees. The kids would make crafts, write to Santa and pick their favourite trees. Afterwards, we would head to The Old Spaghetti Factory.

Every Christmas Eve, Santa would make an appearance between stops to deliver a present to be opened that night. We watched *Christmas Vacation* and *The Christmas Story*. I wondered how many times Scott and Ryan could laugh like it was new.

On Christmas morning, the kids would walk downstairs to piles of presents under the tree that was bare the night before.

These memories make me happy. They fortify me in these dark moments.

This year was different. Ryan was here in Sun Peaks. We were lucky to do the Festival of Trees, but Christmas was so uncertain. We weren't sure he would get time off.

I worried that he would be sad and lonely. He would miss the traditions that were the fabric of our family.

The month of December passed quickly, and we became aware that Ryan wouldn't be home. This would be the first holiday without all of us together.

I FaceTimed him Christmas morning.

"Merry Christmas, love bug. What are you doing today?"

He smiled that smile that every mother remembers from the moment they laid eyes on their precious child. A look of contentment.

"Merry Christmas, Mom. I'm going boarding today. We are doing a Chinese gift exchange and then my mates and I are cooking a big meal."

"So you are okay? "I asked.

"Yes, I am having fun."

I confess I cried. Partly because I missed him terribly but mostly because I knew he would be okay. He wouldn't be alone.

He has always been surrounded by love.

March 6, 2018

You know, I love my children, but it was always important for people to like them. That meant manners and respect and kindness to others.

My children are perfectly imperfect.

I am proud of them.

As wonderful as Ryan could be, he could also be reserved, rude and sarcastic, especially to his sisters.

I suppose that isn't surprising. I always thought time and life experiences would shape our children into people who would contribute to their community in a positive way. I thought I was their teacher.

I thought I knew so much … until today.

This is what Julianna, our 12-year-old back at home, wrote today about her brother:

"As most of you know already, my brother has gone missing. My brother was almost always mean and annoying but some rare times he would do something nice. I can say that one of my favourite memories was the night before Ryan left to do his own thing without the family. We did the Festival of Trees together as a little family. Almost every year Ryan would be all mopey and wouldn't do all the stuff with me and Jordyn until this year—his last time doing it with us. This year was different. His mood changed. Maybe because it was the last year, but it was nice. I think that was one of my favourite memories because it was the last time I saw him other than saying goodbye before his big adventure. I miss him, and I hope we can bring him home safely."

Maybe it is me that still has so many lessons to learn from them.

March 7, 2018

They say the definition of insanity is doing the same thing over again and expecting different results.

And maybe that is what we are: insane.

Day after day. Twenty painful, tortuous days we wake up hopeful of the new day. Will this be the day we find him? Will I finally be able to see my son and speak his name and look upon him? Will I finally be able to give into grief or will I be overjoyed with hope?

And night after 20 painful, tortuous nights, I lie awake incredibly aware that we haven't located him. Did we do enough? Did we somehow miss him? After three long weeks, does someone have knowledge that places him somewhere else?

And in between the morning and the night is the waiting and the planning and the second guesses.

I don't know if what we are doing is right ... but I don't know how to do it any other way.

The dogs did not find my son today.

And now I have to uncurl myself from this dark, dark place and find the strength to do this again tomorrow.

Insane.

\*   \*   \*

The dogs came March 7. After much discussion and preparation, the Canadian Search and Disaster Dog Association (CASDDA) travelled from Alberta to conduct a two-day search. I thought they would be my saviour. I had been impatiently waiting for them for so long. I had put all my hopes on them to find Ryan.

With high expectations, we went through the mapped areas we had tentatively set as good starting points.

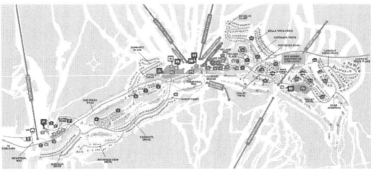

It was an all-female crew, and the sight of them gave me an unexpected comfort. Surely, they could relate to my pain, a mother's desperation to find her son. Silly, I suppose. These search and rescue volunteers joined because they feel a need to help. They were compassionate to the core, no matter their gender.

As they gathered their equipment and readied the dogs, I felt hope swell in my breast for the first time in weeks. Their case manager had assured us in previous conversations that if Ryan was there, they were 90 percent sure that they would find him.

Can you imagine? I believed it. It was such a welcome thought to believe that by the end of their two days, I would know where my son was. We would finally have some closure and could perhaps move on to the next chapter in this journey.

There was nothing to do for the first day, as the searchers had requested that we refrain from sending volunteers out. They feared that more boots on the ground would interfere with the dogs and their work. For the first time since February 19, we were on our own, left to our devices. We had a day off.

I had arranged for Scott, Julianna and some of our friends to go snowboarding for the day. After twenty days of constant searching, devastating setbacks and a growing weariness, I wanted them to have a break. To do something light and fun. I should have known; Scott couldn't step away from the search area for long. The need to find Ryan and bring him home, so deeply entrenched in every fibre, led him to offer assistance to CASDDA. The terrain being much more difficult to traverse than they had anticipated, so Scott's offer of help was greatly appreciated.

I sat quietly with some friends at the house, anxiously waiting for some word. It felt the same as Sunday, February 18, and the stuffy room in the makeshift command centre. Except this time my hope wasn't for rescue, it was for recovery. For finite, concrete closure so that we could continue on with the next stage of this lifelong journey.

The day waned on with no word other than a few texts from Scott outlining their progress. I waited. The butterflies in my stomach fluttered uncontrollably. My brain had trouble tracking and responding to the simplest questions.

Around 6 p.m., darkness had descended and the search had ended for the day. Scott came to pick up me, Lyette and her husband, Denis, for a briefing. There are moments in everyone's life that we feel like we excel beyond our wildest expectations, and there are moments of disappointing behaviour that will haunt us for years to come. This was one of mine.

The people at the fire station had graciously allowed the CASDDA team to operate as a home base from there. We stored water and snacks for the team to stock up on and delivered lunch so they could carry on the search with few interruptions. It was here between the giant fire trucks that we held our meeting.

Their manager unrolled a heavily marked map that highlighted the search areas with different colours. It was evident that they had covered a lot of ground. She meticulously went over the day and the reports from each dog handling team. They had searched all the areas that seemed significant, hoping to find some trace, some scent of our son, but they were unsuccessful. Her quiet voice was full of confidence as I strained to hear the actual words because it was important for me to listen, reflect and process what she was saying.

Certainly not at all times—I am a parent, after all, and we tend to pick and choose words that align with the battles we wish to fight. But on this day, I wanted to hear it all.

My husband has many excellent qualities, and putting up with me is his best. However, his one flaw might just be that he has a tendency to interrupt. Not always, but when he does, it is not between breaths but while they are speaking and usually it is a parallel question that throws them off their original train of thought. Not a deadly failing to be sure. Not even a particularly annoying one. But this day, my frazzled nerves, my exhaustion and hearing my hopes of Ryan's recovery dashed forced me to be sharp. In front of them all, I chastised Scott for interrupting. OK, that might be a generous description of the harsh words I said to the man that had been out each day searching for his first born; a man who never complained and who propped me up on the days that I struggled. But words spoken, however regretful, are impossible to take back.

He said nothing but did not ask another question. A father should feel enabled and supported as he processes his own grief journey. I took that away. The debriefing also revealed that an accounting that was reported to the RCMP may be incorrect, and the person involved may be lying. It was a conversation in which a person living on Burfield said that two young men had mistakenly, most likely drunkenly, entered their house. They had told police that it did not match the description of Ryan but then told a CASDDA supervisor that they believe it could have been. (This later turned out to be proven false.) Another blow to my already fragile self.

The car ride back to the house was quiet, only livening slightly when we picked up my brother Kevin and sister-in-law, Donna from their rental. Having travelled from Edinburg, Scotland, largely due to the generosity of WestJet, they would spend their days searching and their nights at our house to regroup and connect. I walked into the house to the rare sounds of supper being made, glasses tinkling and low conversations sprinkled with laughter. Noises I couldn't bear. Looking into the faces of our friends and family and pretending that I wasn't monstrous was unimaginable. That I had treated Scott so terribly was a heavy weight that I could not get out from under.

There were many nights that tears found me. Soft waterfalls of sentiment. A life lived. A life lost. Memories fell down my cheeks to remind me of what had changed. The tears that night were filled with hot shame, tightening my throat and allowing the floodgate of sorrow to escape. My shoulders shuddering, I curled my body onto the bed and sobbed endlessly. It wasn't just the interaction between Scott and me. All marriages have failings and recoveries—it was to be expected. But the culmination of the entire day was like the cracking of a dam. The natural movements that begin so innocently, so innocuously, but in reality, cause breaks in barriers so carefully constructed. Catastrophic. Every alternative reality that I had imagined, or someone had suggested to me, came rushing forward.

Ryan should have been found.

This should be over.

We should be at home mourning our son. Instead, we are on this mountain, so far from our life.

What if he is not here?

What if someone harmed him?

Over and over, the agony of those last moments reared its ugly head. my chest heaving as I imagined how he felt. Was he scared? Was he hurt? Did he call out to me as he took his last breath? Torturous thoughts and a harrowing, unproven truth that prevailed upon me as the night wore on. Scott brought me water and rubbed my back as I stared blankly at the window to the outside and cried. There was only love and compassion in his eyes, which shamed me further. His forgiveness was my undoing.

In the darkest hours and my lowest points, if I look closely enough, there are always signs of rebirth. Not everything is meant to be destructive; some things are designed to be built anew. Dawn peaked through the blinds and shone its golden light. The tears long spent left me tired, but they washed away and left resolve in their wake. Scott stirred beside me and wrapped his arms around my waist as he whispered, "I love you." I looked in his eyes and told him how sorry I was. He smiled softly, kissed my lips and said, "I know. You love Ryan as much as I do. It's okay."

"But you didn't get to ask your question," I replied.

"Babe, they are here for another day and a half. I will ask today."

So simple.

We never spoke of it again. In truth, Scott probably doesn't remember it quite as vividly as I do. His ability to forgive, forget and move on just might be another of those qualities that make him irreplaceable. I accept that my anger and frustration was misplaced. Setting myself up for an outcome that was not guaranteed forced me into a defensive corner instead of managing my expectations. I am human. Today is another day.

# Living Amongst the Shadows of Memories

March 8, 2018

I understand that people want to know what is going on. I understand that.

I also know everyone, including myself, wants these search dogs to be miracles. And maybe they will be. But what I have discovered is that they will find what they are looking for if what they are looking for is in the areas they are searching. This area is vast. There are too many places here to search and they only have 3 days to search.

I do pray that today is the day we find him. Or tomorrow is the day, and agonizingly so on and so on. Each day can bring such hope, and each night, disappointment.

I do promise that I will post. You will know.

You have decided to travel on this journey with us. It is not an easy journey. At the end is not necessarily a happily ever after.

But there is a limit to how much I can do. Please recognize that. I cannot always give you what you need. You want answers. Scott and I desperately want answers. But we have come to the stark realization that even when we find Ryan, we may never find the answers that will soothe or comfort us.

And that will have to be enough for all of us.

All I can do is continue on with what I know, and what does provide me some comfort ... my stories about Ryan.

March 9, 2018

I wrote this once:

Our lives are made up of a series of moments. If you are lucky, you will have hundreds, even thousands, of them. There will be small moments. Mundane ones that you won't recognize is a moment until you are in it. There will be big moments. Life changing ones. Those moments that make you re-evaluate all that came before and all that will come after. Each moment is precious. Hold its value, for it will not come again.

That is the thing about memories: precious to have and sometimes hard to remember.

I am trying so hard to capture all my memories of Ryan and scared I will miss one.

Last night we went as a family on a sleigh ride. As much as our focus is on finding Ryan, we want to make sure our beautiful, strong and amazing daughters also have good memories in the days to come. Let it not just be tragedy.

It was hard. Oh, I am sure that Ryan probably would have rolled his eyes and asked why.

"Why do we have to do that? Why do I have to come?"

I also know that as he moved on in his life, our family memories would have changed. They would not happen so frequently.

I just thought I would have more time.

Because I tell you right now, I would remember every little second of it.

Today, the dogs finished, but Scott and I will not give up. We begin again tomorrow.

March 10, 2018

We are on our own again today.

Our fantastic CASDDA volunteers left after searching a bit this morning. Their leader apologized for not finding him. I thanked her for all their efforts.

"You might want to consider going home."

I appreciate the sentiment. Makes a lot of sense, really. They are trained and found nothing. Nothing in the areas they searched. Not every area here in Sun Peaks.

I am sure there are a lot of people that may echo those very thoughts.

I am tired and Scott is tired and my volunteers are tired.

But I believe.

We bore this child; we watched him grow, and we love him evermore. He deserves to have an advocate. He deserves to have us look until we are 100 percent sure he is not here. And then search this earth for him if we have to.

And even when we might falter, I look around and see our friends and family believe. We see the volunteers that drive from Alberta and Kelowna believe. We hear our new friends here tell us to hold fast.

So, while I appreciate the sentiment, I believe, and so I shall stay.

March 11, 2018

Saturday, February 17th, our tragedy began.

Sunday, February 18th, the earnest search for Ryan began.

But it is Monday, February 19th, that I want to tell you about.

Kamloops Search and Rescue volunteers spent almost 14 hours Sunday searching for any sign of Ryan. They were amazing on both occasions that they spent looking for my son. I am at peace with their efforts. Their manager that dealt primarily with me is a great man, and I felt his heartache when he told me they hadn't found him.

This post isn't about him or them.

This is about the quiet and solitude that Scott and I experienced on Monday. Five of our friends ignored our concerns and drove throughout the day to come to our assistance. Many more arrived on Monday and Tuesday.

But it was with these 5 that Scott and I went to the original command centre to see how the search for Ryan would proceed.

There was no one there.

Does that sound shocking to you? Inconceivable even?

It was with these 5 that Scott went searching for our son. That was the first time that it became clear that finding Ryan would be our priority and no one else's.

We weren't trained in search and rescue. What parent is? We were woefully ignorant about what equipment to use, how to map out or set up grids, that we would need a command centre and even how to muster volunteers.

We learned by our mistakes each painful, futile day.

We are getting smarter each day. We learned to ask: If this was your child, what resources would you want to have, need to have or pay to have?

We are so far behind the eight ball.

And that needs to change; not just for my child but for anyone that is missing. They deserve to know that everything is being done to find them. Anything less is unacceptable.

What if this was your child?

\*     \*     \*

That night in our hotel room is a moment I tend to go back to often. The room was crowded with our friends, the RCMP and the KSAR manager. The whole day was spent looking for Ryan, and we awaited news—any news.

Sitting on my hotel bed, tired, grief-stricken and sacred, I heard the RCMP constable say, "So Mr. and Mrs. Shtuka, on your way out of town, either today or the next day, please stop by the rural detachment and we can go over the next steps."

The words were tinny and far away. Unsubstantial. I do remember her saying them, but, in truth, I didn't recognize or respond to them until much later. Scott looked at her, though, and said, "We are not leaving until we find our son."

The KSAR manager, solemn and holding back tears, went over the day. I knew the odds, so hope left me as the sun went down. Already slim now became impossible.

He said, "We have completed all the tasks that the RCMP have requested. We will not be back until the weather changes or there is a tip that will point us in a new direction."

I nodded and said, "OK, so I will see you tomorrow."

Irrational perhaps, but in my mind, I couldn't grasp the idea that we would be alone after this one day. Nothing prepares you for such a tragedy, and with so few instructions on missing people cases it seemed unfathomable that there isn't a liaison for the families still desperately searching. Logically, I can understand that these groups of volunteers can't stay on one case for its entirety. So many people have great need for them. Emotionally, I am a mother. I wanted everyone, all hands-on deck, until Ryan was found and we could bring him home.

What parent or loved one has the intuitiveness or necessary skill set to undertake such an operation? We desperately needed advice. There was none to give.

"If this were your child, what would you want to have done?" "What would you need to have done?" "What would you pay to have done?" These were questions that I asked every RCMP constable, superintendent and Search and Rescue manager that crossed our path. "And then tell me who and what they are."

Empty questions that were given no response. That disappointment still lingers. We started from square one. We were introduced to non-profits that had resources we could use. One of the people instrumental in changing the way people look at missing persons' cases was Shane Michael, founder of Wings of Mercy, a non-profit group that works with families, Search and Rescue as well as law enforcement using drone technology to help locate missing people across North America. The group started with a modest number of volunteers interested in using their equipment to help others but has quickly grown to over five thousand members. Their Facebook page and website shares posters of missing people and houses drone footage of searches for experienced eyes to look for anomalies that may provide answers.

We met Shane through Facebook Messenger. His offer of help seemed far too advanced for my brain to comprehend, so my brother, Kevin, an avid drone operator, quickly took over communication. What Shane was suggesting was unlike anything we were aware of. Of course, drones were present in the initial searches for Ryan beginning on Sunday, February 18, to cover vast amounts of terrain necessary in Search and Rescue, but as you move towards recovery, what does drone support look like?

Shane was actively involved in the case of Ashley Simpson, a thirty-two-year-old woman who went missing from Yankee Flats Road in the Shuswap in April 2016. It was assumed that she may have been carrying a pink suitcase on the day she went missing, and that suitcase became a catalyst for Shane to take his knowledge of industrial automation and robotics programming to the next level in the search for missing people. He used the pink suitcase to write a program that can identify a certain colour and sort those images captured by the drone. The program goes through the images and can include multiple ranges of colours. With the GPS coordinates attached to each image, it allows images that may match the criteria to be easily accessed and searched.

This type of programming gave Wings of Mercy the opportunity to look for Ryan in "real time," not historically. Shane used Ryan's jacket and hat as colours in the range. Seeing how this worked was absolutely awe-inspiring. The colours matching the description were sorted to the top. Most, upon closer evaluation, could easily be identified as pop cans or headlights. Some were buried in snow with only a small splash of colour. With the GPS coordinates, Scott would go to the area and clear the item.

It is a program that can be utilized anywhere a drone is possible. And it evolved. Shane has worked through the program to also allow degradation of material and colours through exposure to elements and time, which allows volunteers to assist in those historical cases.

Such a powerful resource that began with a simple pink suitcase.

We also sourced out civilian services that were willing and able to help. We arranged accommodations, food and donations for travel. There was little backlash from officials except for one—a Search and Rescue group from Alberta volunteered to come to Sun Peaks. Permission was granted through RCMP, however, we were told that Emergency Response BC declined their offer. Their reasoning was that resources from BC should be contacted first before allowing interprovincial services. Quite the conundrum, isn't it? No one with the resources or expertise would willingly give us those contacts, but the organization would balk at ones that offered their services.

I think of all the time searching only to discover how inefficient we were. We had maps of the Sun Peaks area. We had mapped out our highest priorities: where Ryan was last seen and his rental house became our number one focus. However, all areas in Sun Peaks were given a grid number. Each day, volunteers lined up to receive a map, a group leader and whatever supplies and equipment necessary. We fashioned probes out of old or discarded ski poles to go through snow eight to fourteen feet deep. Each leader was equipped with a walkie-talkie if they were venturing into a zone with limited cell coverage. These leaders could have anywhere from five to ten people that they managed. It seemed a proper way to conduct a search. At the end of the day, group leaders would drop off the maps, marked complete. We took that information and relied on it to target the areas still unsearched for the next day. The snow made it so difficult. You could walk the village after hundreds of people were combing through the banks, paths and trees and see no disturbance.

We were frustrated and at a standstill. Everything had been searched, but there really was no telling how accurate or complete it was.

Three weeks after Monday, February 19, I was out walking this path behind the golf course with Julianna, Lyette and Nancy. Locals used the steep path that had a huge decline to the frozen creek to bypass the road to get to the village. It looked untouched. I paused and wondered if this area had ever been searched. When I looked to the others, the question must have been apparent in my eyes because Nancy suggested we search. We started at one end and dug snow by hand, clearing the area down the sloped path until we almost reached the bottom. Julianna was standing at the top, and the three of us were a shoulder-width apart—for companionship as well as for safety—as we navigated the steepness. Scott had just finished his section with a large group, and soon everyone joined us. We kept the same line, on hands and knees, as we dug and dug that entire path. When we were finally done, I looked at the decimated snowbanks, and for the first time since Ryan went missing, I felt like we had accomplished something. We may not have known where Ryan was, but I could say with full confidence one place where he was not.

It changed the way we looked at searching. It was not enough to send a couple of people to several places searching the whole area at 10 percent capacity when we could all go as a group and search that 10 percent with 100 percent certainty. This was the first of many lessons we learned during the search for our son. The way in which we searched would be dependent on the location, the seasons, the terrain and the number of volunteers. We needed to adapt continually to the conditions and properly plan to make the best use of time and resources. Over the next several months we continued to refine our skills and spent hours researching techniques and fashioning specialized equipment for the heavy snowfall and changing weather conditions.

I am proud of what we have learned and what we have accomplished.

But the question remains ... should we—the families of a lost loved one—have to?

# Reflections of You

March 12, 2018

Today is about friendships and family.

I grew up with a military father and, as such, we moved around a lot. I learned to make friends with regularity. Some have endured, others were lost. We celebrated almost all holidays by ourselves in my early years. Family was our immediate, and friendships were at times transient.

Scott, on the other hand, grew up with close cousins and friends from birth. He stayed close to them throughout the years.

Until I met him and saw the value of both, I didn't realize how important relationships of this nature were.

You don't miss what you don't know.

I wanted that same connection for our children. That feeling of being part of a community and belonging somewhere.

We have lived in the same house in the same town since Ryan was 6. Our children have gone to the same schools, competed on the same teams and played in the same playgrounds with the same group of kids. We celebrated holidays with an extended family.

And when Scott and I needed friends and family to help search for Ryan ... they all came.

Our friends, Ryan's friends, Jordyn's and Julianna's. Family on both sides. All here. All searching.

Those connections we made along the way have brought us to this juncture. But then I see that the ability from my upbringing to make new connections is just as important.

We have met new friends. My angels I call them. They have become equally as important.

And I realize our friendships, old and new, will always be the blessings that will come from this tragedy. Our families will grow stronger.

We will endure.

March 13, 2018 (Scott's birthday)

Oh, my heart ... I wish that today—of all days—I could grant you your greatest wish. To find your son.

It seems extraordinarily cruel that you should still be searching for answers.

We are blessed that you are the steel that makes up the foundation of our home. I am proud that our daughters will forever know what it means to be loved by the way you love and cherish them.

Our son is the man he is because he has the best role model in front of him. The lessons he learned on what it means to be honourable comes from the man he looks up to. Steadfast, determined, gentle-hearted and loving comes from you. You had my heart on the day we met, but you kept it by being a man that will go to the ends of the earth for his family.

Love, you have moved mountains. I could ask for no more. Your son could not either.

I know that your strength will bring our son home.

I pray it is soon.

Happy Birthday.

March 14, 2018

Seasons change. Winter comes hard and fast, but as the months go by, we see the tiny buds of spring blossoming.

Our spring is coming. I see it in the sun that shines and melts the snow. I feel in the warmth on my face. I hear it as it sloshes about my feet.

I know it in my heart that spring comes. And I am grateful.

Summer has always been my favourite. I was born as a daughter to the beach and the water. Felt it in my bones.

Watching my children embrace the summer is a joy to me. Every weekend at the lake was a balm for life's challenges.

Our babies made forts in trees, rode bikes over makeshift ramps, learned to ski, wakeboard and surf.

Evenings of Mantracker and Capture the Flag, followed by fires and s'mores. I loved it all. My memories will last beyond this moment.

I realize that snow can't last forever.

All things lost will eventually be found.

March 15, 2018

I wouldn't say my parenting skills have always been so refined.

I like to use humour and sarcasm when dealing with kids whose ages span 8 years between the first and the last.

I will say I tend to be relaxed and fun … until I start to count.

I begin at one. "That is one, I am going to ask you to stop."

At 2 … my voice lowers, and in the most articulate way, I say, "That is 2 … Do you really want me to get to 3?"

We never usually do. I was proud to say that I could still stop Ryan in his tracks at my number 2 count.

Not sure if that had more to do with my parenting skills or if my number 3 was a little off the charts.

I tried to use humour to get my point across.

I hadn't realized that my sarcasm would rub off on at least 2 of my children. I suppose I should have guessed.

Ryan at age 8, sharing a hotel room with Nana and Papa. Nana complains to him that he took all the blankets and she was cold.

Deadpanned he responds, "Well you could always pull up those wrinkles and use them as a blanket."

Now please don't think he was rude. Nana and Ryan share a fun-loving relationship. They tease, but he would never hurt her feelings.

My Christmas presents are usually addressed: "To my birth giver."

He texted me one night while he was studying biology

Ryan: So wait, did you or did you not eat the placenta after my birth?

Me: What?

What is wrong with you?

Why would I do that?

Ryan: I hear it's very healthy for you though

Me: No, I did not

Ass

Hey. You drank my breast milk

Ryan: Alrighty and that's where this conversation ends.

I am glad I am not so soft or fragile. I am glad I can think of my son with humour. I am really glad that these dark days have spatters of light moments. I want to remember it all.

Sarcastic and funny ... I wouldn't want Ryan to be any other way.

But I promise that at age 21, I will stop counting to 3.

March 17, 2018 (Ryan's birthday)

Now I don't want you to get the impression that Ryan was solely a mama's boy. Sure, I am cool and funny and smart. Absolutely, I swear as much as a sailor. (In my defence, I exhale on the f\*\*k part so it feels gentler.)

But Ry loved hanging out with Dad. Hockey nights, PlayStation playing hockey nights, Scott coaching Ryan that eventually led to talking about hockey.

However, November was always the beginning of Scott and Ryan time.

Hunting season.

When Ryan was a baby, I dreaded November 1. I fondly refer to it as "The time of abandonment."

But as Ryan grew older, it was clear to see that those two enjoyed the time spent together.

Early mornings with Ryan sleeping all the way to the farm, pushing bush and listening to the usually mild-mannered Scott swear at every second word.

They sat in tree stands, ate home-made cinnamon buns and drove around country roads.

My basement and his room resembled a taxidermist's dream.

Moments are moments and memories are forever. That is what I have discovered as of late, even the moments I wasn't part of become my most precious of memories.

I think of hunting especially now, baby boy, because I want you to remember that your dad has the patience and the skill to move every inch of this snow to find you.

March 17, 2018

Well, my baby boy, you turn 21 today.

I wish you were here with me. I know you wish it as well.

We would pretend that I forced you to look at the baby photo albums. And you would come downstairs to a Happy Birthday sign, your favourite breakfast, and the first gift of the day.

I don't suppose you could guess that you were always my gift.

Last night, we looked through albums, and in almost every one you were laughing or smiling. I love that.

That means you were happy. That means you were loved. That means you knew it.

So, baby, maybe that is your gift to me today.

It is enough.

*I love you forever. I'll like you for always. As long as I'm living, my baby, you'll be.*

\*     \*     \*

I am not sure how I expected his birthday to go. Lots of tears, I imagined, but I had no idea there could be so much laughter. Hardly surprising, I suppose. Ryan had been in our lives for almost twenty-one years. A life well-lived, certainly well-loved and deserving of memories not steeped only in tragedy and loss.

I think we achieved that.

People kept coming into the command centre all day. An event for his birthday increased the number of volunteers that came to celebrate and to search for him. We were overwhelmed by all this support. I couldn't help but look around me constantly and be amazed by the impact my child had, not only on people that knew him, but on complete strangers that travelled great distances to help bring him home. A dizzying thought.

My cousin Neil and his amazing wife Debi owned a bakery in Airdrie, Alberta, and they contacted me to ask if they could design a cake for the celebration. What they created was nothing short of spectacular. Three tiers, with a dinosaur cut out on the top, pictures of a snowboarder with a mountainous backdrop, and a team jersey for The Nor'wester's rugby team, complete with their logo. The final tier consisted of hunting and fishing images. An absolutely stunning work of art. But Airdrie is another nine-hour drive to Sun Peaks, a trip that Neil undertook late at night after working all day. Another miracle to help celebrate baby boy's birthday.

After another long day of searching, friends, family and remaining searchers gathered at Masa's Restaurant, which helped organize a birthday party. I had always thought we would celebrate such a milestone in Las Vegas or Key Largo, Florida, but Ryan was quick to shoot that plan down once he was settled in Sun Peaks. This was where he wanted to spend his birthday, and, like all parents, we were determined not only to honour those wishes, even in his absence, but to do so in joy. The restaurant and bar were full. Ryan's friends came out to help celebrate. Even though our son was dearly missed, he was deeply remembered.

That night, Julianna and I went back to the house as the festivities continued with Scott staying and leading the way. If my dancing were to be an ode to childhood embarrassment, then it was Scott's telling everyone dad jokes that would be icing on the cake, if you will.

A moment of bittersweet reminiscence came upon me as I read messages from Ryan's friends back home that honoured their relationships. A party was being held in his name at The Nor'wester's Rugby Club in Edmonton. Drinks lifted and resounding cheers to the birthday boy. In our hometown, our favorite restaurant, Chartier, raised a glass and toasted Ryan.

Messages from strangers filled my feed.

> 21 years ago, you gave birth to a baby boy that changed your life forever. You raised him up to be a great man. I never had the honour of meeting the beautiful human you created, but I feel like you have introduced me to him. Your strength is inspiring, Heather. Your love is contagious. I hope that I can be half the mother you are to my 3 beautiful children. I need you to know that our family is thinking of you today as you celebrate your baby boy's birthday. We send you all our love and prayers. Keep faith that your family will get through this.

From parents of Ryan's friends:

> I'm Matthieu's Mom Cynthia from St. Denis, Saskatchewan. I'm never very good with words, but I hope you get the message I'm trying to send. We knew Ryan thru our son. Ryan was pretty special to have our son keep a long-distance friendship since 2010. From playing Xbox all day and night

marathons and from hearing my son have some of the best deep down belly laughs. I would hear this from the basement and would put a smile on my face. Their friendship was strong. The next summer he wanted to take his first plane ride to go see Ryan at 13. I was a little nervous, but after speaking with you (Heather) I was reassured and all was good. Right after Matts turned 16 on October 9th, he got his license and said right away, I'm going to visit Ryan and the guys in Beaumont for Halloween. He drove all by himself!!! My husband and myself are very thankful for Ryan!! He showed my son what a true friend is. He is a sincere and loyal friend to our son and Matts looks up to and respects Ryan. Matts was so happy that Ryan came out to the farm this past October before Ryan headed up to Sun Peaks. Ryan impacted Matthieu in a very positive way. Ryan was the older brother Matts always wanted. We know how special Ryan is, just from how Matts acts!! I'm sure you know this but, we want you to know that you and Scott raised a great young man! You gave him the family values and good morals, and he took it and grew into a great young man. The little span of times spent together and creating memories moulded my son into the great young man he is!! Ryan had a part in that, and he will be forever grateful! It breaks our hearts that you and your family are going thru this, and that this happened to Ryan. We hope some of the stories help you. We pray that you soon have answers and can hold your son again! Matts' heart breaks for Ryan, but hurts even more for you all!! Sending you lots of love and strength.

And from WestJet work colleagues:

> Heather and family. We just wanted to let you know that we celebrated Ryan today in YXE. We have cards made up with the RAK-Osaurus message on them for our team to do random acts of kindness and pass the card on to the person they RAOK. Linda, one of our OPS leads, brought her famous, only made at Christmas butter tarts for Ken as a random act of kindness today to honour Ryan and your family. We had green Slurpees and talked about being kind and passing it on, especially today on Ryan's birthday. Our hearts are with you, from our YXE WJ family to yours. Hugs to you and your family.

So many people performed random acts of kindness in Ryan's name on his birthday. There were gift cards for groceries or coffee, donating to a charity in our son's name or doing a RAK-Osaurus (Ryan's Act of Kindness). It was a way to celebrate a young man turning twenty-one. It was a way to honour his life with concrete examples of good deeds. Are all these gifts of service, words and messages extraordinary? Perhaps, but not singular. In the days and months ahead, I felt the full weight of love encircling me along with the many faces of this vast community that showed such humanity. Today, I shed happy tears. Ryan's gift to me on his twenty-first birthday was to tell me that he was loved and that he matters. It will be a reminder of an everlasting love for the rest of my days.

# The Strength Within

March 18, 2018

Yesterday was not all about grief, uncertainty or sadness. It was a beautiful day filled with hope and wonder. Love abounded.

I laughed and smiled and hugged. I am pretty sure I embarrassed Ryan with my dance moves along with all of my "mom" friends. No fears baby boy ... your friends from here witnessed it. So, I think we are cool. I came home and cried reading all the birthday wishes and random acts of kindness. And honestly, I wouldn't have it any other way.

We can't always live in the grief. Sometimes we need to smile and to find joy. We should pass the gift of love and good fortune to others when we can.

The greatest gift, though, came today when we opened the command centre. It was filled again with volunteers. The gift of kindness and engagement came through the messages we still received today.

Sometimes I think you must be tired of me.

But my heart expands because it seems you still believe.

March 19, 2018

I think we are in a constant state of forgiveness. Wanting to be forgiven, asking for forgiveness or deciding whether to forgive or not.

This past month I have struggled to forgive myself.

You don't have to be a parent to doubt the absoluteness of the love or even the time you have given to another. You just have to be human.

In the early days, I was in this dark place where I begged you, Ryan, for forgiveness. I was sorry I had cross words. I apologized for the times you asked for me to play and I didn't. I wished desperately for time to be rewound when you wanted to tell me some important story that you were so excited about. Why was I so busy?

And then a new and now dearest friend told me, "No one is perfect. You are human. If you don't judge Ryan for that night, he won't judge you."

And in that moment, I can proudly say that not one day went by in any of my children's lives that I did not say "I love you. It does not matter where you go or what you do, there will always be two people that will love you unconditionally."

I was not perfect. Tomorrow I will not be perfect. When this is all said and done, perfection will still elude me.

I can live with that.

But for me, forgiveness is the final act of love.

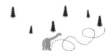

March 20, 2018

Life in abundance.

That is what I would call our state of living at this moment. A state of grace.

Each day I am reminded that I must find the blessings. I think if I couldn't then this would be just a tragedy, and I refuse to believe that Ryan's life up until now has been anything less than a beautiful blessing.

And honestly it is not that hard. I have met so many angels.

From fundraisers to words of encouragement, sharing the posts, to donating services so that I don't have to leave the hill. There is nothing that hasn't been offered.

I find it so difficult to accept. It has never been in our nature to take more than we can give. I feel awkward and uncomfortable. How can we ever repay everyone? Where does one even begin??

And then ... I read the random acts of kindness posts. You are still giving. You are still sharing your generosity in spirit and deeds. Every day you are contributing to this world in a positive way. You are loving and beautiful.

You are my blessing. And when I can, I will take all the love and do my part. I will be the continuation of what you have begun.

Ryan will never be just a tragedy. He will forever be remembered and valued.

Abundantly.

March 21, 2018

The problem with memories is that they are often one-sided. I remember the details that I believe are important; you remember the details you think are important. If we are lucky, in the remembering we can paint a whole picture.

I am now left with only my memories. I hold them tight because right now they are the only things that will not change.

But what about the memories that are made without him?

Who were you, my son, when you weren't with me? Would I find you kind, funny or a bit of a jerk? Did you make someone's heart melt or make them smile when they needed joy the most?

I find myself scouring for any memory or picture that shares more of Ryan with me. I am selfish and greedy. I am like an archeologist whose life's work is to uncover the mysteries of my first born.

You will never know the value of the memories you share about him.

For in those memories, it is still possible to know my son.

\*    \*    \*

I met so many people during my days at the command centre. I was the first person they saw as they came through the door. I signed them in and referred them to their team search leaders. I hugged them for all their contributions and thanked them with sincerity. People marvelled at my ability to stay strong, but in reality, it was all just a flimsy façade designed to keep my grief and heartbreak at bay. During the day, it seemed I represented one image. At night, I could unfold all the tightly-woven strings keeping me together and be more like myself. Two different versions and not always visible to the public. Message after message would fill my inbox with well-wishes and encouragement. Comment after comment flooded Ryan's Facebook page and offered loving support. I read them all and understood them none. Their description of me seemed unlike anyone I knew. I was not courageous nor a bastion of strength that withheld my tears. I was a heartbroken mother afraid to break down when my child needed me the most.

March 22, 2018

I am not that strong.

I read what you write, and it seems like you are talking about someone I don't know. Someone larger than life.

It's not me.

Five weeks ago, I wasn't spiritual, and I will even venture to say not particularly faithful. I believed in something, but I couldn't explain what that was. I still can't.

I desperately want to believe my son will be with me always. In flesh or in spirit. That is not unique to me.

God, when did I become someone who would take whatever meager offerings that came to me? Why am I not raging at the injustice of my plight??

Because I want to believe that I still have lessons to teach Ryan whether he is with me or not. I also believe that Ryan still has the ability to teach me to be a better mother.

Do you really want to know why I try so hard not to cry?

Because if Ryan is only with me in spirit, he will know the torment that Scott and I are going through.

Being who he is, it will grieve him so.

I am his mother. I never want to add to my children's pain.

He will understand my tears of grief when he is finally found. Until then, I will be his protector.

I will be stronger than I have ever been before.

March 23, 2018

Scott tells me today is National Dog Day.

Now I don't want to place too much importance on every holiday that passes. There will many firsts that we will have to experience. Scott's birthday, Ryan's birthday and then mine coming this week. Too many I suppose.

But Ryan would love today. He loves his puppies.

Maximilian Bartholomew Scruffy Shtuka was our very first puppy. Scott won on a lottery ticket and decided to surprise Ryan and Jordyn with a puppy. Now you will never know the value of such a gift unless you knew that my husband is allergic to most dogs.

The look on their faces will be a cherished memory.

We described Max as 75% cocker spaniel, 25% bichon and 100% handsome.

Max passed away 3 years ago suddenly and we swore that we would never get another dog. We are busy, active and selfish people. Dogs don't play into our now grown-up lifestyle. 😒

So ... a month later, Ryan did some research and was quite insistent that we needed to go "take a look" at this puppy.

Imagine: "Mom, Mom, Mom, Mother, Mother, Heather, Heather, Mom, Mommeeeeee ..."

Yep, we went to look. Honestly, at that point, I was considering sawing my own ears off to gain peace.

Let's not discuss the fact that my son was 18. If he annoyed me greatly at that age ... it will be a pretty good indication of his early years. Stubborn boy.

Off we went, and we came home with Oscar Alfonzo Bruce Shtuka.

I want to tell you his parentage but I'm afraid his mother may have stepped out during her pregnancy. He doesn't appear to be a Shih Tzu, Lhasa apso and terrier: the lineage of both parents. But we made no judgements.

So now my house is filled with dog hair and Scooby Doo barks. And Ryan loved him. If I wanted to get an immediate response from him, I just sent Oscar pictures.

So while Oscar is waiting here for Ryan's return, a part of me finds comfort in knowing that Max is waiting for my son to play catch.

\*   \*   \*

The injury that had sidelined me was beginning to heal. I was able to walk more without the hated limp, my strength building enough that I could participate in longer search periods.

I found myself with the same debilitating injury through my own stubbornness and refusal to accept my limitations. Fourteen years previously I was living what I thought was my best life. I was physically fit and happy with my outward appearance, and my children were growing, healthy and needing me a little less. This allowed me to return to soccer, a sport I love. It was such great fun playing again as an adult. After a couple of years, I tried out for several teams and settled on a team that was more competitive than the I one was currently on. Sure, they were younger, but instead of finding that daunting, I took pride that I was one of the faster players on the team. In our first game of the season, we were facing my old team, and I was determined to play with heart and soul. Do you hear my competitive spirit?

It went well until the beginning on the second half. I was last man back, and the ball was coming towards me as I ran to meet it. Suddenly, it felt like someone had taken a baseball bat to the back of my leg. I wildly looked around to see who attacked me as I fell to the ground, but no one was around. I'm told you could hear the pop in the stands. I knew it was serious.

My friend helped me limp to her car where she drove me thirty-five minutes to the nearest hospital. I must have been in a great state of shock to get through what was the worst physical pain I've ever experienced. I then took an ambulance ride to another hospital where surgery repaired my torn Achilles tendon. The doctor said it was a complete rupture. It was several days until I could manage the pain and they could release me.

It took almost eight weeks of healing, including an infection that had me at the hospital twice a day for weeks to receive antibiotics. My full strength didn't come back for almost a year. So, I knew the cause, the effect and the struggle to regain my mobility.

And yet, here I am in Sun Peaks years later with the same injury on the other leg. How you ask? Apparently, I am stubborn, forget easily and hate beyond reason when someone suggests I can't do something.

In August of 2017, I was running every day. I felt strong and capable. It was most certainly a lie, one that I was not entirely aware of. The flimsy tendon was waiting patiently for just the right moment to break in its entirety.

"So, I am joining a soccer league in October," I told Scott with a confidence that I find cringy now.

The look of disbelief on his face gave me pause.

"Do you really think that is wise?" he asked.

Even though I furrowed my brow, he was brave enough to continue.

"You know that your Achilles are both weak. And with your age, you will be prone to injury."

I was indignant. It was like a bullfighter waving his red flag, and I foolishly rushed towards my doom.

"First of all, that is not true. And it's rude. Secondly, I am not playing competitively. It is a fun league." I may have ended with, "You don't own me ... you don't know what you are talking about." That part is blurry to me.

As I played last man back at the beginning of the second half—at the exact same soccer centre!—I had the eeriest sense of déjà vu. Actually, it was me falling again as I clutched the opposite leg. This time it was Nancy that carried me off the floor and had the unenviable task of calling Scott to tell him what I had done. To his everlasting credit, my darling husband never said, "I told you so." However, the screeches in the background from my mother gave me insight of the potential eye rolling that must have been occurring. This time we eliminated the car ride and called for an ambulance instead.

So I now have scars on the back of both legs, and I was struggling to get my strength back as we continued to search. I had religiously seen a physiotherapist in Beaumont, so Lyette, in her infinite wisdom, arranged for me to see someone in Sun Peaks to continue with my rehab. I will credit her for doing something I couldn't even imagine organizing, let alone really wanting to participate in.

"You need to get stronger so that you can go out searching," she said.

Those were the magic words that motivated me into anything. I flatly refused to leave Sun Peaks, so any help would have to come from within the community. Luckily, my physiotherapist's office was right next door, so there could be no argument. I walked into the medical centre for my first appointment and was introduced to Kim, my physiotherapist. We went through the initial assessment, an explanation of my injury, my progress so far and the challenges I was finding with recovery. All very normal. She said she knew why I was in Sun Peaks and was incredibly empathetic, which is something I came to expect from this small and lovely community. She told me what treatments she could offer, and she added that she was intuitive. *Of course, you are*, I thought dryly. *Everyone in this community seems to be spiritually tied to this mountain.* While most might assume that a ski resort would draw a certain type of adventure seeker, Sun Peaks seems to attract an equal amount of laid-back, perceptive and instinctive personalities intent on discovering their connection to themselves and their environment.

I was never a spiritual person, but these last couple of weeks had made me feel very exposed. The moment Ryan went missing, I was bombarded with suggestions and offers from mediums or intuitive people from across Canada. It left me so confused. I was willing to do anything to find my son, but these intuitive experiences and offers of spiritual readings were so new to me, and I was not sure how to navigate uncharted waters. Who do you believe? Could this be real? Were my natural tendencies allowing for me to embrace something completely on faith? I have always been tied to results: You perform an action and see a negative or positive outcome. From that basis, you adapt and adjust so that you change the outcome going forward. Intuitiveness is understanding or knowing what cannot be proven. I suppose a fair argument would say we do that with many forms of religion, but I have long struggled with faith. How can you align yourself with one community if you see the beauty and rightness in others? A theologist I am most certainly not. And until then, that distinction did not play a huge part in my everyday life. But now I found myself confronted with all the things I did not know. I wanted to feel hope, grace, peace and mercy, but I was at a loss on just how to get there.

I looked at Kim with hesitation because my stock responses would not help me. She smiled and nodded to the table to begin my treatment. She was a professional foremost, never intruding. We talked about family and life, and the session progressed in routine fashion, though I was waiting for her to say more. What I came to realize is that, for most people, intuitiveness is a statement like, "Hi, my name is Heather. I like to read, enjoy wine and love the colour blue." It is a part of who we are, how we define ourselves. When telling our truths, we don't normally expect others to respond with, "Blue? Weird, tell me more about your fascination with that." It just is. Kim is a mother, wife, physiotherapist and intuitive.

I was curious. I told her about my experiences with the search for Ryan, some validating and new for me and some so painful that my heart broke just reliving the invasions. She nodded understandingly and sympathetically. She did not offer an opinion on Ryan. I felt comforted in her presence. There was a gentleness that prevailed in her spirit that I was drawn to. When I left my appointment, I felt like the progress I had made was more than some stretches to help my Achilles.

I continued to see her for the next several weeks, and my leg was getting stronger after each session. Walking was easier, and I could search longer. One day, she mentioned she did reiki as well. Of course, I had no idea what that is—some sort of massage technique? Sounded heavenly to me. Her office was pristine, the floors immaculate as I lay down on my stomach to have my physiotherapy first. Without anything to distract me, how the room looked was the first thing I noticed as we went through the treatment process.

Finally, she began the reiki treatment. For those who don't know (like me), reiki is a Japanese form of alternative healing, in this case energy healing. Most practitioners use palm healing or hands on healing to promote emotional or physical healing. So, not a massage. Most times, I was not even aware of being touched. I found myself lying face up, eyes closed. My thoughts were as scattered as the wind—swirling around and not quite landing. *How many people would be at supper that evening?* I wondered. Our house was always full, some leaving each day, more coming each night. We never quite knew, but we never turned anyone away. I thought about lunch. I thought about where we were searching. I thought about the girls. All these thoughts. I was not really relaxed.

And then I felt a light touch on the inner part of my forearm and also my hand. Suddenly my mind was still. I could hear my son. Not his voice. It was mine, but I knew without a doubt that it was Ryan.

*"Mom?"*

*"Baby is that you?"*

*"Mom …"*

*A sigh.*

*"Oh, Ryan, it's you. I am so sorry baby. I don't know where you are. I can't find you. I am trying so hard."*

I was sobbing in my mind and my voice caught, but there was no visible sign of distress to Kim.

*"Mom, I'm okay. It is peaceful here."*

*"I was so worried, baby,"* was my shattered response.

*"Mom, Mom, I know you loved me most of all."*

I laughed at that. Always a contest in our house over the hierarchy of love that I possessed.

*"But I need you to give all that extra love to the girls now."*

*"Okay, baby, I can do that,"* I promised.

And as quickly as my mind stilled, Kim's hand lifted and my thoughts scattered once again. I struggled to put my experience into words after the session. She knew when the conversation took place, she said, because she felt a shift. That's when I let the tears really fall.

I sat up, and as I looked down on that pristine wood floor, something caught my eye.

"Kim, do you have a dog?"

"No," she replied.

"A cat?"

"No, why?"

I pointed to what looked like a white fluff of hair now sitting on the floor—right where my eyes had rested for the therapy session. Kim bent down to pick it up, and it was not a piece of fluff but rather a white feather. I read after that a white feather is often a symbol of mourning and that it is a loved one's presence watching over you from the afterlife.

Life offers us the most unexpected surprises. We exist and try to make sense of the world around us. So many of us struggle against those things that are unexplainable or undefinable. We draw a line that we are not willing to cross. Us vs them. I don't ask anyone to believe my experiences, and I don't want to convince anyone that one thing is truer than another. I hope that I can continue to open my mind to what I may not know and hope that I can understand more as I live and I learn.

Once I was one person. Now I am another.

# *All Things Endured*

March 24, 2018

A bus full of angels came up today to search. There were some people I knew and some that I did not, but they all came for one purpose: to search for our son.

I didn't get a chance to personally thank everyone for coming.

I saw your faces. You didn't fail Scott and I, and more importantly you didn't fail Ryan.

You did something extraordinary. Something outside of your comfort zone. I have never met the likes of such unselfish people. Because you came on behalf of a stranger.

And for all your searching today, in this tough terrain, we can say that in your area ... Ryan isn't there.

32 days later, we haven't always been able to say that. So, while we may not have found Ryan, we did have success.

We couldn't be prouder.

Thank you.

March 25, 2018

After 33 days this is what I have learned so far ...

1) Did you know that you do not have to wait 24 hours to report someone missing? I didn't. Literally, you could be out of my sight for seconds, and if I called, the RCMP or the police would have to respond. (Disclaimer: this does not count for wives making beelines to the mall or wayward husbands heading out for a beer.) It does not matter the age.

2) Make sure there is one person out there who knows your password to your Apple ID if you own an iPhone. Ryan had a two-way authentication on his phone. You couldn't change his password with just an email address. Because we couldn't answer his security questions, Apple would only text his new code to his phone 23 days later. Even RCMP intervention could do nothing. So, we will never know if we could have looked at his Find My iPhone app and found his last location.

3) There is this void when local volunteer search and rescue teams fulfill their tasks. Who is left to take over?

4) In places like these that attract adventure loving people, there should be safety measures and protocols put in place.

Is it possible to have some marker or beacon added to staff IDs that trigger a beacon once activated?

What about having a procedure in place if employees don't show up? Have a detailed plan that involves an emergency contact and an escalated plan that involves the authorities if merited.

This is what I have discovered. There are several reasons why some people go missing. There are the willing, the unwilling and the unknowing. But in almost every case, there is someone left behind that grieves at that loss. There should be resources that these loved ones can access to help them through this process. People should never wonder if what they have done is enough.

I am very aware that in our case all these measures would be reactive and reflective actions.

The shame about tragedies is processes that are developed will only be proactive for others.

But what I have learned, most importantly, is that my son was happy here.

March 26, 2018

A worthy life always leaves behind those that love and grieve.

You watch your children grow and hope they thrive and succeed. You weather the storm of childhood and the teenage years. You rejoice in the adult stages that should bring so much growth and wisdom.

Our parents have lived through all these milestones with Scott and me. Now they watch us suffer and they grieve so.

What can they do? They don't know how to help us just as we don't know how to help our son.

They want to wrap us in their arms and take this all away. I wish they could, if only for just a moment.

A grandparent is meant to spoil and cherish, to teach and to value. From sleepovers to marathon weekends of *World of Warcraft*. From hunting to movie dates, our parents have done all this and more.

We have been so lucky to have a supportive extended family that have shaped our children into people that can contribute to society.

I always thought, *I wish I could be as lucky as them; to be their age and to have all my children healthy and safe.*

We never imagined that we would be where we are now.

Parents without their child, grandparents without their grandchild.

March 27, 2018

I'm not going to lie ... Ryan was the centre of everyone's universe for 3 whole years. He revelled in the love and attention that he received. Who could blame him?

Until suddenly all that changed when a beautiful baby girl was born. Big blue eyes and white blonde hair. My niece was and still is a wonder.

Ryan, in his 3-year-old self, was fairly magnanimous in accepting new baby Ava into the fold.

I am also pretty sure that when his new baby sister Jordyn came 10½ weeks later, his generosity ended.

Two babies squealing, hair pulling and gumming up his toys was too much.

You could see the gleam in his eyes as they grew older and fought over My Littlest Pony and Pet Shop toys. He was such a monkey; he would instigate the fights and sit back and grin.

Then along came Carson. If babies must come, then a boy would be welcome. A cousin that looked up to him, followed him around, and was an automatic playmate. And Ryan was lucky, he got a perfect companion for that. Except when Carson followed him around (go figure) and messed up his LEGO or Bionicles.

8 and 9 years after his singular entry into this family, he was resigned to the fact that he would not be alone. Good thing because along came Julianna and Reid.

The two families, Scott's sister's and ours, were complete. We went on our ways. We lived in the same town, but with such busy schedules, we only saw each other occasionally.

I thought that was normal, maybe even enough.

But as my niece celebrates her 18th birthday today, I realize that being part-time families is not enough.

Scott and I have the pleasure of being related to an amazing, intelligent and kind woman. You are destined to do wonderful things.

Ryan would be so proud.

Happy Birthday.

March 28, 2018

We are so grateful that the RCMP did an aerial search of the Sun Peaks area. As the snow melts and the ground becomes more visible, having this type of search is important.

We have always been pleased that the RCMP have been engaged in the search for Ryan.

It is important to note that today's aerial search changes nothing in regard to our efforts.

Scott and I are still alone. The volunteers that come and search each day are organized by us and our faithful and dedicated crew. Kamloops Search and Rescue will not be able to return until one of two things happen:

1) A new tip that changes the location of the search

Or

2) An environmental change

The sun is shining and the snow is melting. We will be so grateful when that time comes and they are able to come back.

Until that time though, we still need help.

\* \* \*

Kamloops Search and Rescue did come back for a day here and there to do soft searches and plan for a bigger event once the snow had melted. The last official search that they would do would come in May. The insignia on the trucks driving through town or the helicopters that would do pass bys always gave the impression that KSAR was mobilizing in our area, so people would send messages asking if help was still needed. They assumed that Ryan must have been found or a tip had been discovered, but the fact remained that we were still woefully all alone.

March 29, 2018
I lied.
I said that Ryan did a year of work and a year of school and was ready for a year of adventure.
I forgot we already did that.

The year that Ryan was in kindergarten, Scott and I decided to head to Key Largo, Florida, with my parents. We left in a motor home on Christmas Day night heading for the border.

The adventure part is travelling with my parents. Papa is many things, but a calm driver is not one of them.

Nana drank amaretto as the sights passed us by. I understand now how the road trip became more enjoyable for her.

We stopped in St Louis and Nashville. We visited the Grand Ole Opry and the Country Music Hall of Fame. 18-month-old Jordyn sang Keith Urban's "I want to dub somebody, dub somebody like you."

It was a trip of a lifetime. We pulled Ryan out of school and lived in the sun for 2½ months.

Scott came and went, but we stayed.

Oh god, I loved it.

Each day we swam in the pool. Ryan learned to dive from Steve, our next-door neighbour. He fed the rainbow fish in the lagoon outside our back door.

We had day trips to the alligator farm where he teased Nana with the snakes being fed rats. We stopped at Robert's Fruit Stand where they made the best fresh fruit shakes in the world. (Ryan liked chocolate 😌.)

It was where Ryan learned to ride his bike.

He hated doing anything he wasn't automatically good at.

"Baby boy," I said as he fell off each time and grudgingly got up, frustrated and mad, "you did the hardest part. You got back up. That's all you ever need to do my love, is get back up."

I never wanted it to end. Memories filled with sunshine and love.

We were so lucky.

And maybe that is the joy of adventures: the memories you look back on. You were different there and you came back changed.

I know that my son is beside me whispering, "Mom, you can do this. The hardest part is getting back up."

So, I will stand.

March 30, 2018

You know I stayed home for 12 years before I ventured back to work part-time.

Contrary to what my youngest daughter, Julianna, might think, I used to bake and do crafts all the time. My house was filled with play dates and freshly baked cookies.

Oh, please don't think I was this sweet or perfect mom who dedicated her life to her kids. I mean, yes, I did, of course. But I learned early on, play dates meant less whining, "Mommy, can you please play LEGO with me?" and, "Mommy, we are hungry." I was oh so clever. The path of less resistance was my motto.

Were there drawbacks? Well, I may have done more for my kids than I initially intended. They were well-behaved but perhaps not as independent as one would like.

After all, Ryan was 8-ish when he finally learned how to tie his shoes. In my defence, that is a stupid skill to teach and they made super cool Velcro shoes.

In the first couple of days after Ryan went missing, I wondered if I had taught my kids enough. Was this somehow a result of my not preparing him enough?

I don't suppose it will come as any surprise, but I wanted to analyze where this all went wrong. And if there is no one to blame, then perhaps the fault lies with me.

But as time goes by and the weeks drag on, I have spent a lot of time reflecting.

Ryan was brave enough to venture from his home to embark on a dream. He had confidence in his ability to navigate the world.

My seventeen-year-old daughter has the strength and courage to be at home and go through Grade 12. She pays bills, shops and is growing into this beautiful, confident woman.

Julianna continues to be funny and bright and fierce. She listens to the heaviness of the adult conversation and yet still manages to be a kid.

Maybe I didn't do so badly after all.

March 31, 2018

I was born to birth babies with ease, just not to carry them the same way.

From the moment I became pregnant with Ryan, I was sick every day. It was so bad that the blood vessels in my eyes would burst. That continued up until the day he was born.

But from the first fluttering of life, any discomfort was forgotten. I was completely in love.

Ryan decided to make his entry into this world 3 days early. Hardly a push from me and barely a cry came from my beautiful son.

And all the love I had held while carrying him became a whisper to the roar of holding him for the first time.

I tell this story now because it is 6 weeks. 6 long weeks of searching of discomfort and pain. 6 weeks of unknowing, uncertainty and overwhelming fear.

But everything is temporary.

I believe that I will once more hold my son. That I will once again gaze, if only for a short while, upon his beautiful face. That is my right as his mother.

I believe that the lesson Ryan taught me is all things can be endured when you love.

April 1, 2018 (my birthday)

So many "first days." Scott's birthday, Ryan's 21st birthday, my birthday and Easter have all come and gone. I want to say we managed these days of celebrations without our son, but in reality, we haven't found him. So, we will have to experience all these moments again once we know.

I woke up prepared to be unable to face the day ahead. In the past—we shall call them the days of feeling whole—the kids would wake up and make me breakfast in bed. Ryan would be of little to no help. He would stand off while the girls handed me their presents. And then with great flourish and a half smile, he would hand me his gift. Since he worked, he was confident that his present would always be better than his sisters' and their home-made gifts.

Today was different, I won't lie. Except it was the same.

Scott and the kids, including Maddy, Cohen, Nike and Dany, made me breakfast. These beautiful babes gave me gifts and home-made cards. I smiled through my tears, and they comforted me with hugs.

The rest of the day was filled with love. People stopped by with gifts—beautiful, heartfelt presents meant to lift my spirits and soothe my soul.

And still they searched.

The evening ended with everyone coming together for a birthday dinner.

As I sat surrounded by amazing and giving people, I realized that my son had done it again.

He waited until the all the gifts were opened before giving me his own.

He can't be with me, but he gave me the gift of all of you. You filled my day with love and light.

And I know that in the dark days ahead, the gift he has given me will be my solace.

April 2, 2018

Some days I feel like we take 2 steps forward only to go 4 steps back.

Sun Peaks has experienced a record snowfall this year. So wonderful for weekend getaways and local ski enthusiasts, hell for Scott and me.

15 cms fell the night Ryan went missing. It continued to snow the whole first week.

If that wasn't enough, it was bitterly cold. -26 in the early morning of Saturday February 17th with little warmth to follow.

In the six weeks that have followed, the sun will shine, the snow will melt and our hopes of this nightmare ending grows steadily.

And then ... like we are trapped in a giant snow globe, someone shakes us up.

The clouds ominously appear and billowy snowflakes fall like my teardrops, steady and constant.

I just want it all to stop. Please stop. Haven't we done enough, learned enough, fought enough??

I wish I could love it like you do, Ryan. Full of adventure and discovery. Winter wonderlands yet to be discovered and explored.

But I can't find you until it stops. You are like a needle in a haystack that continually gets covered. Like nothing has passed this way ... no marker, no steps and no trace.

"Please stop snowing," I beg.

I would give all that I have, all that I know, to be able to control this weather.

How long must my son be lost?

When will we have suffered enough?

When will our steps move us forward to seeing you again my son?

Soon, I pray. Soon.

April 3, 2018

No man is an island.

As we navigate through some of the most trying times of our lives ... I am left with this thought.

Since Sunday February 18th, Scott and I have never been alone.

We have never had to wonder what it is like to learn this process of search and rescue without support. We have never had to, in our moments of quiet, wonder if the other has done enough.

We have been surrounded by love, by friendship and by unending support. We have learned to lean on others to find our strength.

They have let us cry, dried our tears and made us laugh. They have put their lives on hold, searched without complaint and continued to come back because the thought of us being alone has become unbearable to them.

We never knew.

Oh ... it's important to love your partner. Your greatest joy can come from this singular relationship with another that shares the same goals and dreams.

But I believe that this is not enough.

And although you may never experience the kind of tragedy that we are now facing ... having someone to have your back is paramount.

It is important for your growth. It is imperative for your soul.

To know that there are people in this world who believe in you, love you and give you unwavering support brings this unending peace. Life gives us too many burdens not to also give us the opportunity for comfort.

Our friends, new and old, don't have to love us the way they do, but they do.

What I realize is that it is never too late.

Everyone needs a tribe.

April 4, 2018

Brenda, what a great auntie you are.

I have never had a sister, but the moment I married Scott, we inherited each other.

I think I was the lucky one.

You have this infectious laugh and a joy of life that I envied. We won't talk about your style. I used to joke that I would take scissors to your beautiful hair. I didn't, but I wanted to. Kind and thoughtful ... you epitomize it all.

It wasn't until Ryan was born and I saw you hold him that I understood there would be other people who would love my son almost as much as I did.

He was lucky to have you.

We considered ourselves fortunate that you offered to take Ry for weekends but never thought that it was you and him that benefitted the most.

You snuggled him and took him on adventures in Hinton that brought him such joy. As the years went by, you continued to love him through the all stages. He always knew you were a safe haven.

I remember him as a baby, pointing at you and saying "Doooooo." We would shake our heads and wonder, but it wasn't until we caught you saying to him, "Whatcha dooooooooing?" that it finally made sense.

You have been Auntie Doo since.

Thank you for being our children's biggest champion. For dropping everything to always be there for them.

If there was a definition of what an aunt should be ... it would describe you.

Happy Birthday Beautiful Auntie Doo.

April 5, 2018

So, we have moved locations based on information we received during the first couple of days of Ryan being reported missing. Did we go and look at that time? Absolutely. However, not having the skills or knowledge, this would have been a cursory check at best. For the last 6 weeks, we have focused on the area where the party was as well as his house. But what if he walked towards town???

That is what was reported as a last sighting. So, this is where we will try next.

To someone who has not been here, it may seem overwhelming. New location ... starting over.

But I look at it as a new possibility. The opportunity to check off another area and come one step closer to bringing Ryan home.

I really want to thank the volunteers that come each day. We always seem to have a minimum of 10 people that are searching at any given time. We are an organized machine now. Volunteers that come are asked to sign in. We give them a lesson in the search process. We give them the tools to search with, and we send them to where the group is. No one is ever alone.

We are grateful for any time that someone has to give. Just show up.

April 6, 2018

Snowbombing 2018.

A huge concert with several outdoor venues and lots of artists. Tons of events happening along with my favourite activity of people watching makes Sun Peaks the place to be.

Ryan would have been here for this. And he would have loved it.

The irony is not lost on me that I am enjoying the things he would have participated in with reckless abandon.

I am reminded of this commercial I watched where a transplant recipient completed his donor's bucket list items. It made me think. There are so many events Ryan will never get to experience. That is certainly true.

He didn't know the value of what was given and how quickly it could end. Who really does?????

Even for me, it wasn't until last year that I decided to create a bucket list. Places to visit, books to read, people to meet, experiences to make memories out of. I set off checking things I have never done from this list. So much fun!

Why did it take so long to start? I was waiting. Waiting for the right time. Waiting for the funds to do so. Waiting until I looked a certain way.

All that time wasted.

Nothing will ever be perfect. No time will ever be right.

It has always been about creating this time capsule of yourself for you and others to look back on and remember.

So maybe in my bucket list items, I can include some things that Ryan would have loved to do.

Like snowbombing.

And maybe a river cruise to see the Christmas markets (😂😂—okay that one is just for me.)

\*     \*     \*

We had settled on searching in areas near the house where Ryan was last seen and the route that he could have taken to arrive at his house on Sun Peaks Road. With the amount of snow that fell and continued to fall and the densely forested areas, it was slow going. We spent nights with our small group of volunteers pouring over the map to determine the search for the next day. We were meticulous. We were thoughtful, and we were well-organized. We knew exactly the pattern that we would follow, and we would set forth each day to execute that goal. But as each night drew to a close, the map became a little smaller and we found ourselves wondering where to go next. Sitting around the dining room table, we debated our next strategy. Conversations or information that was relayed to us at the beginning that seemed to hold no significance now seemed relevant or at least worthy of discussion. We knew exactly where we were going next and why we wanted to search certain areas, but any change in location brought forth a flurry of activity and comments on Ryan's Facebook page.

April 6, 2018

I want to give further insight on the "new" information.

We knew about that location within days of Ryan being reported missing. We probably would have known about it right away, but the description of Ryan that was given to the RCMP was incorrect. He wasn't 5'9", 19 yrs of age or 160 lbs. The accurate description should have read: 6 ft, 180 lbs and 20. Small details but still held significance. That was easily rectified with them and Kamloops Search and Rescue but not with the public until days later. As soon as that became available, the sighting of someone matching the description at this location was given to us as well the RCMP.

And yes, we did go look. But honestly, the first few days—and maybe the first week—we were all so desperate. Desperate to go out all day, desperate to stay out as long as we could, desperate to find Ryan.

Except.

We didn't really know how to do that. We weren't knowledgeable. We weren't organized. We didn't have the skills or the training. We were desperate parents scrambling.

We looked but didn't find.

Why did we go back? Because the information about this new location didn't go away.

Nothing new has come to light.

We have just become more organized. We have had searchers look in the one area. We have spent weeks there. And because we have been so methodical, searching takes time. But in the areas that we have searched, we can say Ryan isn't there. Nothing is 100%, but we feel good about going to a new area.

Are the RCMP involved? Absolutely. They haven't left this case since the beginning. They have been in constant contact with us. They keep us up to date with what they can. They readily take our calls and emails and get back to us with answers.

Do I wish it was more? Absolutely. But that is because I am a parent.

I want Search and Rescue to bring hundreds of qualified searchers to this area and to never leave until my son has been found. But that is not realistic. And so it is not fair to place my anger that sometimes surfaces at the inability to find Ryan solely at their feet.

The snow is too high and too thick. What should have been a simple walk home has led us to several trails, paths and roads.

It is all too much.

But before you start posting ... he is probably not there ... I dreamed or I see that he has been taken ... please take a moment.

The snow has not melted. Until it does, I'm not leaving. Those comments have no value to me unless followed by concrete facts. All they do is distract. And that is not fair. Not to me, my husband, our family (including our daughters) and the hundreds of volunteers who have come here for over 6 weeks to search.

We believe Ryan is here.

April 7, 2018

So much tragedy.

Today, for the first time in 7 long weeks, I thought about something other than just Ryan.

Today, parents of the Humboldt Broncos are going through their own personal hell. Some have lost their own life's blood. Some will begin a very long road to recovery. And some, although they are physically okay, will never be the same. I can't even begin to imagine. I can't even begin to express my deepest sorrow. And for all those parents and loved ones who are experiencing this tragedy, there will be the legions of friends and family that want to offer help and to comfort.

Don't be afraid.

One thing that I have learned from my own experience is that I want to talk about my son. I embrace your hugs and prayers.

It is okay to make me cry with memories of my son. He is never far from my thoughts.

I cry because he matters. To me, to his dad, to his sisters and to all of his family and friends.

I cry with sadness over what could have been.

I cry with frustration because I can't find him.

I cry with joy because he was a pretty amazing person.

As were all of these boys.

Make us cry. Just don't forget.

April 8, 2018

My father taught me so much of what I know to be true. His values were important in how he conducted himself. It was how he saw himself and how others would see him that mattered dearly. He forged the man he is today through the traditions that he learned from his father and his father from his. And so on and so forth. Ancestral and strong. Positive and negative.

He passed this legacy on to me, and I have gifted my children with the same knowledge.

Today, on my father's birthday, I witnessed a lifetime of traditions and ancestry.

It was beautiful.

We took part in a pipe and drumming ceremony. It was powerful and so moving. Chiefs, elders and leaders of the Secwépemc Nation and the Neskonlith band came to pray to the Creator and call Ryan and his spirit home.

In that moment, I felt the trueness of us being the same. I felt it in my bones. I felt it in my heart.

They came for a man they have never met. They shared their traditions and their values.

Papa Bear, you would have been moved.

You were right ... we are not so different after all.

April 9, 2018

Yesterday I cleaned the house we are renting. Today I made banana pancakes for Julianna's breakfast.

So mundane ... so ordinary. I have forgotten what normal feels like or even means.

I hadn't recognized the simplest of tasks would forever become my new simplest pleasures.

I long to be normal.

To be utterly bored by my life.

Is it human nature to forever be dissatisfied by where you are in your life? At any given time? To push the boundaries?

I believed that it was important to stand on the precipice ... looking as far as my eyes would go and forever leap. To challenge myself and my ever-changing beliefs.

Now I would trade almost anything to see my family whole, my son safe and my life the way it was. Safe. Normal. Mundane.

\*    \*    \*

The rental was beginning to feel like home to us. Beaumont seemed so far away, a lifetime ago. Scott and I had only one discussion about going back home. It happened in the very first week because it was becoming increasingly clear that this search might take longer than either of us had imagined. One night in our hotel room, Scott turned to me and said, "Maybe you should go home. Be with the girls. I can stay and continue to search." White hot rage boiled within me. Not at Scott but at the circumstance in which we found ourselves. A crossroad with a nearly impossible choice.

"Well, if one of us should go, it really should be you," I calmly replied. "I have hundreds of searchers lined up but no one to man the command centre and organize everyone."

He sputtered a bit. That closed any further discussion on leaving.

But the harder conversation came when trying to broach the subject with Jordyn, our oldest. Left at home in her Grade 12 year, preparing for graduation, she was taking on responsibilities suited for an adult. She was only seventeen, and the burden she was forced to bear was agonizing for me. It felt like we were choosing one child over the other. That Ryan had more importance.

By this time, bringing our son home whole and happy was unrealistic. As parents, we will always hope, but we also acknowledged how many hurdles that stood before us and understood the barest odds that would make this a perfect reunion. The thought of leaving was difficult, but what we had left behind was even more difficult.

But this would be the last physical thing I could do for Ryan. After this time spent there, there would be no more. No more searching. No more posts. Nothing. We would begin to grieve and learn how to live without a huge part that made us whole.

I wanted to pour out my heart to my daughter. I wanted to craft the words that explained to her how very important she was to me. That she, too, mattered. That we were deserting her. I wanted to tell her how very sorry I was that I wasn't with her. How could I possibly explain?

I didn't have to.

"Mom, you and Dad need to stay in Sun Peaks," she said before we could even bring it up. "You guys have to keep looking for Ryan. You can't give up."

*Oh baby, yes, I know,* I thought. *But I worry. I am a mother to three beautiful children. I need to be there for my daughters when this is all over.*

My silence must have seemed endless.

"Max and I are OK," she said. "We want to come up for March break if that is OK. I want to see you and Dad, but we are doing good. We know that you need to be there, and we are OK to be here. There are lots of people around so don't worry about us."

My graceful, beautiful daughter saved us. She willingly gave of herself to allow us to stay. And she was OK. More than OK. She grew in ways that maybe she didn't even realize were possible. She became strong and resilient. She stood on that precipice, looked down on an abyss and leaped. And discovered that she could fly.

April 10, 2018

First child interrupted.

Another child is born to the family.

Everything from here on in leads to a lifetime of accommodating. Sharing the love, your toys and someone else's time. You will be bonded through similar experiences and upbringing. Good and bad.

Who else will know you as long or as well as your parents than your siblings?

If you are lucky, when you need them most they will be there.

The moment Ryan was declared missing, both my brother, Kevin, and Scott's sister, Brenda, dropped everything and came. From Scotland and from Beaumont, they came. We needed them and they came.

I wanted nothing more for my own children than the feeling of belonging. To themselves and to each other.

Ryan, as the oldest, often left the feeling of big brotherly love to be desired. He teased, mocked and sometimes never let up on either. He could be selfish with his stuff and stingy with his time.

But he loved his sisters.

One of my biggest regrets will be not to see the completeness of his relationship with Jordyn and Julianna. They were just beginning to find their rhythm.

But what I know for certain is that, wherever Ryan is, his love for his sisters is strong, true and full of never-ending love.

He will forever watch over them as they navigate through their lives.

After all, that is what big brothers are for.

April 11, 2018

Looking back on all my pictures on Facebook and Instagram, it occurs to me that Ryan was noticeably absent in the last few years.

Was it because he was getting older? Was it because he was trying to prepare us for a future of memories to be captured without him? Quite possibly it was because he got tired of the numerous retakes 😩😩.

That child was a disaster trying to take family pictures. He purposely ruined almost all of them with his eyes closed, side smirk and goofy looks. He irritated me with these lengthy photo shoots. I just wanted one good picture. Is that too much to ask??? Apparently so, with this boy.

But it made us roll our eyes and laugh.

But looking back, here is what I discovered. Before 4 years ago, I rarely took pictures of myself.

I disliked family pictures of all of us. I wanted Scott and the kids. I longed to have memories of all our times together, just not with me.

Stupid now, I suppose. I just couldn't see the sense. I didn't love my smile. I was most critical of how I looked. Aren't we always?

By the time I came to my senses, it was too late. Ryan was well past wanting to sit still or take time from his teenage life to take "selfies" with me.

Memories lost.

It shouldn't matter where you are in your life or how you think you look. You have only a short amount of time that you are able to capture theses rites of passage. Seize them. Make memories.

If not for you ... then for your loved ones. You mean something to them. They deserve to have what you think are meager offerings of yourself.

Just know that they aren't. Don't be in the background in your own life.

I wish I had taken more.

April 12, 2018

My life has become a series of numbers.

52 days or 7½ weeks that Ryan has been missing.

453 centimeters of snow that has fallen from December 1st until April, the entirety of the time Ryan was here.

31 centimeters of snow that has fallen since February 17th alone.

520 is the number of volunteers that have signed in to search for Ryan.

Over 364 of them have returned more than once.

1000 is roughly the number of granola bars, water bottles, muffins, cookies and meals that have been provided to us from our generous donors and meal train angels.

25,000 people have joined the Missing Ryan Shtuka page.

12th of May ... the day that Search and Rescue estimates they will be able to come back to conduct a full search.

I have never been particularly strong in math.

But what I do know is that:

21 years Ryan has gifted us with love, laughter and light.

You have taken these numbers and exponentially expanded upon them to create a community that I am proud to be a part of.

One humanity. Infinite possibilities.

April 13, 2018

*There ought to be a room in every house to swear in. It's dangerous to have to repress an emotion like that.*

- Mark Twain

I realize that I am my own house. A perfect combination of swearing, sass and sarcasm.

Oh, I have tried to use my background in English and history to curb my natural tendencies towards cursing.

I have failed.

Ryan, at 2, was very precocious. I remember him sitting on the ground playing with his matchbox cars. He was getting extremely frustrated with the one. I could hear him muttering "These frickin' wheels don't work."

"Umm ... pardon me, Ryan John??"

"Mommy these wheels don't work. See????"

My angel. Of course, I was wrong. Until later ... he says clearly in front of the entire family, including the grandparents, "Look at that guy with his frickin' moustache".

In my defence ... he used it correctly.

Despite my best intentions to speak in a mature, motherly way, I knew that ground rules would need to be established.

This is what I have told all my children.

Yes, you may swear. However, the rule is: You must be able to read the dictionary back to front and tell me all the words you could have used instead of the word you are using.

Again, note my cleverness. Being as well read as I am, I can get away with my intermittent swearing. Scott may have been a little nervous. He tends to swear outside the house.

I think it has worked well.

The consequences were a mouth washed out with soap.

Being an I-said-what-I-mean-and-mean-what-I-said kinda of parent meant I followed through.

I think back to one day when Ryan skipped school and we went to the movies. It was a great day. We got home and were playing a game, and in the middle of it, Ryan let out a curse. He looked at me and I looked at him. Both our faces fell.

"Love bug," I said sadly.

He looked distressed and said, "I know."

I think I may have felt worse as I handed him the liquid dish soap, but I did look away just in case he only put a drop on his tongue.

My son ... you can create your own house. I think you earned the right to swear.

Love you.

April 14, 2018

Volunteering is an act of unselfish kindness. To care, even a little, forever shapes the fabric of our community.

I confess I wasn't always a volunteer by nature. I mean, what can I do??? I am not extraordinary. I don't have a "unique set of skills" that makes me desirable for volunteering or that I stand out as an expert in helping people.

Except willingness.

In the beginning, I was a stay-at-home mother (I preferred to say "retired") who made cookies and organized play dates. That seemed to be enough. In fact, some days it felt like a lot.

However, I have this guilt that happens when people ask for help. I look around, waiting for others to put their hands up. And when they don't, I feel obligated to raise my own.

That's how volunteering happened at first anyhow.

I didn't expect to feel so good about it. I certainly didn't think it would change my perspective on my community or my place within it.

It started with helping out at Ryan's school. I would do the weekly reading book bags. I would photocopy and cut out laminated shapes and words. I felt it kept me in the loop about any potential misbehaviour.

And how can you not like a kid whose mom volunteers??

Then came the coaching jobs and various board member positions. I convinced myself that it was a night out … time away from the kids.

By the time I turned around, I was the chairperson to fundraise and build a $267,000 all-inclusive themed playground.

Oh, the stress! So time consuming and I had just gone back to work. But the end product was simply amazing. Beyond my wildest expectations.

And lo and behold … I discovered I loved volunteering. I could see the difference I was making.

I met people that became lifelong friends. I had an appreciation for my neighbours. I was invested in my community.

But most importantly, I showed my kids the importance of doing something for others. Outside of themselves. With no thoughts of repayment. To relish the feeling of selfless giving.

This has become so prevalent now as I watch people come from far and wide to help us search for our son.

Even now, Ryan, you have the power to create ripples.

How amazing is that?

April 15, 2018

Ryan once had to write a paper for his university English class about the importance of home. His thesis was "Home is not a place but rather a feeling."

Home: It's all I could think about today.

I find myself far from home in a place I never expected to be in for so long.

It is now, for all intents and purposes, my new temporary home.

I am not sure how I feel about that.

Of course ... this community has been a godsend. The residents have been incredibly kind and loving. They have embraced us from the very beginning, and we have felt such comfort as well as a sense of belonging. But they know full well that I don't want to be here. That I long to be back in Beaumont with my daughters and my husband. To wake in my own space, to have moments of quiet or even quite simply to do something other than search.

And while Home may be a state of mind, I miss everything and everyone in it. Before all of this.

Yet ... when the time comes to leave this place, I will miss it for all its joy, blessings and ultimately its tragedy.

Today, the winter season for Sun Peaks comes to a close. Everything will be quieter and slower. In a perfect world, Ryan would be packing up and making his way home. His year of adventure finished but filled with a lifetime of memories.

With that in mind ... we took time to enjoy our temporary home. A group of 12 of us took the chairlift up and walked down. The steepness of the run made traversing it challenging. Oh my, the fun we had. I felt such lightness that on most days escapes me.

This was Scott's doing.

We are, of course, always searching, but Scott gave us a way to do that and have some moments of joy. My husband has learned that a home cannot survive pain and sorrow without equal amounts of love and laughter.

So, when it is time to leave here ... the home I return to will most certainly be different than when I left. My son will not be there. I am terrified of what that will mean.

April 16, 2018

I wouldn't necessarily call my son a hero.

He didn't perform a heroic act ... or have any heroic qualities, really. But I will say, for one person in particular, he was a role model.

Carson Anthony was born into this crazy family 16 years ago today. We were all so delighted to have another boy after a succession of girls. Ryan was especially thrilled to have a male cousin.

Now he had someone to teach all the wisdom of his tender 5 years to. They would play toys, ride bikes and rule the world ... well, our tiny corner of Beaumont anyways.

And wouldn't you know it—it takes a newborn years to grow. Time to walk, run and bike. Sure, Carson grew, but so did Ryan.

Ryan's toys required precision to put together ... and a 3 year old can't always master the bike tricks. But little did Ryan know what a stubborn boy his cousin Carson was. Athletic, smart and determined,

Carson followed Ryan's lead. Soon he could keep up and sometimes even surpass him.

I loved watching them together.

Despite their age, they enjoyed each other's company. They had a similar sense of humour, and this adventure for life. I suppose the adage that cousins are friends for life describes the two of them perfectly. However, I truly believe that Ryan and Carson would have met and been great friends no matter the family connection.

Like with all things lately, I am left with regret that Ryan will not be able to continue to grow in his relationships ... with his sisters, his cousins, his family ... and with Scott and me. Who would he become given enough time?

Maybe heroes don't always have to perform heroic deeds in order to be celebrated and remembered. Maybe it is just enough that one person believes in you and sees you as extraordinary— flaws and all.

So perhaps I am wrong after all.

Ryan, my son, my hero.

Happy Birthday Carson.

April 17, 2018

Some girls have dreamed of their Prince Charming the moment they twirled around in fancy gowns and dress up shoes.

23 years ago, I thought I had found mine.

Hmmmm ... I wonder if you will judge me if I confess that in the last 8 weeks, I have found myself so many more.

Wait, wait. Let me explain by telling you about two and maybe you will forgive me.

On day 16, I wrote asking everyone to believe. I asked for your faith in our knowledge of ourselves and our son.

And you delivered.

The very next day, Wilf walked in to the command centre and has never left. He believes with a ferocity that bolsters me when my own faith wanes. He smells like sweetgrass and sage. And I feel peace and light radiating from him each day.

And then there is Gerry. Strong and determined, fit and tireless. Gerry has been with us for the last 4½ weeks with little to no time off. I think we might be growing on him. He seems a bit gruff and, let's be honest, he did fire me, but he has a heart of gold. He can always tell within 10 mins who has come from Beaumont to search. And yet, he shows up every day. He walks every new volunteer through the ground search process. Over and over, with such patience and confidence. We would be lost without him.

I adore them both.

I will let you in on a secret I only recently discovered:

Who you are is who you are.

You will have the chance to grow over time, influenced by life experience and your environment. If you are lucky, you will be someone that people gravitate to because you are good and you are kind. You can't just expect people to rise to the occasion and be more than they were before because tragedy has struck.

These men were heroes before they came to me. They were loved and respected before I happened to need them.

They will be my Prince Charmings well beyond my time here.

I pray that what they do for others will forever be multiplied upon them.

Because of them, I am able to rise. Because of all of my Prince Charmings I can do this one more day.

April 18, 2018

Today is April 18th.

I watched Ryan's roommates pack up their cars. They performed great feats of logistics to arrange snowboards, snow gear and clothing. It is like watching a giant jigsaw puzzle, everyone trying to get everything to fit.

In a perfect world, that would have been Ryan.

My son would have been coming home today. Four and a half months spent away from home. The longest he has ever been away.

I remember so vividly the day he told me he wanted to go to a ski hill for the winter season. It was clear that he was looking for a change. To be honest, I was surprised.

You see, my son has always been most cautious. Never treading beyond what he was comfortable with. Introspective and mindful. And I loved him for it. He was true to himself even if he didn't always know it or even appreciate it.

And that's okay, after all that is what my role as a mother is for. I will be your biggest champion and your fiercest supporter. Always. Forever.

If not me, then who?

When he was offered a position here in Sun Peaks, it was like watching him on Christmas morning. Barely contained excitement radiated from him. I was so proud.

He did everything I didn't. He followed a whim and made it happen. As parents, we pray fiercely that our children become more than we ever could have been. To reach for the stars no matter how far away they seem. Ryan did that even if for a brief time.

He never knew my fears or how much I might miss him.

And he was happy. That is what I will remember most in the days I am overcome with grief. My son was happy with his life here.

Tonight, if life was perfect, he would have made the long trek home.

I would have been full of anticipation, wanting to hear all about his life here. Did you meet anyone? Did you have fun? Would you do it again? Tell me all about it. My perfect imperfect son would have looked at me nonchalantly and replied, "Ya … it was good. K, I'm heading to Gage's."

And then slept in for the rest of the week.

April 19, 2018

The landscape has changed so drastically since the day this all began.

Not enough certainly. If that were so, perhaps Scott, Jordyn, Julianna and I would have the answers we so desperately crave.

But seasons change. Winter casts off its icy grip, and the soft buds of spring slowly emerge.

Despite all that, our days remain the same.

Each day, every day, we head to the command centre to open up. This will be the third one we have operated from. I hope it will be the last.

We go through the maps to determine the areas of focus for the day. We organize our volunteer sign-in lists and log the snowshoes and the probes.

And we wait.

Rarely have we had fewer than 8–10 people searching. The response has been amazing. How can words ever express the gratitude? I want to write the perfect words but they escape me.

Our volunteers, outfitted with equipment and armed with what knowledge we have to impart, head out to do ground searches. 2 hours, ½ day or full, it doesn't matter. Anything can happen in a second or in a span of a minute. I know that well enough.

On the days I feel well enough to search, I search. More days than I like, I stay in the command centre.

I greet. I plan. I feed. I worry. I wonder.

Scott digs, probes and prods. I don't know what he thinks in the hours he is by himself. But I do know he is enough. He has done enough. And tomorrow he will do more than enough.

The snow falls, melts and falls again.

Day turns to night to day again. And the weeks go by.

But we don't lose hope.

Because the landscape changes and we are one step closer.

April 20, 2018

Once upon a time ...

There was a young man, tall and handsome who yearned for an adventure. Excitement filled his head, longing for the unknown soared in his veins. Little did he know the tragedy that was about to unfold ...

I suppose it will come as no surprise that I like to read. As a child, I would spend hours with my head in a book. When the fairy tales failed to end the way I wanted them to, I wrote my own.

As a child, Ryan loved to read almost as much as I did. Some of our best moments were spent reading together.

As he grew older, his love for make-believe changed from books to PlayStation. I regretted the hours spent on something that I felt didn't engage his brain.

Until ...

Ryan introduced me to *World of Warcraft*.

"Mom," Ryan said excitedly while were visiting my parents' house, "Papa has this game. You would totally like it."

My look of disdain was evident as he continued.

"You create characters and go on quests. You can play with teams. It's so much fun. Can we get it?

My silence caused Ryan to rapidly rethink his strategy.

"You can be like an elf. They are so pretty ... just like you."

Well, now my curiosity was piqued. And buying the game became a must. After all, who can resist a pretty elven creature uncannily just like you??? 😉

I admit I did like the game. I will also admit that, as with my book reading, I may have become a little obsessive with playing.

It didn't occur to me just how involved I was in the game until one particular day. It was a PD Day. The girls were at a sleepover. Ryan woke me up early, pleased we had the whole day to ourselves. We quested throughout the day, barely stopping. Ryan, growing hungry, went to make macaroni. I think my call to action interrupted him. It wasn't until later that I went to the kitchen and discovered that he had put the hot pot on the counter top.

Oh yes ... you guessed it ... totally burnt the top. A huge scorched mark was evident to Scott when he came home from work.

I am not proud to tell you that Ryan and I made a pact that day. We would lie about how much time we, mostly me, spent on the game. He allowed me to "express my disappointment" in him in front of his dad. I shook my head and told Scott I would take care of it.

The price was completing the hardest dungeon with him so he could get something epic.

Like in all things, our attention shifted and our interests changed.

But my belief in fairy tales still exists.

Every tale has a hero and a villain. I want to believe in a happily ever after.

April 21, 2018

Ryan, I wonder if you will ever know how much you have done?

For me.

For your dad.

For Jordyn and Julianna.

For our friends and family.

But most importantly, for other people.

Yesterday, 55 people, the majority we have never met before, stepped onto a bus. 15 hours of travel time to head through Edmonton and Red Deer.

They came.

And they searched.

Because you inspired them.

For some it was to support our family during this tragedy. For others, perhaps, they will have stepped outside what is known or comfortable to accomplish something they have never done before. How amazing is that, baby boy?

People told me in the early days that you would change the world. I will confess, that seemed slightly outrageous.

And then it struck me.

When people commit to helping others, often they are scared of the response. Will it be accepted? Will the person understand my intention? Is it even wanted?

However, the moment you give of yourself, the scariest part has passed. And you realize the reaction is less important than the pure intention behind the good deed. And it becomes commonplace. Something extraordinary becomes normal.

Wouldn't that be a wonderful world, where random acts of kindness become the norm? Where having empathy and compassion for your fellow human is as natural as breathing? Where we become a global family tied together with kindness and love?

I suppose all it takes is one step. And for my son, I am willing to put my foot forward and walk.

Thank you each and every one of you that move forward each day. You volunteer, you pray, you donate, you share and you organize.

Ryan may have made a difference in the way we now view the world, but don't kid yourself—it is because you wanted the world you knew to change.

You just needed a reason.

April 22, 2018

Rites of passage.

We all go through them. Learning to crawl, taking your first step, leaving Mom's grasp as you walk into school or taking the training wheels off.

So many firsts.

We know now that growth requires challenges. Ready or not, here I come.

I couldn't wait to turn 16 (Ontario raised girl) and take my test for a driver's license. The sense of freedom was empowering. The lack of a vehicle was somewhat debilitating, however. But from the moment I learned to drive, I knew the world was my oyster.

Scott likes to tell me that he was driving on the farm at, like, 11. He says this because he may be slightly younger than I. Don't ask. It's rude.

"If you only harrowed what I plowed," is his most favourite expression.

I have no idea what that means. If it isn't clear to you already, I don't do snow and am not much for farming (it's a farming reference, right?).

You would think Ryan would be similar in his quest for freedom.

And you would be wrong.

The week before Ryan turned 15, I said to him, in no uncertain terms, "You have one week to get your learner's."

He wanted to go with his best friend, Ryan G., to Banff, snowboarding. However, he stubbornly dug his heels in about going to write his test.

By putting conditions on his trip, I was clearly outsmarting him.

You are starting to think like him, aren't you?

He got it. And then refused to drive. His 16th birthday passed him by with no desire to get his driver's license. He didn't ask to practice and avoided the car at all costs.

"So, you are okay with your girlfriend driving you everywhere?" I said in my pitiful attempt to parentally embarrass him.

His response was a shrug of the shoulders and a "Yep."

Finally, at age 18 years and 5 months, Ryan went to driver's training. Having absolutely no experience at all, the instructor told him after 3 lessons he was good to go.

One week later, he took his test and passed.

And took his sisters to Burger King in the city.

By the next month he had bought my parent's van. The "Shaggin Wagon." 😊

This past September, he went with his father to purchase his first "newer" car. He was so proud. He loved his car. He left for Sun Peaks in his car. And here it remains.

Perhaps freedom takes time, but once gotten is hard to give up.

All rites of passage are a bit messy and full of struggles. In the end, though, you soar like the wind never held you back.

Oh, my love, continue to soar.

April 23, 2018

I am what is considered a foodie.

Definition: someone who enjoys food for pleasure.

I seek food experiences as a hobby rather than just necessity.

I wasn't always that way. When Scott and I first got married, I would make lunches and suppers each day. I wanted us to be a proper family.

Except I wouldn't say my food repertoire was refined as of yet. I did make lots of bread from our new bread maker. So good, but it left us 17 pounds heavier.

I settled down when Ryan was born. We were going to eat family-friendly meals in preparation for his introduction of solids. Starting him on sweet potatoes ... perhaps a parenting fail.

Ryan's favourite line to everyone (much to our horror) was: "I don't like delicious ... I like junk food." I still shake my head in abject embarrassment.

Parenting is like a reoccurring nightmare sometimes. With children, you always feel like you are having that dream where you are walking in public naked.

Scott and I grew in our kitchen adventures to a more sophisticated palate. Crepes to beef Wellington, we (Scott) made it all.

And yet everyday was the same.

"What are we having for dinner?"

Finally, my response to the neverending question of the dinner menu was an automatic, "Yuck I don't like this and I can't believe I have to eat this crap. Honestly, my darlings, we have the same thing every night."

Imagine my everlasting joy when Ryan and his taste buds expanded. Finally!

One of my most recent memories is sitting around dinner with Ryan, who was enjoying his favourite meal and a bottle of red wine. Ah ... the sophistication! Okay, I will grant you the wine was free and included with the meal.

Despite my passion for food, the first 2 weeks that Ryan was reported missing, I could eat nothing more than soup. In my mind, if my son couldn't eat, be warm or sleep, then neither shall I.

Such things are not sustainable. Nor would Ryan want my grief to encapsulate me.

Such irony: I love food but can't taste the pleasure as of late.

Food can be nourishment for the body but also for the soul. Memories made from the gatherings of friends and family.

So ...

Each night, we place a food offering out for Ryan. To call his spirit home.

Baby boy, it's time to come home.

April 24, 2018

A legacy is more than a gift from the past. It is a continuation of how we want the world to view us.

I want to believe there is a purpose in all that we do, otherwise my loss will be too unbearable. I want to believe that we have the power to change our involvement within the very fabric of our society.

A call to action is more than just a call for volunteers. Our time will pass and another will sadly take its place.

Whether someone has gone missing willing, unwillingly or unknowingly, there is always someone left behind that loved them.

Let Ryan's legacy be one of kindness and community gathering.

If what you can do is all that you can do, don't be afraid to do it.

April 25, 2018

We stole your friend, Ryan.

I never thought that your value could also be summed up by the people who love you.

Oh, my love bug, if you only knew. You have made the best of friends. They admired you, spoke highly of you, dropped everything to search for you and, my son, they have grieved for you.

Friends that have weathered the years, the distance and the separations.

There are so many. I couldn't count them if I wanted to.

I want to.

I see you and I know you loved him.

You are all mine now.

But we may have stolen one away. I wouldn't use the word hostage, but I would ask that you ignore his mouthing "Save me."

I am not sure Dany had any idea what he was getting into when he first met Ryan. Soccer aficionados and PlayStation gurus, you boys were fast friends. From the age of 8, Dany, you have been a fixture at our house. Weekends at the lake (I am still paying for you and Manny's food bill) to after school dents in my newly-painted wall from you climbing out the window, and sleepovers every weekend. You did it all.

Not even moving to Saskatoon could separate you.

The night that Ryan was reported to us as missing, Dany, you called us in a panic. I could hear the disbelief and fear in your voice. You knew your best friend and because of that you knew the dire circumstances.

You came.

You searched.

You stayed.

I think you needed us as much as we needed you in those first few days. You felt normal. Like we could pretend that Ryan was just away.

It was hard to have you leave. And yet you continue to come back. We insult you, tease you and love you.

You feel normal even now.

No, Dany, you aren't Ryan. You are this wonderful man that has so much to offer the world: compassion, empathy and a huge capacity to give of yourself. You will always be yourself. But I hope you don't mind if we steal you from Ryan. I think we might need you more than he does.

This is just the story we know of one of his friends.

But I am honoured to know that for this one I write of, there are tens that I haven't.

But don't fear, I will.

Ryan's story will be told through the love of his friends. All of them.

As a parent, you want your children to have friends to love, support and raise you up.

My god, Ryan, you were surrounded by the best.

April 26, 2018

I want to tell you a story.

It's not a fairy tale but rather a love story. Completely predictable and incredibly boring except for the two people it involves.

Scott and I met 23 years ago February at a bar in Edmonton (who hasn't?). I will admit I thought he was cute. He asked me out and I, having no other immediate options, agreed.

I remember him picking me up in his old green pickup. He came to the door and, upon opening it, I discovered my "cute" date was actually very handsome. Shhh … don't tell him; it will go to his head.

Fast forward the first date, the first kiss, the first of, well, everything.

We moved in together April 1st, he asked me to marry him in July and we said our vows September 16th. 7½ months after meeting. You can only imagine the side glances everyone gave me as I sipped on wine throughout the evening. 😵

However, Ryan did not bless our lives until 2 years later. The suddenness, I suppose, was shocking, but we just knew. Not sappy movie love but rather a quiet, enduring love that has more ups than downs, more joy than anger. The kind of love that can overcome this type of tragedy.

Scott had just turned 21 the year we got married. The irony is not lost on me that Ryan was almost the same age, and yet I can't imagine him following in Scott's footsteps. He seemed so young. Not quite immature but rather inexperienced in life.

But do not despair; for my son loved.

He was blessed to have fallen in love and been committed to another. He had his first kiss, first dance and his first "I love you." He had butterflies, longing of mutual attraction and the euphoria that comes from someone sharing the same feelings.

In essence ... my son had the capacity to experience love in all its beauty and receive it so deeply.

How many of us can say that?

Not all love is meant to last. Some will teach us what it means to love another, some will break our hearts so that we may learn to love better, and some will just fade away because we neglected to treat love like the treasure it is.

Each love story has a beginning and an ending. It does not matter how long you love or who you love, only that you do.

How wonderful that Ryan had his own love story.

April 27, 2018

It's National Superhero Day tomorrow.

I suppose it won't come as any surprise that I desperately want to have a super power of my own.

I mean who doesn't dream of being a superhero or possessing a super power? To have extraordinary abilities and exceptional skills that are designed solely to impact another in a positive way? To stand for something when everyone around you falters? To be admirable and strong, conscientious and caring?

Is this a fantasy in a world so mired in harsh reality?

Not so.

Over the past 10 weeks, I have encountered more superheroes than in any movie I will ever see. Living, breathing, walking definitions of what it means to be someone's hero.

The best part of being a superhero is that they know their own strengths. Superman couldn't spin webs. Batman wasn't using his hulk-like strength to fight bad guys. Wonder Woman wasn't wearing baggy sweats and sneakers ... well, you get the picture.

And yet, every superhero is remembered and revered because when called upon, they used their extraordinary abilities to make the world a better place.

Tomorrow on Superhero Day, look around and see what you can do to better your family, yourself, your environment or your community.

It can be small acts of kindness or taking time to be present with loved ones.

I promise that you will never regret the moments you take to be more of yourself.

If life is a series of moments, make yours memorable.

Oh ... my super power? It would be to turn back time.

April 28, 2018

I forgot to tell you ... not all heroes wear capes.

The best superheroes are the ones who quietly go about their day doing un-herolike things: grocery shopping, paying the bills or raking leaves. They work their jobs, raise their kids and greet their neighbours.

But still ... in the moments when they are needed most, they will rise to the occasion.

I am starting to believe that if I look closely at night into the far distance near Mount Morrisey, I will see a bright beacon. A green "R" shining strong and true calling on all superheroes to heed the call to action.

Because you come.

Every day you come.

You pray.

Every day you pray.

And you save us.

Every day you save us.

Not because we are worthy. How we would fall short if this was based solely on merit. So imperfect are we.

No ... these heroes hear our cries of desperation and come. Because to stand by and do nothing is unbearable. How extraordinary! I have never really experienced the likes of all of you. And when our time here comes to an end, know that we will gladly join the ranks of all our amazing volunteers who have given so unselfishly of themselves. We will go forth and do the same.

But I shall want a cape. Maybe green in honour of you, Ryan. You have changed me more than I ever thought possible.

Thank you, baby boy.

\*     \*     \*

So many volunteers. Over the course of the many weeks, there was a constant stream of them. Those who could search, came up to search. Those who could provide supplies, meal trains, equipment and resources gladly gave in whatever capacity they had. I am not sure Scott and I will ever be able to properly express the true depth of gratitude that we have, not only to our friends and family but to complete strangers. How do you tell people that they saved you? Every encouraging word or blind faith they gave to us kept us going. In all of this unending sorrow and heartbreak, the steadiness of support and love given to us and Ryan can never be described.

April 29, 2018

The road less travelled often leads to destinations unknown and experiences unmeasured. I find the very thought utterly delightful.

"Mommy did you know that Australia has like 9 out of 10 of the world's deadliest creatures?"

"Well, yes, love bug," I replied as we sat watching *The World's 10 Deadliest Creatures*.

"Man, that sounds so cool. I think we should go there," said my confident 10 year old.

Now I am going to be completely honest: Going someplace where there is a strong possibility I will get eaten or bitten has never been high on my list. That and anywhere the average dress size is 0. However, Australia has an unparalleled beauty that does appeal to me.

So, it always surprised me that the moment Ryan turned 18 and was working for a living, he didn't jump at the first opportunity to travel. After all, I work for an airline. That's what we do: travel.

"Ry ... you should go to Amsterdam. Land of awesome coffee shops and the Red Light District."

He shook his head.

"What about Scotland? Go visit Uncle Kevin and Auntie Donna. Great stopover to anywhere in Europe."

"Nah ... I'm okay."

I learned to stop asking. After all, my dreams cannot be my children's. They need to pave their own way.

Maybe Ryan discovered that you don't need to travel so far away to find delight in an adventure. After all, Dorothy discovered that very fact after clicking her ruby red shoes.

Today, we explored the area that was Ryan's temporary home. We hiked to these beautiful waterfalls. And in the middle of nowhere, there was this rock perched as though precariously teetering. How deceiving it was. Although it looked like it may come crashing down at any given minute, it was more solid than I thought.

I travelled 10 minutes from my temporary home to see what Ryan wants me to know: Beauty can be found anywhere.

You are stronger than you think.

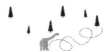

April 30, 2018

🎼 It's not easy being green ... in a world that is so blue 🎼

I want you to picture me singing that one little line. A little throaty and maybe a little bluesy. I am not saying it's accurate, I am just saying I want you to picture me in tune.

I like to make up little songs to sing to my children.

At first it was to hear my own voice after being with babies all day.

"Stretchy monkeys, stretchy monkeys," I would coo to them as they lay there in the crib peering up at me.

Oh, how their eyes would light up and smiles would spread across their faces.

My being green song was meant to coax the kids out of their "woe is me" moods. I mean ... come on ... who can stay grumpy to a Kermit the Frog ditty? Simply impossible. I could see the makings of a smile as they muttered, "Fine."

I suppose the real reason I sang funny songs to them was to see my children smile at the silliness of a grown-up. After all, as life goes on and our responsibility grows, we stop being childish.

Why do we do that, do you suppose? Lose the ability to laugh at ourselves or find the simple joy that life can bring?

I wish I had been more free and less consumed by what others might think. There is still time, I remind myself. My journey is not yet done.

I confess, though, these days feel particularly heavy.

On the one hand, the snow is melting. I see dirt and ground and less snow. That is promising. On the other, is the dismal fact that we haven't found Ryan.

Yet.

Logically, I know that the places that are now bare wouldn't be the areas Ryan would be in or we would have found him by now.

But still I suffer. Fear, regret, grief.

And then like a soft flutter, I hear the whispers of a song stirring in my head ...

May 1, 2018

Saying goodbye never gets easier, I think.

Today, I watched as Gerry and Sharon (two of our most steadfast volunteers) left for their summer in Florida. After 7½ weeks of continuous searching, Gerry is finally getting a break. But if I know him like I think I do, the drive down might be the only rest he takes. They have done so much and been such a big part of our life here. I am glad that adventure awaits them elsewhere.

But my biggest tears fell for Coco.

I have decided that everyone needs a Coco in their life. Someone that is so kind, loving and truly funny. Someone that has the ability to comfort and connect with others. Someone that is strong and gentle all in one breath of being.

Someone that makes you feel like you are home.

Coco is a wonderful wife, daughter and auntie. But I think her biggest relationship will be the one with her sister. Never have I seen two people that love and care for each other more. They have spent their lives building each other up and being this amazing support system.

I know this to be true by the way Coco loved all of us here.

Her friendship is loyal and fierce. I have known Coco for years but only on the periphery. We met through our good friends and then again with her beautiful sister Michelle.

She came Tuesday, February 20th, and stayed for eight days. Every day she set out with her husband Gord in miserable temperatures and searched. Every night, she came to me with tears in her eyes and heartbrokenly said, "We didn't find him." And the next day, they would do it again.

When she left, we said our goodbyes reluctantly. I was grateful and sad. But it was time for her to go.

Coco came back March 16th and stayed until today. It wasn't planned, but she knew that I needed her desperately for this small amount of time. Not just to search but for everything else she offered.

The funny thing is, she thinks she stayed for herself. I don't think she knows just how wonderful she is.

As we stood there and said our goodbyes ... we stared at each other, heartbroken through our tears. I am so very grateful and I am so very sad. But I know it was time for her to go.

Goodbyes are the hardest because they feel like so many things are left unspoken or undone.

I have come to realize that some goodbyes are not forever.

But I hate them anyways.

May 2, 2018

The soothing sound of water. Tendrils of steam curling and rising. Candles flickering softly, warm and comforting.

"Mum ... Mum ... Mummmmmmmmm ... whatcha doing in there? Can I tell you a story? It's just a small one. Mummmmmmmmmmmmmmmmm ...."

And that is why young mothers never take baths.

We show up dishevelled and chaotic with pieces of food sticking to our backs where little hands have gripped tightly. We grin brightly as we try to follow grown-up conversation. Nodding our heads like we are listening to foreign tongues speaking strange languages.

Ahhh the woes of those early days.

I remember you well.

Waiting desperately for Scott to come home from work. I am not quite sure who was more anxious for the day's end, Ryan or myself. I was like a puppy sitting at the window with my tail ready to furiously wag at the sight of the red truck coming into the drive.

"Daddy's home! Daddy's home!!!!!"

I am not ashamed to say that high-pitched squealing came from me.

Night-time routine was Scott's time. From the moment he walked in through the door until 7:30 p.m., he was on the go. And he did so with such gladness.

Bath time was their favourite time together. I could hear giggles all the way downstairs. There were coloured crayons that marked the tub, dinosaurs littering the floor and cars resting on soap bars. Make-believe adventures were nightly affairs. I loved that about Scott. I was more about getting the kids in, washed up and out. On to the next task. He made baths fun and childlike.

At the end, always and each night was the same.

"Daddy ... can you make me a dinosaur egg?"

"Sure, Ry."

Scott would then wrap a big towel around Ryan, with another covering his head. He carried him to the bed, wet towels soaking the comforter, and tucked his feet in so that he was completely covered.

"I'm cracking."

And like a baby dinosaur, he would break free of the shell of towels. Each night a new dinosaur emerged, cheeks flushed and eyes bright.

I may not have liked bath time routines, but I loved that moment.

I look each day at the snow, hard and crusty. White like an egg.

"Ryan, it's okay to crack out now, baby boy. Time to go."

May 3, 2018

Once I was the fastest in the family.

This is how it went according to 8-year-old Ryan: Mommy, Ryan, Max (the dog), Daddy and Jordyn.

Don't laugh, it was proven. We ran races at the lake all the time. I always won.

Then I ruptured my Achilles tendon playing indoor soccer, and my reign was over. The doctor told me no running sports for 9–12 months.

"What am I supposed to do now?" I lamented.

Scott, with a mischievous glint in his eye, replied, "Oh, I know."

10 months later, Julianna was born.

I sat on the sidelines watching as Ryan got faster. Playing soccer, my game. I may have been petulant, but still I cheered him on. God, he was like the wind. Soccer, baseball, football or rugby ... it was like nothing could stop him.

If nothing else, I am stubborn. I worked hard to run again. Each day, on holidays, at the lake, I ran. I may never be as fast as Ryan, but I can still beat Scott.

Until ... my latest Achilles injury.

I will get strong again. I did it once, I can do it again. But even if I could run fast or run far ... I will never be able to outrun the grief that dogs my every step.

In my mind, I still see Ryan, laughing as he chases after me.

Baby, I pray the paths are wide and soft and you have miles to run with Max at your side.

May 4, 2018

Schrödinger's cat is a thought experiment where a scenario presents that a cat may both be simultaneously alive and not. What a paradox it is. For once the box is open, you will know that this is not the case. The cat will either be one or the other.

Now, before you applaud my intelligence, it was explained to me by Sheldon on *The Big Bang Theory*.

But it stuck with me.

I feel like we are living this paradox in a never-ending Groundhog Day.

While we are here, we don't have the answers we so desperately seek. Sometimes, most days, I suppose I have been afraid of what the day will bring.

Because right now, Ryan is alive.

I can believe that for I know nothing beyond that premise. Oh, I am aware that there are theories, scenarios, realisms. But if I close my eyes real tight and empty my mind, I can believe what I wish.

That will change, quite certainly, in the next while. But for now, that is what is true.

We search each day. We wait for the snow to melt and go home to do it again the next day.

We hope and we grieve.

We have tragedies and we have blessings.

We laugh and we cry.

Love brings joy and pain.

All of these are paradoxical.

And then it comes to me quite clearly. In order to truly appreciate one, you must endure the other.

Ryan will always be alive.

His friendships, his connections to others, the love we share and all of our collective memories make him larger than life.

And what a life.

May 6, 2018

What do you want to be when you grow up?

Everyone asks and most don't know. Such a heavy decision.

As a young girl, I had heady dreams of what my life would look like. Reality is so much harsher.

Scott always knew, I think. He likes working with his hands, building and constructing. One of his greatest qualities, and one I take such comfort in, is his ability to find solutions, no matter the difficulty. I suppose one could argue that this will be the first time he can't. But this isn't his to fix.

I, on the other hand, had no idea what I wanted to do.

I went to university to become a high school teacher. I did a bit of substitution and didn't love it. So instead, I went to college and took early childhood education. Not for me either. I did payroll management and then stayed home to raise my kids. It's not that I was flighty, I just couldn't find my passion. It wasn't until I went to work for WestJet that I discovered something I loved to do. Training new staff and travel—what could be better? It filled my heart.

Then.

Before this.

Before Ryan.

Now I wonder ... what will stir my passion? Will anything?

Ryan often dreamed of being an archeologist. If not that, then a zookeeper. If not that, maybe working with Daddy. I used to sit and watch him as a baby and wonder, "How extraordinary. You can be anything." It wasn't the actualizing that is important, after all. It lies within the dreaming. The moment you dream, you believe you can do what otherwise might seem impossible.

How beautiful is that?

I regret that we won't see what Ryan would choose to be when he finished exploring life.

But what you are is so much less important than who you are.

And for that, my son, you were everything you were meant to be.

And more.

May 9, 2018

12 weeks ...

God, who knew? Who could guess this would be my reality? Who knew that Sun Peaks would become a prison of expectation and cruel existence?

I can still vividly see our last weekend. I didn't know. I wasn't aware that it would be my last moment of true happiness and peace. I didn't treasure it, didn't value it or even recognize it.

Because it wasn't extraordinary.

It was my normal.

We were invited to dinner. Our dear friends John and Stevens were up from Calgary and staying at Niki and Brandon's. Bailey, Nicole and Brian joined us for supper. It was like old times. We dined and drank and toasted to new beginnings. We laughed with our recollections of memories past. It was fun. It was normal.

In the middle, a Snapchat came from Lyette. *Odd. We haven't talked in a bit*, I thought. Sure we "like" everything but it's usually not Snapchat worthy.

"Heather, my beautiful friend. I just want you to know I love looking at your posts. I can see you on TV. Maybe a blog. Maybe something with food. Thinking of you."

Ahhh so sweet. I loved hearing from her. You see, I admired this woman so much, I was in awe she reached out. Unexpected.

It was a beautiful evening.

I didn't know.

I went to bed. I slept the peaceful dreams of someone who had it all and had everything to look forward to.

It was such a lie.

The next day was filled with ringette. Both girls had games. Jordyn had two. We spent the day driving back and forth, and it seemed never-ending.

At 9:15 p.m., we finally got home.

At 9:30, our lives changed forever.

"Heather, Ryan never came home last night. He didn't show up for work today. We filed a missing police report."

Never have words swarmed before me and caused such deep, all-consuming fear.

We left for Sun Peaks that night at 11:00. I don't remember the drive. It was fast. It was too slow. I prayed. I begged. I negotiated.

*Please let this be okay.*

As the night wore on and the sun began its steady rise, I knew.

My life as I knew it was over.

I would readily accept it, but never in my world would I have thought the price would be my only son.

The time draws near, I think. Like a chrysalis. We will leave behind this tragic journey and begin anew.

Missing something vital.

I am ready.

I am not.

May 10, 2018

When did we become so judgmental?

I always said that I was observational, but perhaps those words mean the same thing. Mine is just prettier because I tie a bow on top and call it by a different name.

I am not who I was.

From the moment you start to date it is, "When are you getting married? Oooh, you know men don't buy the cow if the milk is free ..."

You take the plunge.

And then it is, "When are you having children? Ooooh, you aren't getting any younger ..."

The time becomes right. The barrage of questions begins in earnest.

"What did you decide for a name? ... Ooooh, my cousin's ex-fiancée had that name. I don't like her ...."

And, "Are you giving birth naturally? ... Ooooh, I delivered and went to the gym the next day."

You think the judgements will stop. Not true. From parenting decisions to house locations to clothing choices to vacations ... we feel as a public we have the right to an opinion. And the right to express it. Freely.

As we grow, perhaps we wrap it in a sweeter package, but the effect is still the same. In essence we say: You are different from me but we must be the same. How can we have harmony if we have diversity?

I have learned ...

Each person is born and raised with a value system unique to them and their environment. What we consider our top ten may be someone else's bottom five. Why can't that be okay? What if we just accepted it? Freely.

I honestly thought my parenting decisions were based on sound, logical and common-sense practices. How could I, in good conscience, not allow you to benefit from my successes? So, I offered it. Freely.

Except.

I couldn't save my son.

He was a grown adult with a mind of his own. Brilliant and vast, he was able to process and assess his own experiences and choose his own path.

Except.

February 17th, he made a decision that led us all here. Not on purpose. Not to his benefit. Much to everyone's never-ending sorrow.

But I don't judge him for that.

Because I am not the same.

May 11, 2018

Music soothes the tired soul ...

The first concert I ever took Ryan to was Marianas Trench. He was 13. Well, honestly, if we were to really go back, it might have been Bear in the Big Blue House, but my selective memory will appeal to Ryan more.

They were his favourite band. I remember the look of disbelief followed by expectant excitement the moment he found out that he and I were going. The tough part is doing something for your children that you are unsure you will actually like. But for this, I will unabashedly admit ... I am a fan.

I think there is something wonderful in the maturing of your children. So many times we, as parents, deal with the unpleasant and disciplinary actions of raising children. To find a common interest and watch it grow is a beautiful thing. It is more often ignored for the ordinary until it is a passing memory.

For Scott, it was hunting and hockey.

For me, it was soccer and music.

And then he developed different tastes. Pink Floyd, Bon Jovi and, surprisingly, a huge love of the Beatles. Posters lined his walls along with the requisite scantily clad women. Throw in deer antlers and I'm out. I'm a woman of cosmopolitan tastes, but even that was too much.

When he met Juliana, he discovered an interest in country music. Big Valley Jamboree made for a memorable weekend. Of course, I can only guess from the pictures. I feel like I probably wouldn't have approved.

Everything about him grew, matured and developed. It was so gradual that I didn't recognize it until it was fully entrenched and completely him.

Even now, someone will tell me a story or a memory of Ryan that takes me aback. Some parts feel familiar, like a remembering of who he is. Other parts are like revealing a new person, much like unwrapping a present.

There is such joy in not knowing everything about my son. It means that I have so much more to learn.

It is as soothing as the music we both listened to and loved.

\*     \*     \*

May 11–13 was such a busy weekend for us. A fundraiser had been organized in Kamloops, BC at the Red Collar Brewing Co. by a continuing and dedicated group of volunteers from the community. There were auction items to bid on, a craft beer created just for Ryan (a dino-sour, of course) and bands playing throughout the night. Scott and I were amazed at the turnout. It was overwhelming to see so many people in the community who came to meet us and to show their support for our son, Ryan.

It was also the beginning of Mother's Day weekend and the first time since Ryan had gone missing that neither Scott nor I were in Sun Peaks searching.

May 13, 2018

Beginnings and endings.

There is a certain amount of fear and trepidation in both, I suppose. Neither knows what the outcome can truly be. You just have faith that in the end, all will be well.

Tonight, Scott, Jordyn, Julianna, Max (Jordyn's boyfriend) and I had the privilege, along with our family and friends, to say thank you to this community that has embraced us as one of their own.

February 17th was, without a doubt, a parent's worst nightmare. It is not far from my thoughts that our journey has been unforgiving and heartbreaking. Such a tragedy, to be sure.

And yet.

We have become closer as a family.

Our friends, forged of steel and fire, have given us the strength to do what needs to be done. Each day.

We have met some incredible people that we are honoured to now call friends.

We have felt the awakening of this community mindfulness that seems to span from coast to coast.

21 years ago, we gave birth to this beautiful baby boy. He has forever impacted us. But as I watch each day, people gathering to help us and one another, I have come to realize that Ryan has impacted all of you.

Even in endings, there can be beautiful beginnings.

May 13, 2018 (Mother's Day)

> *The sweetest sounds to mortals given*
> *Are heard in Mother, Home, and Heaven.*
> - William Goldsmith Brown

At times, I feel more apart from these words than I would ever have thought.

So far from home, missing the one person that would make the family complete again. Like there is a puzzle piece that is gone, and although the picture still looks beautiful, it will never be perfect.

And yet crystals that are shattered into a million pieces still hold a form and can shine.

So, we will persevere.

I don't suppose it is easy to guess that I love traditions.

Normally, Mother's Day begins with breakfast in bed with my favourite stuffed apple raspberry French toast. The children proudly present their home-made gifts. I feel special and loved.

The grandmas come over later for a dinner cooked by Papa. Decadent and planned by us women.

One year, Ryan found himself grounded. Yes, even on Mother's Day. He begged all day and during dinner to be allowed to go out after supper. The sun was warm and the sounds of kids playing was like a siren sound. This year, Papa had made paella filled with seafood. Normally not a fan favourite for Ry.

"Mom, please!" came the fervent plea again.

"Absolutely, love, if you eat this baby octopus," I replied with a certain malicious grin.

Even I won't eat something that grotesque, but I never counted on his desperation. In goes the octopus. The look of sheer revulsion stays with me now. He tried to swallow. I will give him that. Then up he ran to the patio door and out came his dinner. Well, I will never win a Mother of the Year award. That year, anyways. I laughed until I cried.

I let him go out. His desire was stronger than my will.

Of course, this year was different.

Brunch out followed by an afternoon at the lake paddle-boarding. It was lovely and peaceful.

See, we shattered but still we shine.

Mother, Home and Heaven.

I weep at the words, but it is not only with sadness. There is joy as well.

# The Community We Didn't Know We Had

Volunteers are the backbone of every society, the heart of every community, because selfless acts of service make a difference in the world regardless of the circumstances. Most of us volunteer in some form or another. Scott and I spent countless hours engaged with sports or school activities over the course of our adult lives. In all honesty, it was for the betterment of our children's experiences. To coach soccer or ringette encouraged our kids to continue in the sports they loved and provided extended opportunities for growth and learning. Helping out at school allowed us to stay informed on the day-to-day activities and fostered positive relationships with teachers and educators. Of course, these acts always intersected and benefitted others, but in truth, the primary goal was for us alone.

That is hindsight. At the time, it really wasn't a complicated thought process about why we did it. We had the time, we had the love, and we wanted to help our children in any way we could. Volunteering in its simplest form.

It is through a different lens that I see the volunteers before us. Over the course of the days, months and years since Ryan disappeared, Scott and I have come to understand what true volunteering means.

And how it humbles us. Our friends—some we knew really well and others not as much—showed up in the early stages. Some were not quite acquaintances but people we had known for years, saw in the community and connected with through extracurricular events in school and out. We were on the periphery of each other's lives because life gets so busy, yet they came when we needed them most. When we were unsure of how to get through the next minute, hour or day.

In addition to our friends, then came the community, stunned at the tragedy that was unfolding in their town and wanting to help in whatever way they could. Sun Peaks and the surrounding areas will always hold a special place in my heart. On the drive from our hotel to the makeshift command centre on the first day of searching, I vividly remember Scott adamantly saying, "We will find Ryan, we will go home, and we will never step foot in this town again." Quietly and reflectively, I said nothing. At that moment, I probably agreed with his sentiment. But day after day, Sun Peaks showed up. They mourned with us, they laughed alongside us, and they showered us with grace and compassion. How can you attribute such loss with such love? We do it every day just by living. A two-sided coin that changes the circumstances just with a flick of the wrist.

I find it all incredible but perhaps somewhat predictable. One might expect friends, family and the community to rally behind you in the time of tragedy, but something more miraculous occurred. Strangers from far away heard our story and began this call to action. On Saturday March 24, 2018, a donated bus filled with more than fifty people from Beaumont, Edmonton and the surrounding area travelled to Sun Peaks to search for one day. The volunteers gathered Friday to travel all day to Kamloops where accommodations were provided before undertaking a large search effort the next day and then returning home on Sunday. Up until this point, we had large groups going out each day but nothing quite this large. Hope swelled in our hearts as we saw seat after seat vied for and taken until there was no room left but a waiting list growing.

Then on April 20–22, 2018, it happened again. Everything generously donated: transportation, meals and hotels in Sun Peaks offering free accommodations to a busload of volunteers. This time, the bus began in Edmonton, travelled through to Red Deer as a pickup stop and finally rolled into Calgary before continuing on to Sun Peaks. It was almost twenty-six hours round trip for one day of searching for Ryan. Some of our volunteers were returning, but many were brand new. A bus packed full of hope and a desire to help us.

On Mother's Day weekend, a dedicated group of volunteers who spent hours co-ordinating and fundraising gave me a gift of love I still cannot quite comprehend. They arranged to have a plane fly to Kamloops for the weekend so that volunteers could have two full days to search. The snow was melting quickly, so the urgency to find Ryan before the undergrowth became too heavy was apparent.

Each time an opportunity to come from afar was presented, complete strangers—individuals who did not know us and did not know Ryan but felt this need to do something—signed up or patiently put themselves on the waiting list to join in the search efforts. How does one even explain the selflessness to give so willingly for a family in crisis? It's not a half-hearted effort that requires onc to do the bare minimum and a self-congratulations in the end but a full out commitment that stretched them out of their comfort zones.

I don't know if I was ever a person who would travel hours to help another just because they needed it. I likely would have felt that I couldn't carve out time from an always busy life to think beyond myself and offer the opportunity to give hope to another. Maybe that is not a fair assessment. Maybe I would have been someone that heard a cry for action and felt compelled to go. I guess I will never know.

But what I can say with certainty now is, if you need me, I will be there. Committed individuals can change this world because they care. Because it matters.

May 14, 2018

*There is nothing to fear except fear itself.*

What a moronic phrase, in my opinion.

There is so much to be afraid of.

Fear of pain, being alone, unrequited love, injury, failure, sickness and so on and so on. Most times, fears are deeply rooted in alternate realities. They are just things that COULD happen, not that they necessarily will. Our imaginations will create such fantastical tales, so it is a wonder we ever attempt anything.

However.

Fear can also be what drives or motivates us.

Venturing outside the norm, stepping off the precipice or grabbing opportunities that are just a little past our reach can be incredibly rewarding and life altering.

It is finding the balance, I suppose, between being cautious and being optimistic.

Children seem to be born without fear. Maybe that is a blessing. For a short period of time, before we as parents impose our own fears, children are free. Free to believe, to try, to fail and to cope. Some days, I wish I could curl up on my father's lap with his comforting hand on my head as he gently pats my back.

"There there, Pooh Bear. It will all be okay. Everything will be okay."

Because it won't be.

I fear.

I fear so much. I fear we will never find Ryan. I fear that this nightmare will never be over. I fear the image we present if one of us leaves to go home. I fear the whispering that suggests alternative realities about Ryan's disappearance.

But at least I am honest in my fears. I am not crippled by them yet.

I also know that I will never fear the same things again.

The things I feared before all of this.

I don't fear what comes after. I believe.

I don't fear how much I can take before I break. I am stronger than I thought. I can survive this. I will survive this.

My fear motivates me.

May 15, 2018

*Men succeed when they realize that their failures are the preparation for their victories.*
                                    - Ralph Waldo Emerson

I remember so vividly the day Ryan was born. I want to tell you that Scott and I were prepared, but that would be a lie. Of course, we knew he was coming, but I had read too many books. "Babies don't come early. Expect to go past your due date."

So, I was prepared to wait. Despite being sick each day, I was patient. Surely the end result is worth the difficulties that may arise? The crib was barely set up. His room in disarray. I had time, I thought.

The gods laugh at the plans of humans.

Ryan was early. Okay, not super early. 3 days. My friends laugh at my naivety.

The lesson, of course, is that I know so little. I am well-read and intelligent, but I didn't have all the answers. I don't know that I will ever truly be prepared. So began what will be a lifetime process of self-discovery.

Perhaps being a parent means you stumble through. We have missteps and moments of brilliance. You cry at your ineptitude and laugh at your success. But then I realized that not knowing is hardly limited to parents. It is the subtle art of being human. We grow and we learn. We yearn to do better. We strive to be good.

I am no different. I hope to be humbled. I struggle to be wrong.

I don't have all the answers.

What I do know is that Scott and I are driven. We are persistent. We stand before this mountain and swear it will move before we leave.

We were not prepared for this. But I have learned I don't need to be prepared in order to stand strong. To be immovable.

Every day that we don't find him is not a failure. Not on our part. Not on our loved ones nor our volunteers. It strengthens our resolve for tomorrow and the next day.

I may not have all the answers, and I will never be prepared, but what I know with absolute certainty is that my son will be found.

May 16, 2018

I hoarded all the wrong things.

The stacks of bills sitting on my countertop that were never opened because we do online banking. A cruel reminder that money is owed.

The shoes that line my garage and my front closet and my bedroom. Who knows when red jelly shoes will come back in style?? I am prepared.

The clothes that drape so beautifully in my walk in. Taunting me with visions of smaller sizes and long-ago trends.

I loathe to throw such things away. Their importance is in relation to my unsettledness in everyday life. If I do not open the bill, it cannot matter. If I do not throw the shoes away, then time stands still. If I close my eyes and pretend, I can be exactly where I want to be.

What I should have saved instead was all those heartfelt Mother's Day cards, Easter gifts and birthday surprises.

"Mommy, look at the picture I made!"

I must say that was the most challenging game I have ever played as an adult.

"Oh my, Ryan, that is so colourful. You used so much green there," I would cautiously praise.

Never comfortable with my bland, open-ended statements, Ryan would raise one eyebrow and ask me to tell him what it was.

"Gosh, it's like right on the tip of my tongue. Ry ... what is that thing that is green and like big and you know ... that thing?"

"An apatosaurus?"

"Yes!" I cried in relief.

"No, that's not it."

It is never easy having a clever child.

Those pictures would hang on my fridge, proudly front and centre. Time would pass and they became tattered and stained. New ones would take the place of the old. A circle of life.

I meant to tuck them away. Why didn't I treat them like beloved treasures, priceless and irreplaceable? After all, to me, they are reminiscent of a time when my children had complete confidence in their ability to represent their world.

I didn't know. These trinkets and memorabilia didn't seem that important. There would be more to follow. There always was. I thought that the kids would lose interest in them and their value would diminish over time.

I never imagined how much I would long for traces of Ryan.

What I realize now is that I should have hoarded memories.

May 18, 2018

Caution: Proceed with care.

Some people might say such words about me and they may be right. But no, this story isn't about me.

Every year for the past 15 on this night, we have packed up and headed to our lake property for the weekend. We have never missed a year. Not one.

It is opening weekend. Everyone at their sites, the sounds of us neighbours shaking off the long winter blues and greeting each other. The children excitedly catching up on months past. (Now, I suppose, it is redundant due to our busy social media posts making our whole lives visible to everyone to see and experience.) Dirty leaves brushed off decks and patio chairs set out. First things first: The kids always used to run to the lake to "check it out." May long weekend is the first day of lake season and where we spent most of our weekends until September long.

What I loved most was this sense of innocence that we have long lost. My three would run out first thing in the morning, come back for snacks or lunch or dinner and eventually stagger back for bed.

Friends would be brought. Fun would be had.

Constant for Ryan was Dany and Manny, brothers and steadfast friends. They also were the source of our terrible reputation.

Let me be clear ... none of this is my fault. Mostly.

It's Saturday and I have already blown through $300 in groceries. Growing boys hardly describes the pace at which they consume food.

We decide to take the boys on the boat tubing to slow the consumption of eating. Frankly we can ill afford the rate in which they all eat..

As I comment on the speed and boringness of Scott's driving, he hits a wave. Up fly all 3 boys. Down they come. Manny pops up. He's OK. Ryan's head bobs above the water and yells, "Dany bit me!" And then there is Dany. I can see his 10-year-old face and, as handsome as he is, his front teeth are now sticking straight up. This is a problem.

"Whoa ... dude, that's bad," said Ryan

I quickly interject, "No no, it's not bad. Honestly!"

I'm not sure Dany believed my lying face. I have perfected that look since.

Now I must take them to the hospital and an emergency dentist. Despite our auspicious beginning, Dany comes back to the lake. A move I will later regret.

The boys proudly display the war wounds and then proceed to play Mantracker. Through the boat launch marsh complete with geese feces. If you are thinking ... infection in the foot ... you would be right.

Sunday begins with hot temperatures. Ryan is feeling a wee bit flushed but still game to play. "Sunscreen," my new favourite word, echoes throughout the campground.

At night, Ryan is experiencing a mild fever and Dany is complaining of sore shoulders. Manny is OK.

Cue Monday. By now Ryan is full-fledged sick, foot throbbing. Dany says his shoulders are hot. Upon examination, he has not only glued teeth but bubbling blisters where he didn't quite remember to put sunscreen on.

The weekend is officially over. To be honest, I am completely surprised the boys were ever allowed back. But they were.

However, our neighbours suggested having guests at our place sign waivers. Why? Well, there might be more stories.

I tell you this in hopes that as the long weekend approaches, that you all take care. Be safe.

My greatest wish would for us all to be at the lake. Whole and complete.

As you now know, life offers no such guarantees.

May 19, 2018

I think my philosophy concerning life up until now may be a little skewed.

I am going to be completely honest with you. I don't know how to change a tire. I hate shovelling the snow or mowing the lawn. I'm not really a painter or a fixer. I'm okay with that. In a zombie apocalypse, I feel like I need to know three things:

1) How to ride a motorcycle
2) How to shoot a gun
3) How to fashion eyelash extensions out of mink hair ... or porcupine needles

Despite what some might call my supreme limitations, I have high hopes for my daughters.

Isn't that the way, though? You want the accomplishments of your children to outshine yours. I pray that my girls are stronger, smarter and braver than me. I wish for beauty not only on the outside but the inside as well, and a confidence in how they view and receive the world.

Perhaps that puts pressure on them, but, in reality, I just want them to be happy. Not my version of happy. I want Jordyn and Julianna to pave their way through life and make a mark that is utterly their own.

The irony is, I had no such expectations of Ryan. I have no idea what it is like to be a boy so I thought whatever he was doing was fine. I understand now that the ease of our relationship was based on my complete acceptance of him.

I always wondered if I did my girls a disservice in that regard.

But as I looked around today, I realized my fears are unfounded.

Today as we searched for our 13th week straight, I did it with a tribe of strong, beautiful women. Two of them were my daughters.

If my girls are to learn anything, I want them to know that it is not necessary to move mountains with brute strength alone. Sometimes it is the whisper of a voice that says you are capable of more than you know and a quiet insistence that courage comes when you need it most.

We are uniquely individual. We are all imperfectly perfect.

I can finally see the beauty in that.

May 20, 2018

Everyone wants to be the hero of their own story.

But we all need rescuing sometimes. In our darkest hours we call out for a miracle. Someone to help relieve the burden we are forced to carry. That is the truest form of humanity; the ability to cry out and the ability to heed that call.

I think I am strong ... most days. By now, I know you all so well that you will tell me that I am more than I am. In good conscience, I must let you know that my beautiful friends around me keep me humble. "You are just okay ... honestly, you are not that great," they lovingly joke (I think). 😒

So, it is hard for me to seek rescuing. I am a romantic in thinking the ending is better if I overcome adversity on my own. The realist in me insists that is impossible.

I am slowly understanding my own strengths and the challenges I face. Let's be clear: it won't be playing indoor soccer ever again.

For what is life without lessons? Lessons we learn ourselves, lessons others may teach us or, cruelly, savage lessons that are thrust upon us.

Ryan was 11 or so when Scott took him out to Gido's farm. While Scott and his dad were out in the back forty, Ryan decided to go biking with his cousin. The necessity of wearing a helmet was lost on them while riding down the hill on the gravelly road. Ryan swerved to avoid a divot and subsequently fell off his bike. Scraped and bruised, he lay there in shock, unable or unwilling to move. His cousin ran off to get Scott.

"Please don't go," he begged her, crying. "I don't want to be alone."

So, she sat with him and held his hands as he cried. Until Scott came to find him.

You have no idea how this story wounds me now in the retelling. All of his life, my son had someone holding his hand. Someone to kiss his brow, to soothe his tears, to chase the monsters from his bed. Every day, until the early morning of February 18th. This lesson is so cruel and absolute.

I so want to be the hero. To do what we have been unable to do thus far.

It feels like our darkest hour.

May 21, 2018

There are some words that you cannot take back. They are like little particles of destruction that hover all around you waiting to implode at the slightest movement.

They say the truth will set you free.

Whose truth? Yours? It is not as simple as that, I think. There are versions of truth. Perceptions of what the truth is. And truth can be subjective.

Our capacity for truth telling sometimes gives little consideration to another. "That dress is too tight. You look awful." But it's the truth, you argue.

Isn't it better that they should know from someone who loves them?

But your words are as you see them. Based on your life experiences and your value system. Not necessarily how others might view them. Not even how that person might see themselves.

I remember telling Ryan that I could tell he was lying just by looking at his teeth. They turn colours based on the lies he might tell, I said. In his defence, he was 3. Imagine this sweet boy covering his mouth so I couldn't look in. A beautiful lie designed to garner the truth. Ironic, no?

There are black and whites, certainly. Truths that no matter how you wish to package them up in pretty bows and beautiful boxes remain concrete and absolute. And sometimes you will be given the gravest of responsibilities to be the bearer of the truth. Perhaps then you can think about being kind. If the truth is inescapable, then the gift is in the delivery.

The truth is I am not 100 percent sure what happened to Ryan on February 17th. Maybe that truth will forever elude me. But I know what I believe. For me, belief is not just a stretch of imagination or leap of faith. It is based on the strong knowledge of my son and his character. It comes from living and breathing this experience each day since. It is bolstered by what I know from the RCMP.

So, the question, "Do you REALLY believe he is still on the hill?" is tactless to me. Would Scott and I stay at Sun Peaks for 3 months and counting if we thought otherwise? Would we search day in and day out? Would we welcome our friends and family as they continually put their lives on hold to travel here to help us? Would we allow our daughters to grieve without us each week as we stay here? Would we ask volunteers to drive such lengths over and over if we believed it was futile?

How extraordinarily selfish we would be.

The truth is, we are exhausted. A tiredness has seeped into our bones and placed an icy grip on our souls.

The truth is, we question if we have done enough in our search efforts.

The truth is, we hold the RCMP accountable for investigating our son's disappearance. And they have consistently delivered.

The truth is, the time is drawing ever closer to us having to go home.

The truth will forever be, we will never give up.

Our truth is that we believe.

May 22, 2018

Who am I?

I am sundresses and flip flops. Summer warmth and never-ending sunshine.

I am sarcastic, flirty and opinionated. I tell people that I am dynamic (sounds nicer). I am empathic and sensitive to those around me.

Who am I?

I am winter bred, layered in snowsuits and cumbersome boots. I can probe and shovel with grim determination.

I am a crier, numb with fear and grief and a soother of sorrowful hearts.

Who am I?

I am a hiker, clad in all-terrain boots and walking sticks. I climb mountains, fierce and proud.

I am practical with a steel heart that can separate the painful from the joyful. I have a strength that is unrecognizable but deeply seeded in my being.

I am a source of contradictions. Brave and flawed. Hopeful and realistic. Some days more and some days less than who I wish to be. And I'm okay with that.

Who will I be?

I am content not knowing the path on which my life will now take me. I have to be. The curves in the road come upon me and catch me unaware. No one can brace themselves for all that is to come. Good or bad. I have just learned to hold on tight.

Lest you worry that only tragedy can transform who you are, don't be. I think it is your connectivity to others and your investment in yourself, your loved ones and your community that will continually form your character.

Who was my son?

The best of both Scott and I, perhaps. But I believe, from all of you, that he was so much more.

It is a season of change.

May 23, 2018

*Birth is not only about making babies. Birth is about making mothers—strong, competent, capable mothers who trust themselves and know their inner strength.*

- Barbara Katz Rothman

Birthing is unique and universal all at once. Societal norms, rituals and customs all play a large part in the birthing experience. I have read that in some cultures new mothers are "quarantined," which essentially means the larger family gathers around and pitches in. The mother rests and regains her strength. The women in her family surround her with love and support so that when the time comes, she is prepared for the task that lies ahead.

Ryan was easy to birth. At the time, cell phones were big, clunky work phones so Scott and I decided to get a pager instead. If I thought labour was imminent, I was to page 911. Good, solid plan. Thank goodness we didn't have to use it. Although I will confess—much to Scott's grey hair—I did several practice runs.

Our beautiful baby boy was born, tiny and wrinkly, scrawny and red-faced. I held him for the first time and knew in that same moment that my life was forever changed. My capacity to love, cherish and protect was an inherent trait that suddenly manifested.

The nurses swaddled Ryan with the intention to take him to be weighed, measured and bathed, but Scott refused to allow them to take his son from his sight. He is the nicest guy but ever so stubborn.

He reminds me of an oak tree: solid, majestic and proud but with roots that stretch deep beneath the earth. Ryan never left his side. I, on the other hand, was wheeled into my hospital room—a mother without a child. Waiting.

I suppose I can be honest; I don't love waiting. 911 ... pause ... 911 ... pause ... insistent.

Scott came back perplexed and worried. I was relieved and overjoyed. My son was with me. My family complete. Our lives to begin.

It was hard going. I never knew how hard it would be. Trouble with feeding, sleepless nights and a lifetime of adjustments. Scott's mom and my mom worked. Auntie Doo was living in another city, and we were the first of all of our friends to have a child. What I would have given to be part of that matriarchal culture where such love and care was given.

But perhaps I didn't need it then.

When that beautiful baby boy that I remember so well went missing, I became, once again, a mother without a child. Waiting.

I am not alone, though. My family—my tribe—surrounds me with love and support so that when the time comes, I will be prepared for the task that lies ahead.

What a culture we have created.

May 24, 2018

The silence is deafening.

Footsteps echo in the hallway where only yesterday it was strewn with shoes, tiredly kicked off. The kitchen quiet and pristine, not filled with the bustling bodies intent on feeding everyone.

For the first time in 3 months, we are alone in the house.

I am not afraid to tell you that I thought grief would overwhelm us. There is no one to distract Scott and I from our deepest fears and darkest thoughts. We have been so careful to leave such things unsaid. Not forever, surely, just for now. We have tasks to do.

Our loved ones gave us respite. I am grateful that they were able to rotate for so long. In doing so, we were able to put off the inevitable ... until now.

Oh, they tried to prepare us for this moment. Date Night in Kamloops was strongly suggested and forcibly encouraged.

In our old life, I loved Date Night. There was the excitement in choosing a new restaurant. Long talks where we reminisced about our favourite memories and dreamt of a beautiful future.

But now I always find myself crying. Not because I am alone with Scott but because without the busyness of our friends and family surrounding us ... we must face our grief. We must talk about things that we would rather put off.

Date Night now has a third wheel. Ryan joins us each time and we can avoid it no longer. I am quite the sight, I'm sure. Cocktails and hand holding ... then one tear rolls down, followed by another. I try not to. My sadness compounds Scott's. Boy, he wishes so desperately to take this all from me. I believe he would, you know. If he could bear all these burdens, he would, in spite of the price.

Main course and wine ... remembrances of happier times.

I don't think our servers know what to do with us.

I don't either.

But our friends were right. Each time it gets a little easier. The tightness in my chest constricts less and less.

I do miss everyone, but being alone is kinda nice. Like an old friend you haven't seen in such a long time. Tentative at first but comforting in the same breath.

These are the moments that tell me that however long our journey may be, we will face it together. We are never really alone. I understand that now.

May 25, 2018

*"Love means never having to say you're sorry."*

Clearly, this is misleading. I feel like I am constantly apologizing to my husband, my family and my friends. I don't suppose being Canadian helps the situation either.

Honestly, if I could go back and rewrite my vows, this would be the only one I would want. I understand the importance of the words, but the struggle has always been to say them.

This has been the rule in our house since the kids were old enough to grasp the concept of asking for forgiveness: If you are brave enough to hurt someone's feelings, then you also must be brave enough to tell them you are sorry. The words matter, of course, but not unless accompanied by action.

You must look the person in the eye and say, "I'm sorry."

Oh, in theory, that is a wonderful concept. However, it can get somewhat impractical as kids grow up.

Ryan was the King of Mumblers and Master of Snide Apologies. True titles.

Apparently, I was unclear on how these pleas for forgiveness were to be delivered. Therefore, I needed to adjust the qualifications.

1) Look into the other person's eyes. Do not roll yours.
2) Apologize with sincerity. Telling someone you are sorry they are stupid is considered a breach of apology etiquette.

I never expected my children to follow such a rule without Scott and I also complying.

There was a time that Ryan was 5 and Jordyn was 2. We were in our old house and I could hear Jordyn screaming. The sound, high pitched and shrill, surely brought dogs to the yard. I rushed into her bedroom to find what looked like Ryan holding her captive in the closet. My poor baby girl, traumatized and locked in a dark space. I will admit I lost my temper. I pulled Ryan off and gave him a quick spank on his bottom. The look of disbelief and utter hurt is forever etched in my mind.

I got it wrong.

Ryan hadn't been trying to lock her in the closet. He was trying to keep the door open. Jordyn was the one who wanted the door closed and locked.

It was the easiest apology I ever had to make and the hardest. I betrayed his trust by not taking a moment to see the situation as it truly was, not how I perceived it to be.

Lesson learned but at what cost?

Each day, I go out with the best of intentions and the purest of heart. I look and I search. Nothing matters more.

Each night, I return without what I need the most. And in the quiet of my room, I apologize.

"Ryan, I am sorry that I was unable to protect you. I'm sorry that I cannot take your place. I'm so sorry that I could not find you."

It feels like I have betrayed him again.

May 26, 2018

The average adult will take 12-20 breaths per minute.

Breathing is essential to life. It is the very first act that we take, and it will always be the last.

It is ironic that breathing is autonomous. I don't control it, and yet I congratulate myself for getting through the day if that is the only thing I do.

I think a lot about breathing lately.

Inhale. Exhale.

Wait with bated breath.

Can't quite catch my breath.

Every day, people post. "I pray today is the day you find Ryan. I pray for closure. Let this be the day you bring your baby home."

I honestly never think today is that day. I have wanted it for so long. I have gotten down on my knees. I have begged. I have bargained. I have pleaded. And each night there is a shocked disappointment tinged with unexpressed grief that fills me. I am barely breathing.

I remember my babies. Holding them while they fussed. Crying so hard that they forgot to breathe. Their tiny expressions beet red with eyes so wide and panicked. I would gently blow on their faces, and with an expected gasp they took a deep breath.

Sometimes I feel like I am walking the world in the same way. Waiting for the gentle breath that forces me to breathe again.

I remember scraped knees, owies on elbows and cuts on fingers. With a magical breath, I made everything better. Who will be my saviour?

Breathe in. Breathe out.

Again and again.

Today and tomorrow.

For as long as I take a breath, I will search for Ryan.

While I live, I will be his advocate. I will defend him when others may judge. I will protect his character and his memory, for that is all we have left, to my last breath.

Breath is air. Air is life. I gave you breath when
I gave you life, and now I will breathe for both of us.

May 27, 2018
Today I am less than I need to be. Grief paves
my way and I am helpless to move off the path.
I know it is not meant to last forever, but today
I can't see my way forward.

\*   \*   \*

That was such a difficult day for me. It was the last day that
Kamloops Search and Rescue would come up. They had been up a
couple of times since the very first day of searching. The following
Saturday after February 18, they mobilized another command
centre at the firehall. With our efforts on social media, there
was an abundance of volunteers. They went door to door in the
neighbourhood to show Ryan's poster to residents, and they assisted
KSAR in whatever capacity was needed. They also came another
half-day for a soft search to test the conditions and look at the creek
levels.

As new information became available, we would reach out to
the RCMP and ask about future searches because any undertaking
by KSAR would need a request from them. The RCMP and the
constable that was our liaison were never rude or dismissive, but it
sometimes took some prodding to generate resources to continue
the search.

We had so much information coming into us, and sometimes it
was difficult to say how relevant it was. However, the mandate from
KSAR on that very first night was that they would come out and
search again if there were environmental changes (snow melting) or

a tip that would place Ryan in another location. I took that mandate to heart. I posted asking for something—anything—that would help us. We felt so lost for so long, and our desperation was palpable.

In April, I sent an email to our liaison inquiring about information sent to them and what their response would be in regard to a new search date. This was the tip about seeing someone who matched Ryan's description walking towards the village on the night he went missing at approximately 2:00 a.m. The answer was disappointing. The RCMP felt that neither the conditions nor the tip warranted another search.

We were devastated.

But I am a mother. Fierce and unapologetic. If there was a way to help—if you made commitments that would assist us—then I would demand that you be held accountable. I sent an email response to the constable to express my frustration and disappointment. I outlined a conversation that we had with the KSAR manager and the constable on that first night where they told us quite clearly that they would come back out if there was a tip or an environmental change. With that information we raised the Crime Stoppers reward to $15,000. I went on the Facebook page that had 23,400 people following it and did several interviews to clarify what we needed from the public to continue the search. I could not control the weather, but I could influence a location change.

Were we concerned about the snowy conditions and the safety of our volunteers? Of course we were but continuing the search efforts was paramount to us. Scott was acutely aware of how high the berms were. How slippery the paths were. How much snow there still was after six weeks of melting. We had searched every day with hundreds of volunteers as young as sixteen years old. They probed and did grid mapping. We had heavy equipment that moved and broke up those berms to assist in the effort. None of us were trained to do so. And we were all tired. Exhausted from learning to do what KSAR and their team knew how to do. I struggled with the response, however logical and fact-based it appeared to be, because my mind kept asking, *Why are our volunteers fine with searching and theirs are not?* KSAR had the training to conduct searches in a decidedly safer and more efficient manner. After all, they had been up twice when the conditions were more snow-filled than at this time. I read the commendations from the constable for the great efforts of physically searching each day for six weeks, but the sentiment fell flat. All I could think was, *I can't believe the RCMP, KSAR or any of those volunteers would go back to their loved ones and say the person they were searching for will just have to wait for the snow to melt.*

It was a difficult email to compose because I respected the efforts of both the RCMP and KSAR. I just wanted more done. That is not a singular emotion that only I could express because I imagine every parent of every loved one missing would feel and expect the same. It is important to note that the RCMP and KSAR are held to a standard that includes safety and resources available. They are hardworking and dedicated, but they are, above all, humans. No one wants to say no, but it just seemed that sometimes it was the most common answer based on policy and procedures. It was a clinical assessment but a very unhuman approach. But again, it goes back to the question, "If it was your child, what would you want to have done, need to have done and pay to have done?" If that information was not going to be made available to us, then I would use whatever leverage I had to get those resources. Without compromise.

Whatever discussion came from my email brought KSAR back for Mother's Day weekend and for this final time in May. There was a new interim RCMP superintendent, and he had tactical come with them. The snow had melted, the weather was warm and inviting. With additional volunteers, KSAR were able to cover more ground. For the next two days, they would, like always, give whatever they had wholeheartedly.

I knew logically that this would be the final search. I expected no more. With snow on the ground, there was always the knowledge that we might uncover Ryan by digging deep. I prayed that he would be intact so that I might once more gaze on my son and say the goodbyes that had so far been denied to me. How meager a wish is that? But this weekend, the snow almost gone, time was perilously short to find him. Scott and I had made an unspoken pact that if the snow were to completely melt and we still could not find Ryan, we would talk about returning home. Our nerves felt exposed and raw. Everything hinged on having experienced search and rescue come in and do what we may not have been able to. In the deepest recesses of my mind, I felt the insistent tick tock. The temperature was rising every day in this snow encrusted mountain town, and my wish to see Ryan was fading as the season changed. Reconciliation would not come easy.

They didn't find what they were looking for, nor what we needed. They combed the town proper and the outlying areas around the swollen and fast-moving creek. On day one, there were some challenges with being called out to another critical search. I may be a mother that is desperate to bring her son home, but I'm not so depraved that I couldn't understand that as spring and summer approached, KSAR resources would be called out and tasked to save living souls. As they should be. As I would hope they would be. I just wanted one more time; to feel at peace at what we attempted to do, tried so hard to accomplish and what we would continue to do until we are no more.

But that didn't make my heart break any less.

May 28, 2018

Sometimes the smallest gestures can have the grandest outcomes.

Waves of grief poured over me yesterday, palpable and raw. Before all of this, I can't remember ever feeling so sad. So lost. So afraid.

What would tomorrow bring?

Kindness and love.

Thank you to TasteFull Excursions who graciously offered and arranged a Kamloops wine tour. It was such a wonderful way to explore the Kamloops area. We visited Privato, Monte Creek and Harper's Trail wineries. It was an incredible gesture by a beautiful woman who knew just what I needed today. A sense of normalcy. A day to regroup. A time to make plans without the prison we have found ourselves in closing in on us.

And, wonderfully, we had the opportunity to share this experience with our family and friends. My mom, dad, Cheryl and Stacey joined Scott and me.

That was the kindness.

Now let me tell you about love. A mother's love

There was a young man named Cooper. He met Ryan here in Sun Peaks. They shared so many characteristics, which made them fast friends. Ryan's disappearance deeply affected Cooper.

Stacey is Cooper's mom.

She flew here from Australia to spend 2 weeks searching for Ryan. She arrived in Canada two days after her son left on another adventure to Europe. She knows no one here, but she felt compelled to come.

Because ...

What if it was her son? What if it was any one of her children? Who would help? Who would search? Who would hope and believe?

She is incredible. What she has chosen to do is indescribable. Beyond kindness but full of love.

So today, I felt the bones of my ancestors run through my spine, straight and true. The beating of my heart comes from the richness of their blood. I am whole. Bruised and battered but strong.

Just as importantly, I look around and see that I am surrounded by such kindness and love. From friends. From family. From strangers.

How so very grand.

May 29, 2018

*OH!*
*THE PLACES YOU'LL GO!*
*You'll be on your way up!*
*You'll be seeing great sights!*
*You'll join the high fliers*
*who soar to high heights.*

- Dr Suess

Journeys are unexpected, unplanned and uncharted. They never seem to take you where you think you want to go. Sometimes it will be everything you ever wanted and you will be happy. And sometimes it will take you down a path seldom travelled.

It will be for you to decide how you approach the curves.

No one will ever question the tragedy that has unfolded before us. It is all encompassing and never-ending.

We have cried a thousand tears. We will cry a thousand more.

But our journey is not linear.

There is no beginning. There is no ending. We have lost so, so much. But we have gained as well.

Ryan seems to be responsible for my unravelling. Deconstructed down to my core and rebuilt. Stronger, braver and open to the love and compassion that seems to come my way.

This week is a time of saying goodbye to Sun Peaks as we head back to Beaumont. Only for a short time, perhaps, but every loss is felt deeply. The angels I have met have saved me. Through their belief and love, I have risen again and again. Not quite high enough to soar. Maybe I will never be that close to freedom again. My grief tethers me to the ground from time to time.

But my journey is not over.

I have places to go.

Oh, how I wish, baby boy, that you were by my side. Where you go ... I would follow.

May 30, 2018

Tomorrow is not forever.

I am leaving Sun Peaks for the first time in 14 weeks to head home. It is just for a short while.

Jordyn turns 18 on June 6th, and I want to celebrate the day with her. She deserves to have her birthday amongst friends and family and to enjoy our focus and love without this tragedy taking centre stage. Just for one day. It is the least I can do for my baby girl. She has been so strong and so brave. She has my heart.

Julianna will leave for her French Immersion school trip to Quebec soon, and I want to take her shopping. I want to help her pack. I want to see her off. I want to do all the things I should be doing— that I long to do. It is difficult to assuage the guilt I feel for not being there for her. That she forgives so readily is a testament to her spirit. She has struggled with the heaviness of our conversations while maintaining her childlike wonder. That, in itself, is a miracle. I am awestruck.

So, despite all my fears of abandoning my first born to the shadows that hide him, I am going home.

Scott will follow on Monday and return on Friday.

We won't be in Sun Peaks for 5 days. Interminable, long days.

Will the search continue?

I believe it will. The seeds we planted with Ryan's name have come to harvest. We leave knowing that our community will continue to search for our son. We are blessed.

They will take up the torch. They will help lighten our load. We can leave knowing Ryan won't be alone. He is surrounded by our love as well this community's.

Just for a little while.

May 31, 2018

"There's no place like home."

Fragmented and bruised is what my home feels like now.

It looks the same, sounds the same and smells the same. It is still in the same town. I live on the same street.

Same, same, same.

But deep down I know with absolute certainty it will never be the same again.

June 1, 2018

Today marks 6 months.

December 1st was the last day I saw my son. It was the last time I gave him a hug and a kiss goodbye.

December 1st was the last time 1 looked into Ryan's eyes, held his face and told him I loved him.

15 weeks ago, I left this house in a state of panic and sheer desperation.

15 weeks later, I return, exhausted and fractured.

If I close my eyes tightly, I can almost pretend that we are back in time.

"Mommy, can I go out and play? Please????? I promise I'll do my homework as soon as I get in."

"Mom, I can't find my cleats. Did you wash my soccer stuff? Can you please not yell out during my game? So embarrassing."

"Mother. Mother. Heather, what are we having for supper? Hmmmm, well I'm not sure I'm gonna be home. Why don't you make something I like?"

I can hear him. I listen for the sounds of his laughter. I look for the heavy, muddy footsteps on the floor. I can smell his deodorant body spray and the odour of rugby gear.

I see traces of him everywhere.

The discarded clothes, the medals from sports, and pictures of him fill my vision. I see him in the way the girls tilt their heads or try not to smile while telling fibs. I dream of him lying beside me with stories to tell and books to read. I feel his hugs and his soft breath as he leans in to kiss my cheek.

But my eyes can't stay closed forever.

Those are just memories. It's all I have left.

6 months ... a lifetime ago.

June 2, 2018

I am loved.

I am loved by my husband. The way he looks at me is still something I'm not quite used to. Like he has been given this great gift and he wants to unwrap it slowly to truly savour the moment. Perhaps that is purest definition of marriage ... a gift to be treasured at leisure.

I am loved by my children. They fill me unconditionally. I have never felt the depth of emotion before their arrival into this world. My breath is measured by their hearts beating. Is it any wonder that now I find it difficult to breathe deeply?

I am loved by my family. Their pride and joy in my continuous growth spurs me to try harder. They taught me the importance of values and the wisdom of my own truth. All that I am now is who they raised me to be.

I am loved by my friends. They didn't become my tribe because of Ryan's disappearance. We were bonded by deep friendships well before. We are one tribe forever forged with everlasting respect and caustic humour. It is just that now is my time. They rally because I desperately need them.

I am loved by strangers. A community of people that believe strongly in the power of connectivity to me, to themselves and to those around them. They spread a message of kindness, hope and love so that others may draw strength.

The earth may survive cruelty, indifference and hatred but will humanity?

I am a wife, mother, daughter, sister, friend and woman who is loved.

But I am just one person.

All of you are so loved as well.

Humanity lives in the actions of others. Small, perhaps at first, but growing mightily.

This moment may belong to Ryan, but the changes he inspired in me and you are nothing less than divine.

After all, he was so very deeply and completely loved.

June 3, 2018

Night falls like a gentle hush, its canvas dark and bare soon illuminated with a sprinkling of celestial lights.

Beauty in the eternal vastness that creeps up yet again.

I loathe nights.

I must wait for their end to bring about the dawn of new beginning. And yet each day, my patient waiting is left unrewarded. My prayers unanswered.

It wasn't always this way. I remember bright lights, parties and nights out. Perhaps the unease began the night we brought Ryan home from the hospital.

He was so tiny, all 5 lbs. 15 oz. of him. Even my background in early childhood could not prepare me for the worry and fear that I had when putting him to bed. I wanted to be with him when he fell asleep and be the face he saw in the morning when he awoke. In between, I would watch over and protect him. With me, he would be safe.

Foolish? Perhaps. Unrealistic? Of course.

But we tried. He slept right beside us, nestled in a cradle with the bedroom lights casting a bright glow. Monitor on, staticky because it was close to the receiver. Scott and I took turns watching his chest gently rise and fall.

One night became another and a routine was set.

Ryan didn't like to sleep alone. He wanted his dad to lie beside him, twirling his hair as he drifted off to sleep. We assured ourselves that this time wouldn't last forever.

And it didn't.

But what if? What if I had never taken my eyes off him while he slept? Would he still be lost in the night?

I fear this most of all. Ryan, alone.

Night falls. My tears fall along with it.

June 5, 2018

Every celebration or family gathering is like a burning ember.

It feels warm to the touch while filling us with brightness and comfort. We gather around, closely, cherishing the moments. Time spent catching up, relishing times past and futures to behold.

They mean so much more to all of us now.

Ryan is missing. One less seat at the table. One heart painfully absent. He is the first to take his leave. As the years pass, others will join until there are none left. That is the way of it. We understand the cycle of life and yet we don't.

The ember burns hot and leaves the skin tender if left unattended. We shall never make that mistake again.

Our family is together now; not quite as whole but evermore grateful.

We have relearned the blessing of being a family. Our shared pasts will be forged to create new beginnings. A collection of memories that are precious.

For us, family is joy. For us, family is everything.

June 6, 2018

She is love personified.

More than I ever expected, everything I could ever want, she is my daughter.

18 years old with the world ahead of her, I have so much to tell her.

I don't know where to begin.

I want to protect her heart. I want her to know that her strength comes from within and so shall it encompass all that she does. I pray that the wisdom of my ancestors guide my daughter as she navigates this world.

But I will not pass on my fears or my worries. There is time enough for her to learn these on her own. The world will show Jordyn all its beauty and some of its cruelty. She is intelligent enough to see the difference.

I must trust that this woman she has become will withstand the storms that will blow her way. And that she will learn to take time to enjoy the warm, gentle breezes that always come after the hurricanes.

She is my daughter. She has my soul. I see her bravery. I admire her courage. I feel her ever expansive love.

"You will do great things, precious girl," I whispered to her as she lay her head next to mine.

She already has.

Happy Birthday Jordyn.

June 7, 2018

Today I thought I would do a FAQ post.

I get messages throughout the day from people wanting to know:

"What is happening with the search?"

"Why do you believe?"

"How are you so certain?"

"What do the RCMP say?"

"Where do you go from here?"

Is it a bit nosy to ask? Perhaps, but I created this page to help bring Ryan home and to also create awareness of what happens when a loved one goes missing. Through my posts, I have tried to share memories of my son so that you may appreciate our love for him but to also know his character.

Why do we believe Ryan to be in the Sun Peaks area?

It is not based on mother's intuition. I will say I am trying to be more retrospective when it comes to my spiritual side while maintaining what has always been my strength: my intelligence. I would never be so arrogant to dismiss what is factual because I want to believe.

The truth is, there is no proof that Ryan left the hill. The RCMP have no evidence, and the private investigators that were hired in the first few weeks found no evidence. Does that mean that at some point they may? Of course. When you search long enough, something is bound to come to light. Both are committed to continue searching, and for that we are grateful.

Most people have a backstory—stressors or reasons that could point to why they may find themselves missing. Drugs, alcohol, despondency, jealousy, disconnection to family and friends, or anger. Ryan, by all accounts, had none of these.

But you are just his mother, how could you know?

Well, I can't, in all honesty. But what I will say is that the friends he met in just 2 months are as adamant about his character and routine as his best friends from grade school. That matches what we know of him.

Could something random have happened to him?

Certainly. But up until now, there has been nothing to suggest that or any other scenarios.

But if that is all true, shouldn't you have found him by now?

How desperately I wish that were the case. We have searched as many square inches of the area as we know. It is so vast and completely covered in either snow or now underbrush that makes searching so tedious. We also can't say for sure the direction he took or his level of intoxication. What was going through his mind will forever be unknown.

How long will you search?

Until my last breath. This is my son. He deserves nothing less. Even if he left willing, unwilling or unknowingly, we are committed to finding him. He is my son, and I would burn the world to the ground to find him.

What happens next?

The RCMP continue their investigation. We will go back and search this week before heading back home for Jordyn's graduation. Our plan is to come back at the end of July, in August, September and October. We will come to Sun Peaks each month until the snow falls, and when it melts, we will come again. We will never stop searching.

Can I still come and search even if you are not there?

We would be grateful if you did. There is no specific area. Now it is just hiking the trails and the ski outs looking for articles of clothing.

How long will you post?

I think you must be tired of me. I honestly don't know. I will do it as long as it feels right, I suppose.

Please know you have all had such a huge impact on our family. We are grateful for each blessing you have given us. More importantly for what you have given yourselves, your community and this world.

Ryan's legacy will always be about kindness and the power of love.

June 8, 2018

"Have you ever thought of ...?"

"Have you considered that just maybe ...?"

I get these questions all the time in some form or another.

Usually, they are followed by scenarios of what has happened to Ryan. Most times they include foul play of some sort.

I am honestly not sure if the people messaging me or posting on here think these thoughts are unique to them and therefore must share them.

Yes ... we have thought of every possible situation that could have befallen Ryan. For every one mishap you think of, I have thought of 10 more.

I live and breathe this tragedy every second of every minute of every hour of every day. I have for the last 16 weeks. I have no respite. It shatters me into tiny little pieces that I must sweep up each day and glue back together to start anew.

What do I do with that?

In answering yesterday's questions, there came a barrage of others.

So let me be clear.

All these suspicions—yours or mine—go nowhere.

We can't do polygraphs because at this time there is no evidence of a crime. And polygraphs are voluntary. We can't luminol the house. It is not a crime scene. The residents have always co-operated. I hear all sorts of suggestions that appear to come straight out of a penny dime crime novel. We can't "put the screws" to the partygoers. They have willingly answered all questions.

I know we all want someone to blame. Someone must be responsible because then it makes sense. We can say, "Well, that would never happen to me cause I would never find myself in the same situation." When the time comes, that might very well be true. But it also may not be.

"You need to direct the RCMP to do this and that." For what purpose? My vastly limited knowledge of missing persons or criminal investigations? Yours? To be fair, they have been so engaged in this case. Numerous officers, tactical and canine have poured over and pondered Ryan's disappearance. Perhaps there is more to be gleaned; I trust that they will do that.

So, I am going to ask just one more time: Please send posts, prayers and well-wishes. Hug your loved ones, take time to enjoy the moments before they are gone. Invest in your community and the world at large because it makes your neighbourhood a better place to be. Take Ryan on trips to Hawaii or Mt. Everest. Come search if you can.

But do not post your speculations or ideas of where Ryan has gone. It doesn't move us forward.

Love to you all.

# The Power of Regret

By June, Ryan's Facebook group had grown to around 24,000 members. It continues to receive five to ten member requests each day. As I write this, two years later in 2020, we currently sit at 31,300, which amazes me. These are engaged, passionate, supportive and inquisitive people that may have come to learn the story of my son at first but perhaps stay because of the connectivity with others in the group.

It certainly took some transitions to make this missing person page one that works well for our family. Like everything in the beginning, this wasn't what I imagined or even wanted. To place a spotlight on Ryan and his disappearance weighed heavily on me. What if I was wrong? What if Ryan just crashed at someone's house and missed work? Having Search and Rescue carry out this massive undertaking to locate him initially worried me. If Ryan had screwed up and made a poor error in judgement, would he be embarrassed to show himself with the news media and social media focus? Would he panic that all these resources were put into searching only for him to shamefacedly return home? Would he stay away because of all this? My intuition told me that this was not the case. I have never professed to know everything about any of my children—they are unique individuals that share some parts of their lives and keep other parts to themselves or their friends, which is a natural progression and rite of passage. Still, I struggled in those first days because of my fears of what the alternative might be.

You want to believe in something that would explain and give you back the life you had before all of this. Even if it is contrary to everything you thought you knew. So, I was hesitant to publish anything beyond the initial missing poster that Nancy had created. I did not want to create a Facebook group. I didn't want to draw attention to us or to Ryan. I wanted to create a safe space so that my son would return to me unharmed. That is a parent's prerogative, I imagine.

You can wish for the best outcome even though you know you are headed for certain heartache. It just takes time to come to terms with reality. But I had to be sure. On Monday, February 19, sitting in the new command centre as Ryan's friends filtered in, I asked the question that had been plaguing me: "Do you think Ryan is hiding out now? With all this fuss and attention, do you think he is afraid to come forward and let everyone know he is okay?" The shocked look of disbelief on their faces told me that my instincts were right.

"No, Heather, absolutely not. He wouldn't do that. He wouldn't worry you guys like this."

A relative of a friend initially asked about creating a Facebook page, and I said no. I understood the need for it, but I didn't feel I had the ability or knowledge to create it and, realistically, I didn't think I had the will to see it through. It required more brain power than I possessed at that time. They asked again. I was so grateful that someone who had experience in helping families create groups for their missing loved ones would be taking it on. In my depths of despair, even I could recognize that was an odd arrangement. How does one even get involved in such an emotionally draining quest? Through mutual experience and an empathic need to help it would seem.

After day three, I became an active participant and administrator. I wanted to share memories and pictures of Ryan so that others might know more of him. It was also important that his poster was shared far and wide in the hopes that some information might become available. Appealing to the group members to come to Sun Peaks and help with the search was also a goal of the site.

We went through many growing pains in the first two months. Like all things open to the public, it did not always go as planned. I received messages daily that complained about the way other administrators dealt with requests and posts. Some members didn't appreciate the structure set in place, nor the rules that were outlined. The rules were simple:

1. Be kind and courteous
2. No hate speech or bullying
3. No promotion or spam
4. Respect everyone's privacy
5. No speculative posts

Ironically enough, it was me who directed family and friends to monitor and help alleviate some of my stress. They acted as a buffer, or so they thought. But day after day, my inbox was filled with the same people expressing hurt feelings that their speculative posts were being taken down or that they were being censured. Never in my wildest dreams would I have thought strangers would feel it was OK to chastise me on my missing son's page. It was one of many truths that were revealed to me about social media.

My direct involvement in monitoring, reading and responding to the posts gave me a sense to know what I could control and what would be sane for me going forward. I would not allow speculative posts on what happened to Ryan or who might be involved. That information, if credible, should be given to either the Crime Stoppers anonymous tip line or to the police. To read the most heinous of events that occurred that night based on a dream from someone across the country or nasty comments that suggested my son was being held captive in a basement to have his organs harvested did nothing to move me forward. Not to mention that it is incredibly cruel. Even if I were strong enough to wade through malicious content, my family and my girls were not. It was not that I was naïve in what may have happened to Ryan, but to have that thrown in my face at every turn was insanity.

So, we changed the way members could post. Every post required an approval from an admin. It was such a relief to go to bed and night and not wake up in the morning with hundreds of comments relating to a vicious post. Repeated cruelty and blatant disregard towards our wishes meant we had to block people from our site.

I never minded questions because, like everyone else, I was trying to understand how something like this could happen. I spent hours responding to posts and to members' comments. There really was not any information that I would not address nor rumour that I would not try to clarify. And for 99 percent of our members, it was more than enough. Wading through other's opinions and criticisms of you in a public arena takes a concentrated effort. I have not mastered that ability in any way, but I had more critical things to concern myself with.

Our template for a missing person's Facebook site is quite often used as more cases become known to us and family members reach out to ask for help. The templates involve sharing resources such as how to conduct ground searches, how to deal with ambiguous loss, volunteer sign-up sheets and the like. As we understood more, we added more. As more people joined from across Canada and the United States, it was important to create an album of other missing persons posters to share that may have aided in those families' searches. Members in those affected areas could heed the call to help. Ryan's Facebook site was a labour of love borne out of necessity, but it was completely collaborative and a true testament of humanity when we found ourselves in dire need.

June 10, 2018

How do you celebrate one's life?

Is it through a memorial? A foundation? A quiet spot upon which you can reflect?

I recently met a woman whose husband of many years had passed. The grief lays heavily on her head. I can see such profound sadness in her eyes and the fragile way she holds herself.

I understand. It is like grief is lapping at my heels, whispering, "Surrender. Come, its time."

But I don't dare. There is still so much that I must do. Every day feels like a chore, and I am task oriented.

My head hurts. My thoughts. Others' opinions. One of us will be right about what happened to my son. But I will still lose. Vindication or absolution will never be mine. Not truly.

Ryan will still be gone.

I fear one day that woman will be me.

For now, my loved ones pull me one step away from the waves. This is my blessing: Since the beginning, we have always talked about Ryan. We laugh, we cry and we remember. No one is afraid to mention his name. No one wonders if they should tell a story or share a memory. No one forgets.

I believe memories that are stored in their own storybook will be worn with the rereading and retelling. It is how we hold onto Ryan. It is the way we celebrate his life.

June 12, 2018

Can I let you in on a little secret?

In our house, I am like The Godfather. The kids know my favour is like the golden ticket to a good and peaceful life. My displeasure on the other hand … well. Nothing as drastic as a horse head, but I will admit I have a flair for the dramatic.

Ryan has decided that, with this journey, he is going to teach me to be kinder and gentler.

I guess I can be quite stubborn when I want to be. Scott might argue that I must want to be all the time. Not true. Okay, well maybe a little true. Fine, mostly true.

I always describe myself as "bossy," but that hardly seems flattering. I have adjusted my descriptors as the years have passed; I began at aggressive, moved to proactive and finally settled on dynamic. I have a dynamic personality. It is much more fluid. Adaptable with my mood.

Nancy looks for my cues before warning people, "Ooh, here comes the work voice." Apparently, my head tilts as my finger comes up in a rather stern and pointed manner. My voice lowers and I appear to enunciate my words ever so carefully.

That is for an inconvenience or mild irritation.

My kids have always known full anger is volcanic. There is sputtering, and I would hazard a guess that my hair is aglow in angry flames. It was one of the reasons why, at 20, I could stop Ryan in his tracks. The 360-degree head spin has that affect.

It doesn't quite feel like me anymore. I am still the same, but it is like layers have burnt away leaving me starting from a different place.

Things that normally would upset or displease me seem so inconsequential. I want different results with my interactions. I yearn to see all points of view so my decisions are more reflective than reactive.

It is just a beginning—nothing perfected—only a sense of wanting to grow. To teach my girls to be more than me.

I am finding my old ways antiquated. It is an unravelling of everything I have conditioned myself to be.

Is it possible?

Gradually.

Ironic that my 20-year-old son has taught me such a valuable human lesson. I always thought it would be the other way around.

Well ... except with Scott. That poor man couldn't possibly deal with such a drastic change in this dynamo.

Baby steps. After all, Rome wasn't built in a day.

June 13, 2018

Graduations are upon us.

It is the time of year that our children celebrate the milestones that come with age. For some, it will be from preschool or kindergarten, junior high or middle school. For others, it will be high school and university. Each one miraculous and wonderful. The looks on their faces as they recognize their achievements is nothing short of amazing. Their accomplishments are parallel to the amount of commitment they have put forth.

Skin of their teeth or sailing with honours, all of it upon their shoulders.

We have been down this road several times, and it still has the power to move me no matter the milestone.

I vividly remember the conversation where Scott, likely in shock, asked me if I was spending *that* amount on Jordyn's Grade 8 graduation dress.

"You know it's not high school, right?" he spluttered.

I did. It still didn't matter.

Who decides what celebrations are more deserving than others? Each rite of passage should be noted and remembered, for it is certain that the moment will never come again.

I have invested as much in my children's Grade 4 graduation as I have in their high school ceremony. Maybe not monetarily but always with the same enthusiasm.

At Bellevue, our elementary school, there was, traditionally, a year-end performance where parents would pick a song that was current and formulate a dance routine to perform at assembly.

Ryan's year was *High School Musical*. "We're All in This Together" was the parent anthem and the choreographed dance our deliverance. Okay, well not as dramatic as that. We had like a week to learn the routine and most parents came and went as schedules allowed. We were a rag tag group.

I could tell Ryan wasn't impressed with the new commitment to his year-end assembly.

"Whatever ... it's not like anyone will know who you are. 'S not a big deal."

Hmmmm, I do believe a challenge was issued. And I, baby boy, have accepted.

Game day.

The parents stepped onto the stage to the stifled giggles of the Grade 4 graduates. And we killed it (I'll let you decide if that is a good or bad thing). But I will tell you that as every parent turned around, on their back was a picture of their child. Each had the same caption: Mine, in bold, read "Ryan Shtuka's Mom."

Of course, teachers don't require such debasement from parents as our children grow. We are granted a reprieve of sorts.

But the memories remain. The celebrations were another chapter in our children's lives.

I am glad we took such joy in all of Ryan's graduations.

*Wherever you are, be all there.*

- Jim Elliott

June 14, 2018

I have driven up this mountain countless times.

But coming back here on Sunday night, I felt nauseous. My heart was beating wildly in my chest. A feeling of dread permeated the air. I was overwhelmed.

It's only been a week.

But so much has changed.

If you ever wondered about how the seasons impact the landscape, Sun Peaks is an exacting case study.

Everything is so green. The brush is full, the undergrowth like tangling of branches fighting in beautiful, chaotic harmony. Wildflowers explode in colourful array. Everything hidden and dense.

Nature here is like a thousand miracles, and I only need one.

The rain falls gently since my arrival. The sky, heavy with the weight of memories, sheds its tears for me. I feel them on my face, and I am made to understand. They are cleansing.

The seasons will change, that is what they must do. Ryan's time will come.

I feel peace once more.

June 15, 2018

As the week here at Sun Peaks quickly comes to an end, I wanted to send out some housekeeping items before we head home on Monday.

The searching will still continue. During the week, we actively encourage anyone that is willing and able to search to come up. Areas to search? There is nothing specific at the moment. We suggest that people take the opportunity to hike trails and the area. We will update everyone on areas of interest as they come. Not sure about hiking trails? The Sun Peaks tourist centre will have that information available.

If you see anything out of the ordinary, we encourage you to contact the Kamloops RCMP or Crime Stoppers.

Every Saturday for the next 5 weeks, we will have someone that will sign in/out volunteers. The hours will be 10–4. You are certainly welcome to search outside those hours, of course.

The command centre building will be operational until July 1st. Its location is still at the P2 parking lot. After that, we will have a tent set up in the same place. There may be Sundays that we will have someone manning command centre. They will post on this page to keep everyone updated.

We want to thank everyone that lent us equipment to aid in the search. If you still have snowshoes with us or other items, please take a moment to make arrangements to pick them up.

I will never be able to express our heartfelt gratitude and love to everyone. You have given so much to us whether you came to search, raised awareness, generously donated your homes and equipment, donated to the GoFundMe, prayed or sent well-wishes. Every single thing allowed Scott and I do the one thing we needed to do most in this world: search for Ryan. We are his advocates. You became ours.

We are not done yet. We haven't found our son. We won't give up until we do. Don't give up on us. Continue to do what you do best.

If what you can do is all you can do, then it is all we need.

This is just an update. Nothing has changed. We will continue to search. Our friends and loved ones will be here as well searching in our absence.

I will continue to post.

In great faith and our continuing love.

June 17, 2018

I love this man. He has loved my imperfect self with such perfect serenity. He has softened my edges and guarded my heart.

That would be enough.

Except … he is the father of our children.

I have seen the tenderness in his eyes as he looked upon their faces. I have seen him grow into a man that they could be proud to call their father. He has held them with such gentleness. He has imbued them with the strength of a thousand men. The love he has shown them is a mark that they will forever wear upon their brow.

He is the man who went to every school performance and field trip. He coached every sport that they had an interest in. He went without so that they didn't have to.

He has held our children's hearts with the fragility of hand spun glass. They are precious and worthy.

I wonder about destiny. As we shift through our shared tragedy, he still has enough heart to love our daughters truly. He has gathered me in his arms and protected me when the pain is too much to bear.

This man is more than I ever deserved but everything our family could have wanted or needed.

His love is the reason I breathe.

His love is the reason Ryan was the man he was.

We are so proud.

Happy Father's Day.

June 17, 2018

This post is about a man I am proud to call my father, a.k.a. The General, a.k.a. Papa Bear.

Isn't it a wonder that after all my years growing up, I could still find things about my dad that are simply amazing.

He has this quiet strength and stoicism that I lean upon and learn from, but it is the graciousness with which he greeted volunteers that I am most proud of. He treated everyone like family and showed such a grateful heart.

I am proud. Ryan would be as well.

Happy Father's Day. I love you.

June 18, 2018

Today feels so permanent.

Grief stains my soul as I look at Sun Peaks in my rear-view mirror. I won't see its vista again until the end of July.

I feel like I failed.

On my good days, I am practical and logical. I can see everything we have done, the areas searched, the volunteers that have helped us, and the support we have amassed. I feel strength from my loved ones.

Most days are good. Good enough anyways.

On my bad days, I feel as fragile as tissue paper, worn and creased. I'm afraid to move lest I tear holes where once a whole heart beat. Ragged and gaping.

Today is such a day. No words comfort. No solace can be given. It is not within anyone's power to alleviate my sorrow. I don't want it.

The Welcome to Alberta sign beckons us.

Tears stream down my cheeks as I whisper over and over, "I'm sorry. I'm so sorry. I'm sorry."

Echoing silence is my only reply.

Jen, Coco and Tianna

Denis, Wilf and Brian

Kevin with the poles that
show the height of snow

Lyette and Nathalie
(command Extraordinarie)

Me searching

Scott and the level of snow

Nana and Papa

Searchers out

Stacey and Cheryl

The girls coming for the first time

PART

# Coming Home
*Beaumont, Alberta*
*June 18, 2018–February 20, 2019*

# Which Way Is Home?

I stand before you bare and raw. All my imperfections, failings and frailties laid out so that all may see. There is not one part of me that is free from judgment and criticism, and I claim no immunity.

There are so many fears that we cannot control around Ryan's disappearance. The hows, the whys, the what ifs. I have accepted that. The one fear that has kept me awake at night is that people will forget my son. That he will fade into the distant recesses of our minds, and when Scott and I pass, wither into oblivion. I won't allow this to happen.

I wrote every day since February 19. I poured my heart out the only way I knew how, with words, so that I may commit my son's life to paper, to permanence.

Still, I struggled with the concept of Ego vs Soul. Writing is good for my spirit, my humanity and my heart. But I had long since noticed that I rushed to read the comments that my posts generated. Did I hope my words inspired and denoted my son's importance? Of course, but with that came the risk that my writing would, in the end, be essential for my ego.

It has been a fight within myself as I transitioned home and integrated back into our life in Beaumont. I learned to let go and be okay with less writing and more living. At first, I feared that not posting daily would cause less interaction from supporters, less engagement in people joining the group, and in end, fewer searchers. I had to go home but in doing so, who would continue to search for Ryan?

A fear unfounded.

As in all things in life, once one problem is solved, another stands in line to take its place.

Grief quietly waits in the wings. She can be pushed away for periods of time but until acknowledged and confronted, will be a constant, silent companion. I don't know how to be a grieving mother. Even now, it is a concept that seems foreign to me. I can only imagine the guilt and sadness that permeates the soul of a mother or parent who has lost their child. How the simplest pleasures are marred by the feelings that you are left to enjoy what they no longer can. It is an idea that plagues me, floating around me but never really landing.

I feel guilt every day. Guilt as we searched through snow and now brush to find no trace of Ryan. Guilt as Scott and I drove down the hill to leave for home, each mile that we drove a stake was driven through our hearts; it is impossible to recover from. Guilt that comes from the joy of seeing our daughters and sleeping in our own bed. Guilt from not having to get up at a certain time and have the days meticulously planned to capture the most hours and search areas that the day brings.

So much guilt.

But our guilt does not come from losing a child. It is heavy with the knowledge that while we carry on with our lives, our son is waiting to be found and to be brought home.

There will be lessons that we learnt in the next year. We found purpose. We would navigate through loss and not be battered nor beaten by heartbreak.

June 19, 2018

*It's a funny thing about coming home. Nothing changes. Everything looks the same, feels the same, even smells the same. You realize what's changed is you.*

- F. Scott Fitzgerald

In the yard stands the tree Ryan planted in grade one. Spindly but sturdy. Not full grown but yearning for space to grow. Dreams of majestic heights are within its pine needles.

Ryan's 12-year-old handprint lies forever captured in the concrete poured for the backyard patio. 2009. All of us together.

There are reminders everywhere. In the living room, the yard and the kitchen where his favourite foods line the shelves.

It is ironic.

Because ...

I am not brave enough to go down to his room. Not nearly strong enough.

These pieces of Ryan are enough. They are meant to prepare me, I think, for the onslaught of memories. A gradual descent to the past unchanged.

But what if I'm wrong? What if I go through his things, his room, his clothes and I remember nothing? What if the memories are not that strong or that vibrant? That is what I fear more than anything. I want to believe that his room holds a treasure chest of memories. But what if it's just fool's gold?

Home has always been my solace, but now I fear the uncharted territory that lies before me.

I am home but I am changed.

June 20, 2018

Some days are more poignant than others. There is no rhyme or reason, only a rawness that permeates my soul.

FIFA World Cup Russia 2018.

No significance. Not a holiday or a celebration. Well, unless, of course, yours is the winning team.

But it was ours. Ryan's and mine. It was the sport we loved, and watching our favourite teams was a passion we both enjoyed.

I will admit to being a bit overzealous. Sitting on the edge of my seat ... ready to jump up.

"Woo woo woooo! Ah ...," the disappointed sigh of an unrealized goal.

"Hmmm ... Mom, you sound like a distressed monkey," ventured Ryan.

My withering stare invited no further comment. Well, until he got older. My fierce expression then become a perfect excuse to tease.

"Woo woo woooo ... ah!!!! Woo woo wooooo ... ah."

Sometimes, it is these moments that makes me the saddest. The most regretful. The everyday routines that I remember so clearly. Those memories are the things I miss the most.

A future without Ryan is difficult to bear. All the what ifs. What would he do when he was grown up? Would he marry? Would he have children? What would they look like? Where would he live?

His future will always remain hazy. A blurred expectation where nothing is certain.

I mourn the possibilities.

But it is the certainties that are devastating.

I miss the everyday.

I miss Ryan.

June 21, 2018

I think I must be tired. Not the physical sort. I am running every day. My foot is getting stronger. But my capacity to deal with everyday things is stretched thin.

Just the other night, my youngest wanted to make a healthy snack. She had the recipe book in front of her. I could hear her from the living room gather her ingredients. Suddenly I hear an "Oh Oh." I turn to see Julianna covered in cacao powder.

"Someone left the bag open. I'm sorry. I will clean it up."

Well, that person was me.

The whole pantry was covered. There were mounds of it everywhere.

"Oh no," I whispered.

The sight of it was overwhelming.

"No, mommy. I will clean it up."

But as I watched her sweep it around more, I knew that for her, it would be impossible. The look on her face as she walked away was this naked dejection. Sorrow for causing such a task was evident.

As I heard her leave, I cried. Deep sobs.

"I can't do this," I whisper. "Ryan, I'm so tired, baby."

But, of course, I do.

Moments later, I hear Max calling my name.

"Heather, Heather. I have a surprise for you. We found Jordyn's passport."

The same one that has been missing for a month. I had prayed to Ryan to help us locate it. And in that instance, I thought, *Okay. I got it, Ryan. You are trying to tell me "Get over yourself, Mom. You can do this."*

As I got up to rinse my cloth and come back to the pantry, there was a strong odour of weed. Overpowering and certainly not mine. The only person who ever did that was my son.

This always led to lectures on my part and a sheepish look on Ryan's face.

Through my tears, I started to smile. Okay, Ryan. It is clear he was trying to make me laugh. To see the humour in my cacao covered clothes. To remind me that it is just a mess. Messes happen. Accidents or purposely, there will always be chaos. I just need to find a way through the storms.

I finished cleaning and went upstairs to talk to Jubie.

I apologized to my beautiful little girl. You see ... I don't have it all figured out. I am not always coping well. And I'm sorry for that.

I'm a work in progress.

June 22, 2018

Childhood is often a series of unfortunate events.

Fevers, coughs and sniffly noses. Bruises, scrapes and broken bones. Trips to the hospital.

No one is spared.

I am reminded of this as I sat in the hospital waiting room last night.

Jordyn, cutting up home-made granola bars, slipped and cut her arm. To my infinite dismay, Scott and I weren't home. To my everlasting gratitude, Nancy was and rushed right over.

Three stitches, some tears, a couple of selfies (cause ... well, that's who I am) and one very brave girl. We got through it.

We have been down this road before.

Julianna and Ryan jumping on the trampoline. She was 5 and he was 13. The fact that Ryan was playing with his little sister was heartwarming. So rare and therefore so valued. Until ... Jubie comes in cradling her arm. Ryan trails after, his face ashen.

"Mom, we were jumping and I landed on her," he says. "It was an accident.

"Of course," Julianna pipes up, "Ryan was bouncing me just like the wrestlers do."

His face pales further if that is even possible.

Off we go to the hospital. Julianna's arm, just before the elbow, is broken. Many tears and a bright pink cast were the outcome. But she proudly showed it off.

"Look at my cast. Ryan broke my baby arm." (That, I confess, came from my description.)

The guilt he felt was evident. But we didn't blame him. They were having fun, living in the moment. He didn't set out to hurt her.

We can't control such things.

Perhaps what I am trying to say is, life is full of mishaps. We are not immune to tragedies nor accidents. Being a good person doesn't prevent bad things happening to you. Having something terrible occur does not prevent more in the future.

But I don't want to live always fearful of what tomorrow brings. It comes whether I wish for it or not.

I want to wake anticipating the sun on my face and the gentle kisses that come from being truly and deeply loved. I want to be full of hope and promise.

I want Ryan to know that for every moment I am here on this earth, I am grateful. I will not squander the moments because I am here and he is not.

That is not the way to honour my son.

June 23, 2018

Without all of you ... none of this would be possible. Each of you have shown that love is not limited by blood. That you can make a difference. You have proven that an investment in others, far and wide, yields great dividends. That is the legacy I want for my son. For all of my children.

Ryan's story won't end.

Thanks to all of you.

\*      \*      \*

There is the family you are born into and the family you are born to create. You gather people to you though shared experiences, marital/partnership connections, birthing order and life events. I believe that is family we should cherish and hold onto.

For the first few weeks, Scott and I were hardly alone. Our rental was full of friends, and we were surrounded by volunteers at the command centre. It was dizzying, but not being left alone with your thoughts, especially when they centre around the most horrific visions, is a blessing. Time moves on, though. No one can continue at the breakneck speed and desperation that we created in the beginning; it was not sustainable. There were jobs to return to, lives that must be resumed and, one by one, our numbers from home dwindled. The support remained, it just changed in the way we once operated. We understood and were grateful to have had so many for so long.

It is here that we discovered the impact that good people have on us, the ordinary. The faces of volunteers became a constant, and after a while, the same ones became a fixture. Day after day, we saw strangers continue to climb the mountain to search for a young man they did not know and give hope to a family still needing it. It did not take long for strangers to become friends, and even less for them to feel like they had always been there.

Ken and Cherie knew the pain we were going through intimately. They first heard about Ryan two days after their son, Kenni Jr.'s, thirty-fourth birthday. Kenni Jr. was murdered on April 17, 2009. His remains were eventually located in a shallow grave alongside his friend Damien on a property in Knouff Lake. They had been missing for six weeks.

Cherie could vividly recall the phone call from the RCMP, who explained that they were investigating the disappearance of the two young men. She knew that gut-wrenching panic and helplessness that comes from the first notification to the dull pain and heartbreak with the final outcome. Both Ken and Cherie knew our fear and our grief. As Ken so heartbreakingly said, "No parent should survive their children." Their lives changed forever with the death of Kenni Jr. Each morning dawns with a moment of hope before the blinding realization that their world will never be the same again. They contacted us because they felt if it was in them to help another family traverse those same murky waters, then they would offer whatever assistance they had.

Cherie started to show up with her friend Roxanne by her side on day three. They combed snowbanks, walked the road down the hill and volunteered to help search creek beds. Sharing Kenni Jr.'s story began this relationship, but it was really this connective feeling of love and support that I began to rely on.

Kamloops has a population of over ninety thousand people, but a small-town feeling prevails. It is a place where you can ask what high school someone went to and if they knew so and so, and the answer is inevitably yes. During the many searching days, Cherie met another Kamloops native, Cheryl. Of course, it didn't take long for them to exchange all the "Do you know …?" and "Yes, and how about …?" and they realized they knew many of the same acquaintances. As our volunteer numbers changed, I often found myself, along with Coco, searching with these ladies.

Despite the circumstances and the reasons behind our daily adventures, I enjoyed being in their company. We shared equal parts laughter, care and concern, and muffled curses as we hiked through prickly bushes. I felt safe with them, more of myself than I thought I would ever feel. Maybe it was in part because there was no explaining who I was before and who I found myself to be now. It was not like my friends at home had any expectations around me, but I felt the pressure. Do I try to recoup that which is lost or do I forge on in what I hope to become once I am stronger? Funny, the way we think others might not understand and yet the people that truly love us almost always do.

Day after day, Cherie and Cheryl showed up. We learned each other's stories. I found it refreshing that they already knew my circumstances and they gave me the chance to learn theirs. Cheryl always felt the need to qualify that she was so far outside her comfort zone because she wasn't a very brave person. It made me wish each of us could see the values and strengths others see in us before judging ourselves because we might be very surprised when looking through someone else's lens. I remember standing on this steep embankment that led down to the creek below. I was surveying the road to find an easier way down when Cheryl looked at me and said, "Do we have to go down there?" I nodded and started telling her what I was looking for. Suddenly, she began to slide down the hill.

"What the hell are you doing?" I yelled from above.

"Well, you need to do this, so we are doing this. Let's go!"

Cheryl and I have walked through icy creeks, slipped on rocks, had twigs whip us in the eyes. Together. We have watched the salmon swim upstream and climbed mountains and walked roads filled with flowers adorning the sides. She has stayed by my side as I cried, and she has made me laugh. My girls ask her when she is coming home to see them all the time. I suppose that is right, family belongs together.

Our group of searchers tended to stay the same. Small groups of the familiars. It was safe, and it was comfortable, but we grew just a little to make room for Jo-Dell. Her name was easily recognizable from Ryan's page. Over and over, I would see posts from Jo-Dell as she continued to spread awareness for Ryan down in Kamloops. I would see pictures of two ladies sitting outside grocery stores selling green ribbons and signs with our dinosaur. We talked as a group with gratitude about strangers who showed up to always help others. If there was to be a definition of humanity, Jo-Dell, Trevor, her husband, Jesse, her mother, and Barry, her father, would have a page all unto themselves.

In May, my parents arrived in Sun Peaks from Florida. What a relief to have them run the command centre so I could search every single day. My ex-military father ran that post with such precision, ensuring proper sign ins and a prepared lunch each day. I was initially worried that his gruffness might scare volunteers away, so I told both my parents, "Everything we do is to bring Ryan home. It is to ensure his legacy lives on. We now have to be more than what we ever thought we could be for him." I needn't have worried. On day one, Papa was hugging everyone who walked through that door. Nana fussed over them, occasionally wiping tears of gratitude.

One beautiful day, though, Scott and I had stopped for lunch and were sitting with my parents outside of the P2 parking lot. We brought our chairs outside and ate lunch as we looked up to the mountains on the opposite side. We all watched as a car pulled into the parking lot. I looked to Scott and said, "I think that is Jo-Dell." I had never met her before and did not know what her car would look like, but the entire vehicle was decked out in Ryan paraphernalia so I had a hunch. Out of the car came four people who started making their way up the ramps.

"Hi, my name is Jo-Dell."

I smiled knowingly at Scott. When you live your life each day the way these four people did, kindness shines like a beacon. With the exception of my children, I have never instantly fallen in love with anyone before, but I did that day. In their eighties, Jesse and Barry have more energy than I have seen in most toddlers. Jesse was cradling her side. Apparently the two of them had decided to put flooring in their basement. All went well until Jesse, carrying a flat of pop, tripped over the cord to the fridge that was still plugged in and cracked her sternum. But that did not prevent her from proudly wearing a Find Ryan T-shirt. All of them had one on. This family came bearing gifts. T-shirts for all of us, gifts that Jesse had made for the girls, and Barry handcrafted a keepsake box for Ryan's things, something Scott treasures. Each gift was as thoughtful as the one giving them.

I told them I was pleased to finally meet them. I had hoped to have the chance earlier, but I didn't really leave the hill and hoped they would make their way up. Jo-Dell held my hand and said that today was a whim. They hadn't set out that day to come up. She wasn't even sure if the meeting was going to happen. She never wanted us to think they were doing this for anything other than to help a family in need. They wanted to help because it was the right thing to do, not necessarily to meet us.

So began this friendship that grew with each visit. Jesse and Barry are my adopted parents (mine are okay with it; they have been adopted by Jesse and Barry as well), and Trevor is this funny big brother who just might be nicer than Scott. And Jo-Dell, well, she talks as much as I do but has a much bigger heart. I completely and utterly adore them.

There are always moments when you stand humbled before people that truly define what it is to be extraordinary—not always for acts of heroism or unique and exceptional abilities, but for the strength and resolve to continually give of themselves. Like breathing, kindness comes naturally and intuitively to them. It is a gift that makes this world a place where we can see hope.

All the people we have met through our tragedy have given us so much. I often think of who I was before all of this. I believe that my core has always been the same, the essence of my combined experiences, but almost like a buffer or a cushion, there are tendrils of other things that have not shaped me but that have hung from me. They have wrapped around my core, sometimes helping me and other times getting in the way. Ryan's disappearance has burnt so much away. All the extraneous material that did not move me forward or that directed my focus on the unimportant has faded. So, my core is more exposed. But in doing so, it has offered me the ability to take pieces that can only strengthen me.

I am more myself because of this new family. They have shown me the best of humanity.

June 25, 2018

Every summer has its own story.

Delicious in its telling. The warm summer sun wraps you in comfort almost as if to cradle you. It is my most favourite season by far.

Most of our chapters could be told gathered around the campfire at the lake. Imagine waking to lazy mornings so carefree and full of promise. Or watching as the sun lingered, reluctant to give way to night-time.

It was our time.

It was family time.

It was moments spent with friends.

It was as if happiness was captured on the hardcover of a book waiting to be read over and over.

I never wanted it end.

This past weekend, we headed out to the lake. Our friends, understanding it to be one of our "firsts" came along as well.

It is exactly how I remember it. The sounds of children squealing and their parents' laughter. The clinking of glasses, the mowing of lawns and the smell of wood crackling. It is the coming together of a summertime community.

But not everything is the same. You cannot go through seasons without changes. Ryan's disappearance is not the only loss felt here. Grandpa Bruce also passed away this past May. He was the soul of our community and is greatly missed. Our community stands but just a little bit smaller. Sadder.

Our summer story is no longer familiar in its telling.

The bench that was erected to commemorate our dearly departed loved ones has grown to carry two more.

June 26, 2018

*Travelling in the company of those we love is home in motion.*

- Leigh Hunt

I love to travel. I love the sights that unfold around me, seen for the very first time through my eyes, through my perspective. I love the sounds that come from the bustling of busy lives that surround me. I love the richness of other cultures that welcome strangers to their shores.

I believe I would travel far and wide and never stay long in one place if I had my way. I always wanted my children to have that wandering spirit—to have wondrous adventures before planting roots. Perhaps they will ... one day.

This, we believed, would be our last year to have a family vacation. A chance to spend it together and celebrate so many milestones ... Ryan's 21st, Jordyn's 18th, her graduation, my mom's 70th and my parents' 50th wedding anniversary.

The look on their faces when Scott and I told them our plans is a memory that will forever be etched in my mind. Our children, save for Julianna, had never been to Europe. I had half-heartedly imagined *National Lampoon's European Vacation* where our family would play a starring role. But in reality, it was a trip we felt would be memorable. Pure delight and sheer excitement tinged with disbelief.

Our trip is upon us. I struggle daily with thoughts of going vs staying. I never thought we would be here. I never thought I would have to make such a heart-rending decision. How can I feel peace?

What helps ...

Searching continues in our absence by some of the most amazing people to walk this earth.

Our friends and family have encouraged us to honour these plans for us and for our daughters.

Our girls have been without us for so long and endured so much. Without complaint. Without blame. With so much love and understanding. I yearn to spend time with them alone. As a family.

But not in the way we were supposed to. That I cannot do.

I know I need to go with all my heart. My girls deserve that. I just don't know if I can promise that.

I carry pieces of Ryan everywhere I go. In my breath, my cherished memories and in the faces of my husband and our daughters. This trip will be no different.

Charms with words that say, "love, hope, faith, truth, story, wander and travel" will be engraved with Ryan's initials. We shall leave them everywhere. Perhaps someone will find these charms and the power of the words and the love we have shown will be transformational.

*Two of the greatest gifts we can give our children are roots and wings.*

                         - Hodding Carter.

I pray I do both.

June 27, 2018

The two best days of school are the first and the last.

Today both girls said goodbye to a year full of changes. Jordyn finishing high school forever and Julianna leaving a school that has been home for the last four years.

And so begins the sleep-ins. There are no school lunches to be made. And no homework projects that I must complete. If there was a heaven on earth for parents, this would certainly count.

Today, as we have done for almost every last day of school, the kids and I made a trip to Chapters.

This is one of my favourite rituals. Browsing through books, their spines peeking out as if to say, "Pick me!" It is pure enticement. It is impossible to leave without a book as my newest companion.

When the kids were younger, they shared the same excitement. Choosing their own book, regardless of cost, was a special treat. It was only as they grew that other interests took place of fantastical stories of make-believe and happily ever after.

The girls less so, but Ryan would rather longboard or hang out with friends than spend time with a book. I tried to encourage reading graphic novels, science fiction or books based on movies he loved. He reluctantly complied but often times, I would find these purchases left haphazardly in odd places and covered in dust.

Such is life.

It wasn't until Ryan went to university that a revival in reading came about. He rode the train each day. Bored, he approached me to recommend a book to take with him on the long rides. The novel I suggested was by one of my favourite authors. That night, I asked how he liked it.

"The prologue was a guy who slit his own throat," he said, looking at me incredulously. "It was awesome!!"

I had him hook, line and sinker. Finally.

Next came his passion with Frank Herbert and the Dune series. Not necessarily my genre, but I rallied. Ryan was thrilled when I finished the first novel. For Christmas this year, he gave me a gift card and his own worn copies of Books 2 and 3.

This is why you do rituals and traditions. Not with the hope that every time it will be perfect and pristine, but with the knowledge that someday those seeds will take root. Memories will be made, never to be forgotten.

Happy last day of school everyone!

June 28, 2018

Forgive me ...

Today I want to talk about my oldest daughter, Jordyn.

I watched this beautiful soul walk across the stage to accept her high school diploma. I could tell she was nervous.

What I wanted to tell her is that she already did the hard part. For the last 4½ months, she has been on her own. With her boyfriend Max by her side, she has managed the household. From grocery shopping, ringette games, a part-time job and juggling a full Grade 12 course load, she mastered it all. She did it effortlessly and without complaint.

It would have been so simple to take the easy road. To allow people to step in and take away all the stressors that come from living our tragedy.

But she didn't do that. She rose to the occasion and did it with poise and grace.

My beauty, congratulations on your graduation.

I know you will do amazing things, Jordyn Delaney.

For you already have.

June 29, 2018

I was honoured to be asked to speak at Jordyn and Max's banquet this evening.

This is what I wrote:

As parents, we remember the first day of school; the feeling of your hands holding ours so tightly, afraid to let go. You were nervous, anxious and a little bit scared of being without us. We understand now. The tables have turned. We are the ones holding on, not wanting to let go.

And yet we must.

I have the unenviable task of imparting wisdom on behalf of the parents to all of the graduates here. It is impossible, really.

Even if there was unlimited time or you all weren't so eager to leave here to head to safe grad, I would never be able to fully describe all the beauty you will encounter or the hardships you may face.

Only time and life will accomplish that.

But with the time I have, this is what I want you know:

Be brave. Don't let fear be your only companion on this journey. Have a healthy skepticism, take the opportunity to examine your options but don't become so mired in the "What ifs" that you are incapacitated.

Be strong. For life is full of missteps or failed adventures. The hardest thing you shall ever have to do is to stand back up, but it is that willingness that will determine your course. Know that it's okay to rest. But the world goes on whether you choose to view it from lying down or standing tall.

Be joyous. Find like-minded people that share your passions and love the quirkiness that is uniquely you. Through them—with them—you will discover your true, authentic self.

Be involved. Whether you live in one community or 100 throughout your lifetime, invest in it. Seemingly random acts of kindness can yield the greatest outcome. The world becomes smaller when you connect with those around you.

But most importantly, be proud.

Be proud of who you are and where you came from. Be proud of where you will go and what you will do. Have as much pride in yourselves as we do here tonight.

So, this evening as we celebrate, we lovingly let go.

June 30, 2018

> *You can never plan the future by the past.*
> \- Edmund Burke

Despite having two children that graduated high school, I couldn't have prepared myself for the vast differences.

Jordyn was a flurry of dress shopping, dress alterations, hair appointments and make-up artistry. It was busy and chaotic but, in the end, absolutely perfect.

Ryan ... well, it was a late March remembering, "Mom, I think I need a tux. Can we go sometime?" A haircut, a buying of the corsage and we were finished. It was laid-back with minimal involvement but in the end, also absolutely perfect.

We survived two safe grads. Two 12:00 to 3:00 a.m. shifts. And two 5:00 a.m. sleepy morning pickups.

They both danced. I feel Ryan's sporadic hand movement was maybe more memorable, but that's only because no one in their right mind wants to dance like that. Well, not if they are hoping to pickup the opposite sex. Jordyn's years of dance made her the clear winner.

They both hung with friends on their final day as high schoolers. And what friends they had. Wonderful, supportive and kind friends. So many of Ryan's friends attended this year's graduation ceremony. It made my heart swell to have them come up to give their regards to Scott and me. I felt Ryan in every hug they gave us. Their loyalty, a clear mark of Ryan's character.

It was a wonderful night for Ryan and Jordyn. Three years apart but memories abound. They came. They celebrated. They conquered.

They were different but always the same. Perfect.

There is only one left behind to follow in her siblings' footsteps. If you know Julianna ... you will already be praying for my salvation. 😬😬😅😅

July 1, 2018

Canada Day heralds the beginning of summer complete with the pride and glory of this country we call home. Decked out in our red and white, we host parties, go camping, watch fireworks ... spend well-deserved time with family and friends.

What makes this weekend special?

School's out! No projects to do or spelling words to memorize or crafty objects to hand in. We as parents are finally free. At least for a few months.

Summer is like calorie-free ice cream every day. (Wine for me ... maybe sangria. Could I have both?)

So it is with great reluctance that I ask something from all of you.

Tomorrow, I leave with Scott, Jordyn, Max and Julianna on "The Trip." I call it that because it will be our first. The first time we have been away from searching, the first time it has just been us and I can control nothing about what happens here with the Find Ryan Shtuka Facebook page. To add to my worries, I also made a resolution to post only as often as it feels right without the pressure I place on myself.

I will admit. I am scared.

I am afraid that I won't be able to let go. That I won't be able to give my family the attention they deserve. That my heart will feel empty and bereft of real joy. I fear that my guilt will be ever-present.

And what panics me the most is that the momentum that both you and I have created with Find Ryan Shtuka will come to a halt.

So, I thought, if it was okay ... could I give you a summer school project?

Maybe you could help with the posts?

Is there a post by someone (not necessarily me) that really resonates with you? There have been thousands of posts since the inception of the Facebook site. So many wonderful and meaningful.

A memory about the search? Your experiences or personal meanings since joining this site?

RAK moments?

Your favourite summer vacations or traditions?

With your help, I can rest easy in the knowledge that, for a short while, Ryan is in good hands.

And please know how grateful I am that every day you search when able, that you continue to dedicate sharing the site, posting and caring so much about my son.

Ryan's legacy is because of all of you.

Happy Canada Day!!!

# Destination: Grief, Journey Unknown

W e left on the second of July for what should have been a trip of a lifetime where we celebrated Ryan's twenty-first birthday, Jordyn's eighteenth and her high school graduation. In the back of our minds, it most likely would be the last family trip. Scott and I had discussed the possibility that, with the kids getting older, these adventures would begin to look different. Oh, yes, if we were footing the bill, I'm positive that we would always have eager participants. But timing around schools and work combined with new relationships would present some challenges.

So, we were going to embrace this vacation as our last one. Ironic. I am always reminded that you should savour any moment because you have no idea if it will come again.

It was our vacation to Las Vegas the year before that would have the glory of being the final trip that we all took together. I have since learned that the less stress you put on any event makes for a more memorable experience. Even Vegas in August. We had booked two one-bedroom apartments adjoining with Julianna, Scott and I in one, and Jordyn, Ryan and his girlfriend, Juliana, in the other. We spent a week swimming, playing dice by the poolside, walking the strip and taking side trips to Lake Havasu. It was laid-back, unintentional and relaxing. The kids all enjoyed each other while Scott and I congratulated each other on a job well done—if you discount taking the almost twelve-year-old Julianna to Freemont Street and watching her eyes bulge in disbelief. Located in the heart of downtown Las Vegas, Freemont Street is home to some of the oldest casinos like the Golden Nugget and the Four Queens. But it is so much more than that; it is an experience worth visiting with its neon lights and overhead video screen that is said to be the largest in the world. Block after block of free entertainment, it is a mecca for oddball performers and buxom showgirls.

We had high hopes that this epic adventure would bring about the same closeness and a memorable experience since it would be both Jordyn and Ryan's first trip abroad. Julianna had the opportunity to travel with my mom and dad to visit my brother in Edinburgh two years prior, so I was hoping we could expand on her vast knowledge of navigating the streets of Paris to locate a Gap store for a sweatshirt she no longer wears.

With Ryan's disappearance, I had forgotten about our plans. Hardly surprising. But the flight reminder prompted me, as did the Airbnb notifications about our accommodations. Scott and I sat down in our Sun Peaks rental at the end of April one night to talk about it. For as much as I love travelling, to the point of obsession, I suggested cancelling. Scott, always balking in order to save money, suggested adjusting and going.

"But it won't be the same," I lamented.

He looked at me sadly. Two months into the search and the snow was slowly but continuously melting.

"Nothing will be again, babe."

Different but not without some joy. Changed but ever-evolving into a new normal. Our girls had been through so much. They never complained, and they always moved forward with love and acceptance about what now was. We could make this trip. Ryan would be with us whether we were at home or abroad.

We knew that we would be returning home from Sun Peaks once the snow melted and that we would be in Beaumont in time for Jordyn's eighteenth birthday and her graduation. That timeline was set in stone. When we returned to Sun Peaks to continue, the search had not yet been confirmed, but discussions about the improbability of the ground conditions in the summer months gave us some flexibility without so much guilt. It wasn't inescapable of course. I doubt the guilt will ever really fade until Ryan is found. Even should that occur, I think the guilt of not finding him will really just evolve into what we could have done to find him sooner. But every circumstance requires an adjustment or transition into what was and will now be. We couldn't continue to live in Sun Peaks and search every day for the rest of our living days. We gave birth to more than one child, and they are all deserving of our love and attention. We would have to learn to shift and adapt to include all of them in the days, months and years moving forward.

Like everything I do, my decisions never feel small and slight but rather experienced with a force that shakes me. This trip would such a moment. If Ryan could not come with us in person, then we would include him with charms and mementos that we would bring and leave along the way.

But there still was a ticket waiting. Such an easy decision to bring Max. He had been living with us since October of 2017—a situation that, like with all things temporary more often than not, becomes permanent. And what a blessing he was and continues to be. Calm and level-headed, he supported Jordyn as she stayed behind in Beaumont. They went to school, worked part-time jobs and planned for graduation. We left behind two teenagers—not by design or without regret—and we came home to two young adults that were capable and responsible for making their own decisions. How could we not be proud? Max was part of the family. He is his own, completely different from Ryan. He is not my son. He is not meant to replace what I have lost. He is a wonderful addition to our family, though.

So, our plans for the trip would change. We would leave the second of July and fly to London Gatwick and spend the night. The next day would take us to Genoa, Italy, where we would spend a couple of days before boarding a cruise ship that would take us to such places as Cannes, Corsica, Palma de Mallorca, Barcelona, Rome and La Spezia, Italy. After that, we would fly to Edinburgh to visit my brother and my parents who were celebrating not only my parents' fiftieth wedding anniversary but my mother's seventieth birthday. We would make a return visit to London before flying home.

Ambitious? Absolutely.

Privileged? Yes, but not completely outrageous.

We had saved, of course, but with gifts of flights that all WestJet employees had received that year, deep discounts that come with being an airline employee for the cruise and my experience with booking accommodations through various sites, we were able to travel with perks most people would not be able to get. It is one of the reasons that people that love to travel get into my industry. The pay is slightly above minimum wage and the shift work takes away from normal everyday interactions, but the experiences that we get can be beyond amazing. I suppose every company offers attractive incentives in some form or fashion, ours is just more tangible.

It was always easy to travel with Scott. He is a "flow as you go" kinda of guy. He eats when and where you want. He doesn't have to visit every tourist destination, unless, of course, it offers beer or scotch. We went to Florence for our twentieth anniversary, and despite the bountiful museums and breathtaking structures, the only place we went to see was the Museum of Torture in San Gimignano. I confess that was my choice. After walking the halls, I can say with confidence that Scott was completely amenable to any ideas I had thereafter. I should say he took my point. We would wander the streets, stopping for gelato and coming back to our place for wine and cheese.

I was excited to spend time alone as a family and enjoy the same experience. I should have known better.

July 3, 2018

Definitely a bucket list item for Ryan. Arrived for a short stop in London. How much better is it to see England win in a shoot-out when watching in an English pub on English soil?

Ryan would have loved it.

Leaving our charms everywhere we go. We tell everyone to keep them if they wish or pass them on to someone who might need those particular words of hope and encouragement. In this way, we continue to spread love in Ryan's name.

\*     \*     \*

After a long flight and an afternoon nap to recharge, we set out to find a place for dinner. Exploring the internet for restaurants nearby, we settled on one within walking distance. How hard can it be to follow directions on smartphone maps? I want to say that it was perhaps not the best app for European destinations, and that would certainly become clearer throughout our whole trip, but I now believe it may have been the user's fault. That user was me. At the time, I was fairly sure it must be Scott's. So, if you see him, let's keep my confession between us.

We kept walking through neighbourhoods and hitting brick walls. Literally. We knew the restaurant was on the other side, but there was no way to get to it save climbing the walls. Eventually, Scott and Max found a small, hidden pathway. I was thrilled to be there on our first night, but the feeling of being torn left my happiness in tatters. Regret took the polish and shine off of what should have been the beginning of a grand adventure. It started with a quietening, and deeper breaths with eyes losing focus and gazing into places unknown. We all sort of felt it.

Then we heard the cheers and shouts of the crowd seated tightly in the pub portion of the restaurant. Peeking in we could see the FIFA World Cup on the television. Oh my, it was amazing. Overtime and then a shoot-out with England winning to advance. The celebration was intense. People hugging, beers raised. Scott and I looked at each other and smiled. It wasn't like we felt Ryan's presence, but we both knew then that our son was always with us and that going forward there may be reminders of what we had lost, but there would also be reminders of what we have loved. No matter the years ahead, I would rather put more value on the twenty-one years that Ryan had given us.

July 4, 2018

She looks towards me, turning her head from the airplane window. Her smile is wide. There is joy and excitement that clings to every soft squeal she makes and how she tilts her head.

"Mom, look!"

In that moment, I see Ryan and am transported back in time to another family trip. We are going to Tampa. Busch Gardens is our first stop, and he is tall enough to go on all rides. I know this because my son has done his research. But he has saved his excitement for the holy grail of roller coasters here: The SheiKra, the first dive roller coaster to be built in North America. The floors retract and it climbs to an astonishing 200 ft at 47 degrees. It is like being on the wings of a plane. It waits at the top for 4 long, interminable seconds before dropping you below. The rest is unimportant since my eyes are tightly closed. I hate heights.

"Come on ... Mom, Dad ... please, please can we all go on?" Ryan begs us.

Vomit in my throat, I agree. I feel like I rarely said no, despite my discomfort. After all, I would say most of parenthood is filled with the disquiet of constant growth. We evolve over time, but it often at our own expense. Growth is never easy.

"OK, OK ..." I am rambling.

But in my defence, the ride was and still is super scary to me.

The three of us waited in line. Ryan is a bundle of excited nerves. I am a quivering mess. I feel like Scott is nonchalant. Damn that man.

We sat in the front. Of course, we did. The only two seats that my son wants.

"Mom, Mom! You sit with me."

I am torn. Plummeting to my death with Ryan by my side or violently heaving and wetting myself one row behind? To this day, I am unsure if Ryan chose me to be his seat mate because he loved me or because he had some pent-up anger over my nutritional school lunch offerings.

Up we go. One of the longest climbs of my life. I realize I can't do this.

"Ryan, I'm scared."

"Yah, me too, Mom. But it won't last for long. We will be on the ground soon. Do you want to hold my hand?"

Yes, my son, I so desperately do.

He was right. I AM on the ground. Pushing through some of my most harrowing times.

But in the moment of the drop, I swear I could almost fly. To stretch my hands and touch the sky and heaven above.

My eyes clear, shaking off the memory. I look in my daughter's eyes and realize that I have been granted some pieces of heaven here on earth.

"Yes, baby girl ... show me what you see."

July 8, 2018

La famiglia ...

Family is the word I imagine when I think of what it means to be Italian. Well, that and pasta. But only one will not cause your pants to fit. Mama mia!

Scholars and philosophers have long recounted the bonds of the extended family and the closeness that seems to permeate every social transaction. The bustling, the noise and the traditions. But mostly the love ... all the love.

The kind of family we long to come from and belong to.

I will venture, however, that the scholars never had to use Google maps to navigate Italian streets. Honestly, I am not surprised that most explorers got lost and wound up finding new worlds. It is treacherous out there.

Our family tradition seems to be having wild expectations about the outcome of experiences before they even happen. We build them up, change the landscape and arrive at picture perfect. You would think reality continually surprising us would help change our course.

Not so.

Maybe it is because reality can be harsh so we hold out for something good, something so perfect that it will take our breath away.

I wanted this holiday to be so perfect that for a moment we could suspend our reality. We would laugh and explore new vistas. We would grow closer and define a new sense of what it means to be family.

But we are not entirely new. Some parts have changed about us, but the core of who we are still remains. Softened perhaps but still a bit jagged. We are learning to live with ourselves and each other in this new world.

That is the grace of family, though. Seeing through our imperfections and still loving each other anyways.

That and maybe ... stopping and asking for directions every once in a while.

\*　　\*　　\*

I took some time to come to the realization that our trip was not going to be the magical soothsaying experience that I had hyped up in my own mind. Oh, the signs were there. Five completely individual people wanting a trip that reflected their own ideas and thoughts, and I was apparently the maestro of this ill-prepared orchestra. Normally, I might have planned activities and researched areas extensively, but there wasn't enough time. At best, I thought it would be easy to learn and adapt as we went. At worst, I thought we could wing it. Is there a more intense word than worst?

By now, it was clear that we were a navigationally challenged family. Apparently opinionated as well. And continuously hungry. Whereas Scott and I would wake and have breakfast before stopping for gelato, maybe a glass of Prosecco and a late-afternoon snack at home before dinner, that premise did not work for the girls. Hangriness runs rampant on the girls' side in our family, poor Scott. But the difference is Julianna and I can find something appealing anywhere we stop. Jordyn, however, is a little more select in her eating habits. We wandered the cobbled streets looking for a suitable place to stop every day and got lost each time.

I must have been tired because every part of me was second-guessing our decision. We were not laughing at every moment. We were hot and tired and cranky. Or maybe I was just the cranky one. The girls are sensitive to my mood, which just made it so much worse. No one felt free to do or say what they wanted. Scott, in his ever-present wisdom, held me tight and said, "Talk to me." All my fears, my insecurities, the magnitude of what our lives had become were overwhelming. I was afraid to let go. I was afraid to stand still. I wanted this trip to be perfect, but I knew that nothing will be perfect, so why did I bother trying?

"You are not alone. Nothing is the same for any of us," Scott said.

We have to learn grace. We must find peace in what was, what is and what will be going forward. No, I wasn't alone, but if I couldn't find a way to express myself with the ones who loved me most, then their truths would also be lost.

"What can I do?" he asked in earnest.

There was no judgment or condemnation, just a willingness to support and love me and our girls.

"I can't shoulder the responsibility of this trip on my own. I feel every disappointment," I said.

He could have said that I set myself up for my own failure. They had no expectations. Instead, he said, "We are all in this together. Now and forever."

I want to say that it was smooth sailing after that, but friends don't lie to one another. We still could not find our way around. We still had frenzied afternoons looking for food. But the mood was lighter, and the laughter was more often and so much sweeter.

We continued to learn our new lives.

July 10, 2018

*Keep love in your heart. A life without it is like a sunless garden when the flowers are dead. The consciousness of loving and being loved brings a warmth and a richness to life that nothing else can bring.*

- Oscar Wilde

Cannes, France, is one of the most appealing cities on the French Riviera. It is best known, of course, for the Cannes Film Festival. It is a haven for the rich and the famous. Naturally, Julianna wants to live here when she grows up. Somehow, I don't doubt that she will do whatever she sets her mind to. Perhaps she won't mind me tagging along.

At times, I pinch myself at the places that I have been able to travel to. Farther than my wildest dreams to be sure. I am thankful to my career in the airline industry that allows me to explore the corners of this world. I have only scratched the surface. Every time I travel, I discover somewhere else that piques my interest.

It is insatiable, really.

Scott liked to gently remind me that just because I had seven weeks of dedicated vacation combined with some creative trading to extend each week, I didn't always have to plan to go away. Preposterous! Surely one can see the absurdity in such a statement.

"Vacations aren't free, you know," he would say mildly.

His tone belied the crease on his forehead, the furrowing of his brow.

But I had no cares. Even when things felt tight financially, I always had optimism. I had this steadfast reasoning: It won't always be this way; the kids will grow and leave the nest. Finances can improve. Memories should be made, ones the kids can remember. Explore while you are young and healthy. Time is not guaranteed to anyone.

Funny, isn't it? My only goal was to run away and have my soul soar. To entrench this feeling into my children. Scotts was to provide for our family and ensure their stability.

We both have regrets. I suppose that will always be the way. I wish I had been more conscious of the spending so that Scott could fully enjoy our time away. To know that one does not have to travel far to come back forever changed. Scott wishes he could have stolen some of my optimism (blind, foolish faith). He wished he recognized that time is precious, and that, occasionally, it is okay to let go and embrace uncertainty.

I doubt I will ever be rich.

Life has delivered me a catastrophe and yet I have discovered grace. There is a richness in the souls that surround me now.

And I think I shall never be poor.

July 12, 2018

Anonymity, for me, is this oversized black umbrella. It shields me from the burning stares of grief-stricken eyes while allowing me to fix my gaze forward.

In the beginning, being so far from home sounded heavenly. We would have a chance to rest, to breathe and to grieve. No one would know us. We could be free.

How wrong I was.

Yes ... the world does go on turning, the seconds ticking by, the laughs and cries of the multitudes continue. Life moves forward with nary a thought to those left clinging to the edges.

There is no fault in that. It is after all, what I craved.

However, being anonymous is like a double-edged sword that cuts you to the quick if you are not careful.

"How many children do you have?"

The question so innocently asked by the unknowing leaves an acrid taste in my mouth. The answer so simple. In the past, I never had to stop and think about what I was going to say next. Scott used to have to remind me several times that

I claimed all three as my own, as if his part were inconsequential.

Now there is a sharp intake of air as I ponder how to answer.

Here I am clearly the mother of two beautiful girls. Here I am anonymous.

But it takes every ounce of self-control not to scream to the world that does not know me ... that I have one more. One who is lost and has not found his way home. A son whose absence tears my soul little by little.

And in those moments, I desperately wish that I could cast off my umbrella and come home.

To those that know and understand my grief.

But how can I move forward through the winds of change if I don't firmly plant my feet?

So, I shift the weight of the umbrella and breathe.

July 14, 2018
Ryan John Marcus Shtuka
147 days.
4 months, 27 days.
21 weeks.
3528 hours.
211,680 minutes.

All of them interminable. Unbearable to the ones left behind. Ceaseless to the countless who search, share and pray.

Why do we continue? Because he has value. He is loved. He is so deeply missed.

He is my son. But he could have been your brother, nephew, cousin, grandson or friend.

We search because everyone deserves to be found.

To find out how you can help go to:
www.ryanshtuka.com

July 17, 2018

I remember.

I remember the moment that Ryan was placed into your arms. There was a look of pure amazement on your face that something so pure and precious was part of you. Oh, the love you poured on him from that moment on was a gift that continued to grow with the births of both Jordyn and Julianna.

They remember sleepovers and cuddles, treats filled with baked goodies and time spent focused solely on them. You rarely ever said no. You rarely ever raised your voice. You laughed at their childish humour and listened to endless stories with such patience.

I remember the feeling of contentment that my children had someone in their life that did not criticize, judge or discipline. You left that job to Scott and me. You just wanted to be a safe place for them to land. Someone who would always take their side and protect their heart.

I remember Ryan and Jordyn growing older. Soon Julianna will follow. Their time divided between parental obligations and the need to be free to grow up. You sat patiently on the sidelines happy to see them take their next steps, even if it meant less time spent with you and Papa. You remained proud and full of love. Full of grace.

Those who surround you—your family, friends and strangers just recently met—remember your kind soul and gentle smile. They love you for your generosity of spirit and your zest for life. You have welcomed daughters to our family circle that love you as fiercely as I do. We have grown in blessings and love.

I remember your wish for me. One, that I believe you still pray for each and every day. But you can't change the past or take another's place. I know. Because I would change places in a heartbeat if could.

After all, we are mothers. What wouldn't we do for children?

On your 70th birthday, I want you to know that I remember.

All the wonderful things you are as woman, grandmother, sister and friend.

But mostly as my mother. Who I am today came from the lessons you taught me. The strength that I must draw from now came from the backbone of your experiences and teachings.

You have given so much love. My birthday wish is for you to feel that love a hundredfold.

Happy Birthday Mama.

July 19, 2018

> *I shall tear up trees with my bare teeth!*
> *I shall crush mountains with my fists!*
> *I shall go crazy—for love!*
> - Miguel de Cervantes' Don Quixote

I am destined to climb mountains, it seems.

Arthur's Seat in Edinburgh sits like a jewel in the city centre, an ancient volcano that is over 2000 years old. 251m above sea level, it has amazing views of the city. But first, you must climb it.

It looked daunting at the bottom, often that is the way of all things. You are never sure how to tackle the mountain in front of you. Scott and I climbed rocks and steep, narrow man-made stairs to get to one plateau before surveying our next move. Onward we went, silent and determined until we reached the top.

They were right. What a view!

And upon further inspection, an easier, gradual way up and down is evident. Naturally.

I looked at that path filled with young children and parents leisurely making their way up, and I laughed.

It reminds me of my son.

Ryan has always been smart. Things came to him naturally and with little effort. Whether it was sports, an answer to a test or the luck of a situation, he honestly thought that was the way life worked, at least for him.

"Baby boy, I wish that you will always have this ease of life," I said to him once as he played on his video games instead of studying for finals.

"How so, Mom?" he responded with great suspicion, afraid his playtime was over.

"Life feels like it comes so easily to you in everything you do. Like you are incredibly lucky."

He grinned knowingly (and with good reason; he received 96% on the test).

"But life isn't always so generous, Ryan, and my biggest fear is that you will not be prepared. Do the work, all the work even if it is hard, even if it seems easy, so that your life isn't based on luck alone."

He was young ... perhaps he thought there was more time to learn that lesson.

I'm no different.

I didn't know I could climb mountains. Until now.

July 22, 2018

What's in a name?

Everything.

Often, it is the very first piece of information another will have of us. Impressions are made upon hearing a name, and judgements are formed. Mothers-to-be are superstitious about revealing their newborn's name beforehand lest someone steal it away or cruelly dismiss it.

For me, it was a lesson learned.

"What are your names if it's a boy or a girl?" I was innocently asked.

I instantly puffed up, excited to disclose this highly classified information. Much thought and discussion went into the perfect names, and the world would weep at the sheer beauty. Okay ... well, maybe not. But it was my first child and as such, my interpretations are far grander than my following babies.

"Well. We have chosen Ryan John Marcus if it's a boy and Carson Delaney if it's a girl."

Now preparing to go into great detail about the significance of the names, I am stopped short with the response, "Carson for a girl? She will hate that name."

And maybe they would not be wrong because we identify so strongly with our names. They are interconnected with the life's worth of experiences that we associate with ourselves.

They are important. But they are just one. We, as a community, can add to a long list by which we call others: kind, thoughtful, civic-minded, courageous and generous to name a few. I think that I would like these adjectives to follow me around as well. Wouldn't it be wonderful if I introduced myself, "Hi, my name is Heather, but I am currently known as fair-minded, mostly kind, seriously funny with a bit of bite." Perhaps we would strive to be more than we are now. After all, no one would want to tell people that they are stingy, cruel and judgmental.

Ryan means "Little King."

He certainly acted like his name as a child. I used to tease him and tell him, "Actually, your name means "He who walks like Nana." He looked up at me in horror. They both have a nasty habit of veering into you as they walk. No matter the side or the distance, they will cut you off.

At a store on our vacation, Scott found Ryan's name on a cup. Maybe not so interesting. However, above it was Peter, Richard then Ryan and below Scott. The names of his grandfathers and father.

A sign that names are important?

You have made Ryan's one that he could be proud of.

You have made your own one that people will remember as being kind, caring and compassionate.

We have added adjectives to our names that will last as long as our memories.

That means everything.

July 24, 2018

Our trip is coming to an end.

I am sitting on a train heading home after a long, hot day. In the row of seats in front, a woman is facing me. I can see her face in my window. Her teenage son sits opposite to her. He is chatting away, seemingly happy to be in her presence. His mother's responses are getting slower and more measured. The rocking of the train and the warm sunlight are lulling her into a sedative state. Finally, she says to her son as if he was a small nattering child, "Please, can I just have 30 minutes of silence? It's been a long day. I'm tired and I have a long week ahead. Please just stop talking." She turns her head towards the window and stares absently out. She doesn't see the slumping of his shoulders or the bowing of his head.

But I do. And it breaks my heart.

I have been her.

Exhausted and rundown, she wants to preserve what little energy she has left.

I understand.

Ironic that we tend to be most impatient with the ones closest to us, the ones we love. I suppose it is because we think that they understand us. They see through all the trappings and pretense to see our weaknesses and love us despite them. They will forgive all.

Our moments of dismissiveness certainly will be outweighed by our moments of attentiveness. That is our hope anyways.

But they still leave scars; fissures in our relationships that threaten to break open if left unattended.

But if we treat others with a callous disregard and disdain, it will yield the greatest fractures. Our neighbours, friends, strangers unaware of our burdens and weary souls bear the brunt of our collective frustrations. Most times, we don't mean to be rude. We just don't give as much thought and care in the treatment of others as we do with loved ones.

I will admit, I was jealous of this mother and the interaction with her son. I wanted her to know the precious gift she had in front of her. I wanted ... I wanted ...

Instead, as she caught my eye, I smiled at her. It was a wistful, gentle, "I've been there" smile. She looked away, perplexed.

Moments later, still gazing out the train window, she placed her fingers over his, squeezed and turned and began their conversation again.

Our trip may be ending but the journey continues.

July 26, 2018

*We must not wish for the disappearance of our troubles but the grace to transform them.*

\- Simone Weil

Go after that which is lost ...

Tomorrow, Scott and I are heading back to Sun Peaks to continue our search for Ryan.

There won't be an official command centre, but if you are planning to come and join, you can send me a message.

We are there until Tuesday.

Our searching has gone into a new phase. Moving forward, we will be coming up each month for a period of time until the snow falls. When it melts, we will resume. We will continue until we find Ryan or the search venue changes.

I cannot tell you how that last part pains me to write. I am torn with what is practical and what amounts to a feeling of ultimate betrayal.

We can't stay for months or even weeks on end to search for our son anymore. We have been so fortunate to receive such blessings that allowed us to stay as long as we did. The costs are astronomical, and yet what price would I pay for the return of Ryan?

Everything I own.

Except it's not just me. It's not just Scott. It is our daughters and our family.

Ryan deserves to be found. He deserves to have peace. He deserves to have closure.

All those who go missing deserve this. As do the families.

Ryan has always felt the infinite love that I have for him. He also knows that I will never give up; not until there is not a breath left in my body. So, I know that my son forgives me for the difficult choices I must make.

I'm just not sure I can forgive myself.

July 30, 2018

*Peaks & Valleys: The Search for Ryan Shtuka*

A couple of months ago, Scott and I were approached by three Kamloops filmmakers, Russ, Jared and Allan. We met these young men through fundraising efforts and were struck by how determined they were to tell Ryan's story.

There is an organization called Storyhive which provides grants to filmmakers from western Canada. Storyhive's main sponsor is TELUS, and it has connections to government arts programs as well. If their grant application is successful, the main focuses for the documentary would be to share background information about our son, tell the story of the search so far, and tell the story of the community (both from BC and from Ryan's hometown) that has come together to help support the effort. I am pleased to say they have begun. Currently, they have produced a 60 second video to submit for the grant approval.

I am so incredibly grateful that these young filmmakers want to bring wider awareness to Ryan's case and to continue the investigation

Thank you and much love!

\*  \*  \*

This project needed votes to become a finalist for the Storyhive grant approval. With the support and engagement of our Facebook members, we thought we could help make this happen. It would be a great way to include people in the awareness piece for Ryan. We provided a link and instructions on how and where to vote. Voting took place from July 30 until August 2, a relatively short window, but people could vote up to five times a day. It was as simple as clicking on the sixty-second video. We shared reminders throughout that time period to generate votes and interest in the documentary, and Scott and I were stunned by the level of engagement and interest from others. The comment section of the post was quickly filled with members letting us know they voted or shared the link. It was clear that it was gaining traction, but the final decision would not be announced until September.

July 31, 2018

We are a motley crew by definition.

A group of individuals from various backgrounds, ages and life experiences. What binds us together is this unwavering commitment to Ryan and to each other.

We brave the extreme temperatures, the uneven terrain and the vast search area. Inexperience or inability to find a quick resolution doesn't weigh us down. We persevere. It is not enough to survive this part of our life. We must thrive in spite of it.

And oh how this group has ... they are unlikely heroes. My heroes.

I can't imagine my life without this incredible, growing community. It has been built on heartbreak, tragedy and blessings.

Sometimes ... well, most times, I sit in the woods batting flies and avoiding what I'm pretty sure must be an area filled with rabid beaver covens (is there such a thing?) and say aloud, "Honestly, Ryan???????? Kid, I love you, but you must have been crazy to have chosen me to help lead the search. Your dad ... yep, you are spot on. But me???? Am I the best you could do?"

Yet here I am and here I'll stay.

With my motley group of the most heroic people you have ever met.

Steadfast and resolute.

But just maybe armed with a little bit of bug spray. 😩😩😩

*   *   *

I have often wondered what type of qualities make up a Search and Rescue volunteer. Selflessness is a characteristic we can all agree upon. To give of themselves time and time again, to rush into the unknown and potentially put oneself at risk with only the thought to help someone in distress or imminent danger is selflessness. It is not just having a necessary skill set or an understanding of the hazards of your surroundings, but it is an incredible capacity to adapt, adjust and educate. Combining those personality traits with an overwhelming sense of empathy makes these volunteers heroic.

But not everyone decides on such a career path or this type of volunteer experience. It is not a far stretch for those involved in fire and rescue, law enforcement or emergency medical services to transfer their skills. It is extraordinary to see people go beyond what they thought was possible for them and become such fierce advocates for not only Search and Rescue but for the missing in particular.

In the months since Ryan had disappeared, we had organized hundreds of people who came out to help us search. It did not matter the skills they possessed, they wanted to learn, and they wanted to do what they could to bring our son home. Every single one of those volunteers, no matter the length of time given to assisting us, are and will forever be my heroes. I always said that I just needed the right person at the right time in the right place to do what we had not been able to do up until that point.

As time passed, the number of volunteers and their makeup changed. Over 1100 volunteers signed in with us at the command centre, and still more came from the community. These people did not sign in for their purposeful daily walks, and they changed the areas they walked their dogs or regularly hiked in order to cover different ground. The majority of those volunteers came more than once.

Scott and I always started the day with such hope when we saw people coming day after day for Ryan. It was this balm that soothed our heartache. No one seemed to be giving up. So many people came through our doors, and we met them, shook their hands, hugged them and began to know them more personally. We thanked each and every person for dedicating their time for our son, but I don't remember everyone, and that is devastating to me. It is my biggest regret.

Of course, in the beginning we were barely hanging on. We went through the day on autopilot, our minds holding onto the necessary information and storing nothing else. But these people gave so much of themselves, they gave so much to us, and I want to remember each and every one. I want to have their generosity so entrenched in my soul that were we to pass by one another, my heart would automatically gravitate to theirs.

Each week, the same individuals came, their faces so familiar to us. Their lives an intimate extension of ours.

We first met Colby and Greg, sixteen-year-old twins from Kamloops, when they gave up their spring break of snowboarding to help in the search. It was originally supposed to be only one day, but it soon became clear that these young men were heartier souls whose determination to help others outweighed any one singular activity. Such serious men, they showed up early each day. They were sensitive to the task at hand but passionate in learning what could be taught, so they drank in whatever knowledge they could from Gerry, our resident search leader and trainer and shared it with whichever volunteer group they were placed in. As Greg and Colby returned each weekend to help search, their quiet confidence combined with such intellect had many people assume they were so much older than their years. With their parent's support, they became team leaders with our larger groups, and grown men followed their directions without question. I take nothing away from my son in saying this, but this kind of maturity, empathy, determination and leadership is rare in such young men.

As the months pressed on, our relationship with the guys grew. We settled into a smaller group of searchers, and Greg and Colby came on weekends until school was over and then for longer periods when they could leave work. Along with Scott, they were the epitome of long-suffering. These young men endured raging creeks, fast-moving and biting cold. They suffered bee stings, the prickles of devil's club and blisters from long walks. They managed to smile effortlessly and continuously for every selfie I made them take with me (secretly enjoying it, I am sure).

I sat alongside Colby and Greg's parents watching them walk across their high school graduation stage to receive honour and acclamation, and I felt immense pride in their accomplishments. Watching them grow into such amazing young men has been a gift to us. In the many miles that we found ourselves walking and searching, we talked extensively about the importance of connecting to our community and participating at the ground level to bring about change. Both boys had strong ties within their high school and in Kamloops. They believed it wasn't enough to talk about things such as climate change, but you had to be willing to invest what resources you had even if that resource was yourself in the form of volunteering or by choosing a career path that made change.

So, it came as no surprise that each summer since, both young men have worked in the forestry industry as crew hands and graduated to supervisory roles with the BC Wildfire Service. As they pursue bachelor's degrees in natural resource science with dreams of obtaining a designation of Registered Professional Forester (RPF), I realize that helping our family was the beginning of a lifelong journey to make a mark on this world. Even though they are not our children, we claim them as family because we adore Colby and Greg more than words can describe.

Our motley group also consisted of Melissa and her dog, Caesar Shtuks. I first met her once we finally settled in our last command centre. It wasn't her first time coming to search but by then my brain was adapting to the continual faces, and it was easier to make note and remember. She walked through the door with a present in hand. As I unwrapped it, I saw pictures of Ryan peeking through. It turned out to be a multi-frame with pictures of Ryan and our whole family. I was completely stunned that this stranger took the time to download pictures from our page, develop them and create such precious memorabilia. It was a beautifully thoughtful gesture. Constantly looking at pictures of our previous lives, the smiling faces and the sense of wholeness made me cry, naturally, but this frame on the wall behind me strengthened my resolve and grounded me to our continued purpose. But on a more primitive level, I could feel the love that radiated from Ryan all around me.

Waking early each Saturday morning after a long week, Melissa drove four hours from Maple Ridge, BC, to search with us. Her constant companion was her tiny terrier mix puppy, officially known as Caesar Shtuks. We had the privilege of being introduced to our "god baby" in his puppy stage. Dressed in a tiny dinosaur suit, Caesar hung with me at the command centre on the days Melissa came up to search. Being in the presence of such cuteness was an arduous task, and Caesar endured the endless cuddles. As he grew, he graduated to a backpack so he could join his momma on our searches.

Melissa made the trek to Sun Peaks every Saturday regardless of the weather or the traffic conditions on the dreaded Coquihalla Highway. She gave it her all with us tirelessly all day and then returned home. This wasn't her profession or hobby; it was Melissa's nature to seek ways to make the world a better place. She was designed to offer whatever gifts she possessed to make real and relevant changes. After so many weeks of training and dedication, she continued to search not only for Ryan but she also began assisting families in her area that have had loved ones go missing. My heart swells at the notion that when a desperate family experiences such an unimaginable tragedy, they see Melissa's kind face and benefit from her experience. Once all official resources are exhausted, families are left to shoulder this burden alone, but Melissa stands alongside them.

Rounding out our little engine that could was Dennis. This man has certainly learned that a way to the heart is always through the stomach. He first messaged me in March of 2018 when I was receiving several messages a day. I tried to respond with a detail-heavy message, but more often than not I only had the energy for a quick thank you and a note of appreciation. I suspect Dennis fell into the latter. Thankfully, my memory recognized his name when he showed up at the command centre soon after. Originally from Kamloops, he actually resided just around the corner from us in Beaumont, and he joined the first busload of volunteers from the area.

His intimate knowledge of the land in and around Sun Peaks made him quite valuable and a ready resource. He joined the Search and Rescue team on his first day to help navigate through heavy snowfall and left with the Alberta volunteers the next day. But he came back. Regular visits to see his mother in Kamloops gave him time to come up to Sun Peaks with his quads to search areas that the snow made impossible to get through on foot. His analytical mind calculated the odds and gave logic to my otherwise emotional mother's fears.

If he couldn't make the same nine-and-a-half-hour car ride, he sent baked goods. All my well-intentioned hikes and better eating habits were constantly sabotaged by this man through the temptations of home-made cinnamon buns and cheese bagels. Perhaps music soothes the savage beast, but it is my heartfelt opinion that food made with love satiates the tired soul. Even as we began to volunteer in search parties for other families experiencing similar tragedies, Dennis always had a sweet treat to share with me.

Apart from being an active participant in our searches and an avid baker, Dennis was best known to me as Ryan's wingman. Proudly sporting a Find Ryan hat and sweatshirt, Dennis included our son in his travel adventures. Ryan has gone to Egypt and studied the pyramids. He has laid eyes on the tallest building in the world, the Burj Khalifa, on his many trips to Dubai. He has seen the vastness of the Grand Canyon and partied in France during the World Cup (by far his favourite). Ryan's awareness has spanned the globe, and my son has had the opportunity to explore the world through the eyes of a man he has never met but would surely admire.

These ordinary people have mirrored the extraordinary through simple and singular kindness. It is not within my nature to moralize about how the world could retain its humanity, but it almost certainly begins with a tiny sprout of goodness that awakens one's soul and grows through selfless acts of service. Our motley crew wove their different experiences into a beautiful fabric from the tattered remnants of hopelessness and sorrow. Now, as I look at the well-organized team that continues to use their knowledge and skills to help others, I cannot help but marvel at what a beautiful blanket of love that was created.

August 3, 2018

For the first time in 7 years, my side of the family was together. In Edinburgh, away from everything, just enjoying the opportunity to spend it in one another's company. The love and the laughter were constant and precious.

Scott teases me about being married for almost 23 years. The stress of living with me. Except his face completely ruins the effect. Love rolls off him in waves. I roll my eyes. He looks at me.

"Happy?" he asks.

And in that moment, we look at each other. Tears fill our eyes as we recognize the stark realization: we shall never be truly happy again.

I know there will be joy. There will be times of carefree satisfaction in the lives we will lead. But nothing will be truly or completely anything again.

It is like I'm missing a part of my heart that will never grow back. And yet the pieces that are left grow outward. They expand with all the love we have received, constantly pumping with the blessings of others.

I take stock of my life so far. Around 4 years ago, my life was good. I had a job I loved, surrounded by people I adored, my family was strong and happy and my friend circle complete.

And yet I was unsettled. I struggled to find my place in my own life. I allowed the inconsequential and irrelevant to consume me. I just wanted to be happy.

Ironic that my happiest moments were the ones that I didn't know I was. The diaper changes, the sleepless nights, the homework sessions or the quiet dinners. Time spent with the people that loved me the most; whose acceptance was universal.

Purgatory for me is the ability to remember those peaceful, happy moments and yet not appreciate them or me for what they were or who I was.

I continue to grow and learn. I am forever grateful for the opportunity to be more than I thought I could be.

I only wish that some lessons were learned well before they had irreversible consequences.

I would never have wished for happiness because I would have already had it. I just had to accept it.

August 6, 2018

*My grief lies all within; and these external manner of laments are merely shadows of the unseen grief that swells with silence in the tortur'd soul.*

\- William Shakespeare

Sometimes I lie.

I am a stone. Impervious to the battering of questions and stares. Anchored in an empty and unforgiving sea, watching helplessly as the lives of others drift by. I am stuck.

I am a void. A porous vessel where grief and sadness pour endlessly in, yet it never fills.

Oh, how I envy the young and the bloom of innocence. I long to be a child. The only thing I was afraid of was the bogeyman. Now that I know there are worse things to fear, I am no longer able to close my eyes or cover my ears. I hate pretending to be brave.

I am a sprinter. Barely able to keep ahead of my own thoughts, I dare not slow down. What is chasing me is worse than what lies ahead.

Life has moved on as I know it must. Never in a cruel way, but I watch as normalcy for other people comes slowly back.

However, much as I might envy others, this is not meant for me. For now.

So, when the question comes, so gently and cautiously asked, "How are you?" I merely smile and lie.

"I'm okay."

August 10, 2018

*It's difficult to understand the sum of a person's life. Some people would tell you it's measured by the ones left behind, some believe it can be measured in faith, some say by love, other folks say life has no meaning at all. Me, I believe you measure yourself by the people who measure themselves by you.*

*- The Bucket List*

Oh, love bug, your dad and I believe that to be true.

And yet when I look down, all I can see are the Rubbermaid containers and one treasure box. The accumulated contents left in your room. For a moment, I'm paralyzed.

The aching is so pronounced I can feel the weight of it in my bones. Beautiful hues of life that used to surround and dance about me are monotone and still. Now only colours of grief and sadness seep out as they bleed together. Like sentinels standing guard, refusing admittance.

They are my constant companions and until I find a way around or through them, there they will stand. Imposing and silent.

I will never be able to fully describe the enormity of Ryan's life or his impact. Just as I cannot adequately convey the depth of love I have for my son. The words I write are only that ... words. Pale as the waning moon. Cold without the passion of my thoughts, my voice that gives them some warmth. Words unique to me except I'm not the only one missing our son. I'm a silent witness to Scott's never-ending pain.

But without the words, Ryan would slowly fade into the contents of that keepsake box. Left to be remembered by only his loved ones.

The sum of my life will be forever entwined with Ryan's. As it will be for Scott. And everyone who loved him.

The true measure.

August 14, 2018

6 months has changed me.

I was never as strong or as brave or as civic-minded as I have become. I didn't know the simple act of kindness would have such long-lasting or stunning results. I didn't know that I would matter. Look who I have become because of you.

Ryan, I will wait forever for you. Your father will be by my side. Those who love you will form the ring around us. Know our solidarity. Understand our purpose.

You matter.

You are my own.

I will never give up until you are brought home.

6 months has gone by. But you are not forgotten.

Nor will you ever be.

\*     \*     \*

Settling into a routine a home was a paradox of emotions. We were glad to be home. We relished the small moments of normalcy. We were grateful to be surrounded again by our friends and family. But we felt torn. There still was this hole in our lives, this uncertainty and this longing to be back in Sun Peaks. Searching for Ryan was never far from our thoughts. Six months later and we still didn't feel any closer to knowing what happened. What we did know was that the snow was now gone. The spring run-off had come and gone, and the once raging creek running through Sun Peaks had slowed down considerably. We still maintained monthly contact with the RCMP to discuss any new information that was being brought forth. In truth, lots of tips were still coming in, but, like the creek, they were also slowing. There was nothing new to report.

August 17, 2018

Last night I dreamed of rainbows.

With that came a memory of a night long ago.

The rain was gently falling, streaking down my bedroom window. Cooling the warm summer air that blew against the curtains. Respite after a day of heat and one cranky kid. Resting my head against the pane, I looked out and saw the most perfect rainbow. The colours vibrant and clear. So close, that I almost believed I could stretch my fingers and touch their silky waves.

I stood there. Marvelling in this perfect moment.

I tiptoed into Ryan's room. Sprawled on his bed was my sleeping three-year-old boy. His tiny face flushed from the day, his breathing soft and steady, he looked so peaceful.

"Ry? Baby," I whispered.

His eyes fluttered gently as he focused on my face. My son's face lit up and this beautiful smile graced me.

"Hi Mommy."

"Do you want to see the most perfect rainbow?" I asked my dozing boy.

Ryan answered by stretching his arms up to my neck. I scooped him and drew him close. As we stood looking at nature's masterpiece, I saw the wonder in my son's eyes.

"Wow," he whispered. "It's awesome."

He settled in my arms and soon was fast asleep. As I tucked Ryan back into his bed, eyes still closed, he sighed heavily.

"Thanks Mommy."

I swear I could almost touch him. In the grey light of this morning, I could see his face peaceful with sleep. The tiny breaths of life filling his chest as he laid there. The smell of his little boy scent filled my nose. The rightness of the world in perfect harmony.

It is dawn. The day is like ash in my mouth. I smell the heaviness of smoke. I feel the weight of sadness that permeates my soul.

Six months into a journey that seems endless.

The rainbows I see now are replaced with chaos and rain.

And yet once, I was shown the brilliance of what the world can create.

August 21, 2018

*When the character of a man is not clear to you, look at his friends.*

- Japanese proverb

Humans are such complex creatures; it is almost impossible to understand their reasons for being. We have learned to define each other by a complicated set of life rules that gives us the ability to place each person in a box of preconception.

One of them is character.

Character will always be defined by your actions. It is the intention that comes within your soul that provides others the opportunity to know who you are and what you stand for. It is then up to society to attribute traits to your actions in order to better establish your place in our culture.

Seems complicated and exacting. With plenty of opportunity to get it wrong.

However, in the midst of all that confusion is this absoluteness. The sum of one's life can be tallied through the choices they have made.

This past weekend was the 6-month anniversary of Ryan's disappearance. I'm not sure why this one day seemed more grievous or tragic than the day before or quite possibly the day after. Only that it was.

Left on our own, perhaps we would have settled into a mindset of pondering our son's choices up until February 17$^{th}$. How selfish and cruel to Ryan whose intention would never have been the end result.

Except ...

The support and unyielding love we have been surrounded with from the beginning circled around us yet again.

In the most unexpected way.

We were honoured to have 8 of Ryan's friends come to the lake to celebrate and remember our son, their friend. What an amazing group of men. Destined to do great things in this world. Strong, bright, intelligent men that love my son dearly. And despite the grievous loss they have suffered, it was important for them to come and spend the day with us.

Saturday we were invited to attend a game that Ryan's rugby team were playing in. After the game, we had the privilege of being presented with Ryan's jersey, framed. We now find ourselves included into a new family of individuals that respected our son.

Ryan, you never really had a chance to show the world the whole of your worth. Well, not entirely.

But who you are thus far has captivated so many.

August 28, 2018

I have always been a lucky person.

Not the win-the-lottery kinda lucky. Not the invest-in-this-groundbreaking-company kinda lucky. And certainly not the eat-whatever-you-want-and-never gain-an-ounce kinda lucky.

But I had the sort of good fortune that meant never really studying but somehow what I did remember was always on the test. The type of luck where I mournfully watched my bank account go dangerously low and somehow miraculously a cheque arrived in the mail. I guess the kind of luck where I always felt that I got what I wanted. As long as it wasn't too big or too extravagant.

Now all I want to be is courageous and strong and surrounded by loving, resolute, brave souls that will embrace and encourage me. The definition of who I am must expand in order to survive what is to come. The words I use to describe myself are changing. Like clothing that is ill-fitting, I will need to dispose of everything that no longer suits me. That I understand all too well.

Still … I wonder.

How did I suddenly end up here?

Was the world being especially kind to me? Did it know the trials and tribulations that I would soon face, so up until now it was willing to ease some of my everyday worries?

Or could it be that the world is saying, "Despite all you must bear ... you will endure"?

I honestly couldn't tell you the answer.

If luck is the combination of preparedness and opportunity, how is it possible to reach beyond this tragedy?

Of all the things I feel, lucky just isn't one of them.

September 5, 2018

I want ...

I want ...

I want the life I had before February 17th, 2018.

I want to wake up unafraid.

I want to have that feeling of security and comfort that comes from knowing your loved ones are safe and protected. Not the endless torment of the unknown.

I want to be forgiven.

I want to know that I have done all that I can and so much more to keep my children grounded and with me. Not agonizing about Ryan and what I have possibly missed.

I want time to stand still.

I want the seasons to stop changing. The nights to never come. The ice and the cold to stay away forever.

I want the power of words.

I want people to never forget Ryan. To continue to join and spread awareness. To pray and to search.

I want peace.

I want to conquer my fears, overcome my uncertainty and shed my feelings of guilt and sadness.

I want Ryan to come home.

I want to tell him how much I love him. How much I miss him. That nothing is the same without him.

What I want, I cannot possibly have.

September 7, 2018

I am happy to announce that the documentary *Peaks and Valleys* was chosen for the Storyhive grant proposal. I want to send so much love and gratitude to everyone that shared and participated in voting. I hope the world will know Ryan's name, and the legacy he leaves behind is that all missing people matter. And when communities of strangers turn their attention to kindness and love, wonderful, amazing things can happen.

Thank you.

September 10, 2018

Today is her first day back to school.

I think we are both a little nervous.

For Julianna, it is not only a new school and new people, but almost 7 months since she had a regular school routine.

For me, well, it is always the "Pray everything goes okay" fears. Life is so much a struggle right now that I want the impossible: for the new beginnings to be perfect.

I want her to excel. I want her to feel comfortable. I want the sometimes insensitive comments from classmates that came late last school year to not be spoken or if that is not the case, at least not heard by her.

I guess I want her to brave.

And really, when I say that out loud, I realize that my fears are unfounded.

Julianna is one of the strongest people I know. She will always be brave, not because of the tragedy she has faced but in spite of it. The courage to be herself and live life brightly is a lesson she teaches me every day. I know she will be okay.

However, the yelling at the bottom of the stairs, "Mom!!!!!!!! Let's go!!!!" is so eerily reminiscent of Ryan and something I could live without.

Argh, let the school year begin ...

September 16, 2018

Some people love roller coasters.

The death-defying heights, the adrenaline rush and spine-tingling unease that comes with heart-stopping speed. Full of steep curves, unpredictable and extreme in nature, it brings about feelings of exhilaration and incredible fear.

Others find comfort and joy in the merry-go-round. Intricately designed, handcrafted with such attention to detail, gentle with each rise and fall, it is a ride that is timeless and classic. The pace at which you travel may seem slow to some, but it gives you the opportunity to enjoy your surroundings.

Scott, you have made life with you the perfect combination of both.

Happy anniversary to the man who has loved me through all my imperfections.

Happy anniversary to a man that will always carry the weight of his children upon his shoulders even when it is clear that they can walk on their own.

Happy anniversary to my carousel horse, strong and steady. With the roller coaster we find ourselves on, I find peace, love and grace with you by my side.

September 17, 2018

I find that I don't hunch my shoulders in Sun Peaks.

I am able to walk tall. After all, we have been together since the beginning. This community has watched as we walked in desperation, our eyes hollow and shattered. They have seen us slowly shake off the chains of inability and grief to focus on the task at hand. They have embraced us through our tears and our laughter.

If our anniversary is to be a reflection of love and hope, it is no wonder we felt at peace in this adopted home of ours.

People often ask how I feel about Sun Peaks. I know without a doubt that the people we have met have become such a huge part of our new lives.

There will never be an equal balance to tally our loss vs our gains, that is certain, but perhaps life has a way of continually adding so that you are able to bear your new world.

And for that I am grateful.

\*     \*     \*

Our twenty-third wedding anniversary was spent in Sun Peaks. It was not intentional. We had begun to co-ordinate our monthly searches and visits around the quarter share schedule that our friends Paul and Tianna had for The Residency. The two-bedroom condo was attached to The Grand Hotel and allowed us the opportunity to stay in the village one week each month. As we headed into our seventh month of Ryan's disappearance, we were increasingly aware of the financial burdens that came with searching long distance. We were also blessed to have met a couple, Jen and Brad, that owned a house with a two-bedroom basement suite who offered their accommodations to us. Without the generosity of these four amazing friends, our ability to search would have looked different. Knowing that Scott and I didn't have to make the difficult decision on when or if we could come to Sun Peaks felt like a gift. One we never wanted to waste or take for granted.

September 18, 2018

Thank you to my Unicorn squad for the delivery of the beautiful flowers and chocolate. I may be generous and allow Scott to gaze on their beauty, but I hid the chocolate. Shhhh. Don't tell him.

Also, my messenger is down and out. Same time as the arrival of the flowers ... coincidence????? You decide.

But it has seemed to slow down the pinging of my phone. I'm not totally mad.

Love to you ladies. You truly do sparkle!!!!

\*   \*   \*

Unicorns are legendary creatures, mythical beasts with incredible healing powers and the gift of divining truth. If there ever was a more apt description for a group of women that have become our saviours, I know not what it would be. Monitoring Ryan's Facebook page on a daily basis allowed me to see the names of people who consistently offered support, shared our story and reached out to us to offer any assistance.

One of the regular contributors was a woman named Indigo. This beautiful twenty-one-year from Kamloops was instrumental in identifying other empathic and kind women that wanted to help our family in any way possible. They dubbed themselves "The Unicorns." Indigo was kind enough to share her thoughts on meeting our family and the other group members here.

> The first time I worked up the courage to come and search was on Ryan's birthday. I had wanted to come since the first day, but none of my friends would come with me so I let that hold me back for an entire month. Something was pulling me to be there and to help. I knew after that day that this was a community I wanted to be a part of and a cause I wanted to give my heart to. I wrote a post about going to the mountain and doing a RAK. Sonia sent me a message and asked me to help her with a project. She wanted to do a video about Heather. We started by going through all of her blog posts and pulling out snippets to make the second video (*A Mother's Love for Her Missing Son*), then we just kept talking. It was so easy to talk to Sonia. We worked on the video for days and talked constantly about how to make more people see it. We decided to go through the group and choose people who were devoted to this family and to Ryan. That is where The Unicorns began.

Sonia, a Maple Ridge, BC, resident created the dinosaur logo that we used to spread awareness. The green long-necked dinosaur with white fir trees in the background were perfect and easily recognizable images, and they are the driving force behind the ongoing recognition of and association to Ryan's case. She had stumbled across our story and felt compelled to use her social media, graphic design, blogging, and videography skills to help out. Our only conversations were through Messenger until she finally made her way up the mountain in May.

Amongst the other consistent group members were Laura, Stacey, Claudia, Gina, Pam, Kim and Jo-Dell. Such normal sounding names belie the magical qualities of unicorns, but upon closer inspection you will clearly see that subterfuge is how they manage to remain unique and sacred.

Their criteria was to look for people that kept engaging and that often ran interference when comments became unkind or speculative. They were members that welcomed new people joining the group, outlining resources to read or look at to become familiar with Ryan's story and were constantly asking what more could they do. This is how Indigo described the process for recruiting members to their group:

> We watched the group for those special souls and schemed how to get them to understand what we were doing. The entire goal of the group was to get that video to "work"—more people to see it, share it and ultimately care enough to join a search, put up posters, donate or participate in a RAK. When the video started to get some traction, we realized we could actually make a difference, and it was an amazing feeling. We all believed, as I think many did, that when the snow melted in the spring Ryan would be found. We talked about how we could help other families to get their story heard and seen.

The group was formed to spread awareness and provide support, but I think these women severely underestimated the power of like-minded people brought together with a goal in mind. Theirs was to help our family, so they brainstormed constantly, adapted and grew from an organic beginning into a powerhouse of knowledge and expertise. They joined local community groups and shared posters, videos and search events. They kept meticulous copies of who they contacted so there would be no overlapping. They helped admin Ryan's Facebook page and took over the website to help alleviate my workload.

Lest you think The Unicorns were simply concerned with the logistics that surround a missing person, you should also know they wanted to spread love and light in their communities. They made ornaments and keychains and sent seeds out to complete strangers to grow sunshine wherever they found themselves. They became fierce advocates for other missing person's groups, giving hope to other families so desperately in need.

They may have begun this group from a desire to help our family, but it will come as no surprise to see how much they have impacted others as well as each other. They became connected in a very profound way. As Indigo said:

> We spoke a lot about Heather and Scott. The way they approached this tragedy with grace and determination. We were all drawn in because of Heather's blogs. We each felt that Ryan could have easily held a place in our own circles as a friend, brother, nephew or grandson. Each of us saw Ryan in our own loved ones because of them. We loved and do love Ryan because of the way Scott and Heather told the world about him.

As time went on, we became more comfortable and opened up to one another a lot more. This group of complete strangers from all walks and stages of life shared our tragedies and struggles, passions and joys and connected on a deep level. We had our differences, but there was this common ground that we all stood on in which we supported and cared for each other no matter those differences. If that isn't the definition of family, I don't know what is. I've never felt something so magical or so at home with people I barely knew. Indigo described this phenomenon best:

> We joked about being unique and different. We have all been asked various times why we care about a missing young man we never met and a family we don't know. Our answers are all quite similar: Because we would want strangers to care if it were our family. Because we believe in the kindness of complete strangers. Because we believe the world is one community and we need to look after each other. We're different. We're rare and magical in our own eyes, so the name The Unicorns was born.

The first video we produced was profoundly impactful. It highlighted pictures from Ryan as an infant and through childhood to adulthood. It was filled with heartfelt memories from his friends saying how much they missed him. It was beautifully done and would become the first of many videos Indigo and The Unicorns produced and shared.

> We did quite a few more videos trying to take a different standpoint on each of them to give people a reason to connect to this story. Ryan as the missing piece of a family, Ryan as the missing piece of a friend group, Ryan as the boy who played rugby and hunted with his dad, Ryan as the boy who loved his mom and lovingly taunted his little sisters. We tried every angle and pushed the videos hard. We joined mom groups and ski groups, hunting groups and buy and sells—any group we could get into to push out Ryan's story through the videos.

As Ryan's mother, I was definitely on the outside. I knew they had formed this group, and each time I spoke to or saw Indigo and Jo-Dell, they always referred to The Unicorns. I knew that Claudia was involved as well. She had already been to Sun Peaks twice, making the long trip from Regina to come to search. Laura, with her search and rescue background, was a constant who came from Hinton several times. Those were faces I could use to form my impressions, and I knew everyone's names but hadn't met them all. There was Kim and Pam, sisters from Red Deer, beautiful souls that not only consistently shared about Ryan but are so connected to their communities. Sending flower seeds to spread love and joy to members of Ryan's Facebook group and an involvement in feeding the homeless or displaced through a group called Line of Hope are just simple examples of their goodness. Gina, the organizer and hostess of the group, ever a calming influence in the chaos of chatty women, came from Edmonton, as did Stacey, a strong and fierce presence that made us all take ourselves a little less seriously. They are all nothing short of amazing.

In July, I was finally invited to this illustrious group—I really felt like I had made it! It didn't take long for me to regret that a little. The back and forth from all these women was astounding. Like ping-pong. I soon turned off my notifications because the brainstorming, love and friendship would ring all day and night. Their respect for each other was evident. Their conversations deep and thoughtful with advice and comfort for the personal parts of their lives. I could always count on waking up in the morning to entire threads filled with laughter and support. But little did I know that although I was "part" of The Unicorn group chat, there was another one. Indigo and the other Unicorns had a surprise up their sleeves.

> The pinnacle of our friendships was when we started to plan our Unicorn weekend at Sun Peaks. I remember when we decided to make it a surprise for Heather, so we created a separate group

chat and made sure nothing slipped in the chat she was in. It was going to be amazing!! We were determined to get everyone there no matter what it took by chipping in for plane tickets, sharing airplane points to pull together to get everyone there, sharing grocery bills and throwing what we could into the pot. We organized airport pickups and grocery lists as well. There were times when we weren't sure we were all going to make it, but we were all meant to be on that mountain together that weekend.

Scott and I had no idea. Ironically, as Scott was passing through the airport in Calgary, he ran into Claudia. I can only imagine the look on her face as she tried to come up with a reason why they were going onto the same flight.

"Oh, I'm heading to Victoria to see my daughter," she said.

Plausible, but with my background in the industry, I knew that the airlines don't have through flights for that route from Kamloops. Luckily for Claudia, Scott wasn't really clear on what flight he saw her on. The surprise was complete. One of our volunteers invited us to dinner that evening at their condo. I confess I was tired after searching and hadn't really wanted to go out. I was snuggled in my PJs looking forward to a glass of wine and some quietness, but when I walked through the door, I was greeted by a family I hadn't yet met. For Indigo it was a similar feeling.

That weekend was pure magic. All of us met in person for the first time in a rental house we had never been in, on a mountain only a handful of us had been to, in a place of tragedy and great love. It was like seeing old friends. My friends thought I was crazy for spending the weekend with strangers I met on the internet, but the bond was already there and it just got stronger when we were physically together. Even those who were a little more guarded in sharing themselves with the group let their guard down that weekend. Seeing Heather's face when she walked up the stairs to see us in our silly unicorn headbands gathered around the island just added to the magic.

I remember standing in the kitchen that night and feeling complete, and I could have stayed in that trance of magic for the rest of my life. All these kindred spirits were brought together because of one person who couldn't even be there to see the magic he had created. All these beautiful women gathered around the table to hear Heather talk about Ryan and were hanging on her every word. We shared each tear and light laugh, and I felt completely at home.

Of course, some things have changed over time, as Indigo explained:

Our group isn't what it was three years ago, which isn't a bad thing; it has shifted and changed. Some people have moved on, some don't talk as much in the group chat, but we all hold that magic in our hearts, and when we need each other or Ryan needs us we are only a text or a phone call away. These women have reminded me that the world is full of kindness. They have given me hope for the future in which I want to raise my own children. A future where people care about neighbours and strangers alike and where hope is held in the hearts of people across the world. It is a place where friendship, joy and peace can be found in the most unexpected places.

It isn't all joy these Unicorns feel. Like me, they experience the bittersweetness that comes when discovering a purpose so intertwined with tragedy.

> Behind the magic is a sliver of guilt because these friendships were born from tragedy. I know what they cost the Shtuka family. We would give up this magic in a heartbeat for their world to go back to what it was before February 17. Ryan will always be our reason. I am thankful to Ryan for reminding the world that there is kindness in strangers. I am thankful to the Shtuka family for finding the strength in their grief to share Ryan's light. I am thankful for my Unicorn girls for reminding me of the true meaning of friendship and family. I am forever changed because of a boy named Ryan.

Unicorns are found in so many myths and fables. They are enchanting and beguiling, beautiful and majestic, and they bring hope and peace to those lucky enough to see them. Some would suggest they belong to make-believe, but the modern world could all use a little of the hope they bring.

# From the Ashes

September 19, 2018

    13 years ago, as we waited for the birth of our last child, a girl, we all made a wish. Her mother wished that she would be beautiful and kind. Her father closed his eyes and wished that his daughter would be intelligent and loving. One by one, this little girl's family collectively expressed their own desires upon this unborn child. May she be charming, good natured and funny.

    At last, late in the afternoon, the gentle cries of a baby girl could be heard. As she was placed in the arms of her mother, she opened her eyes to the world. I knew then that our wishes had been granted, but I did not know that her fairy godmothers were also present to bestow gifts of their own.

Strength: to stand anchored in the wind while it blows about her.

Resilience: to know that many things are temporary and to try to find the good wherever it may be.

Courage: to be herself when the world wants her to be something else.

Thoughtful: To show kindness and love even in her darkest days.

She was born a warrior child.

I know that wherever Ryan is, he is wishing "the baby" the best birthday.

I love you sweet girl.

September 21, 2018

What would you do??

If you were me?

If your child had gone missing without a trace?

What mountains would you move??

Every morning I wake up with an optimism that today is the day. And each night I go to bed thinking that I failed my first born.

But oh, it's the time in between that hurts the most.

I remember.

I miss the smell of his baby boy hair just fresh from the bath. The way he snuggled into me like I was a security blanket he was afraid to let go of.

I miss his sarcasm, the way he left muddy boot prints on my newly washed floor and the times that he would run through the house chasing the dog so that the barking and yelling interrupted everyone.

I miss his crooked smile and the pride he felt when he scored a goal, a touchdown or a try. I miss the way my house was a haven for his friends and my pantry was filled with empty boxes of snacks.

I miss his hugs. I miss the way he told me how much he loved me. I miss my son.

The mountain seems insurmountable, and yet still I must climb it.

So, I ask you, what would you do if you found yourself in my situation?

I hope that you will be better than me.

But by God, I pray that you never have to.

\* \* \*

I suppose it is inevitable that for all the love and support we have received that there would be an equal and opposing force of negativity. There was a small number of people who felt we should approach this situation differently and became increasingly angry that we wouldn't allow wild speculation on Ryan's Facebook page, nor would we publicly call out anyone associated in our son's disappearance, even if those people were on the periphery. Blood would be drawn and heads were to roll and if we, as a family, wouldn't be the ones to unsheathe our daggers, then they would do it for us. They acted as if we had the power to control, navigate and influence the investigation. Well, not so much Scott, but certainly me. My daily posts were in the forefront and I was the sole presence on social media, so the criticism was aimed at me alone, but Scott was an equal partner in every decision we made about Ryan that was in our control. *Our control* is the key. What could we possibly do outside of searching and spreading awareness?

That lack of understanding spawned the creation of other social media groups in Ryan's name where all the theories and comments that we couldn't allow in our group could run rampant. Group members shared unique criticism of me by copying my posts then mocking them and tearing them apart. Anyone who defended me were quickly removed and blocked.

Some found sport in joining our Facebook group, making negative and often incendiary comments without a care and then laughing about it in a secret group. Did it hurt? Of course. My posts were those of a grieving mother who desperately wanted to capture memories of her son and make him important to others like he was to us. His legacy was paramount, and I mourned that anyone would find his loss amusing. Especially disturbing was the knowledge that a cousin—someone I had only met on maybe five occasions, and Ryan only three—joined this secret group and set herself up as a family spokesperson. She used her sister's and father's searching help at Sun Peaks in the first few days to provide inaccurate information and then suggested I was creating my posts on Ryan's Facebook page for attention. This struck me as ironic because, whereas I did not have a choice to participate in this nightmare, she actively sought a group and wheedled herself into it posing as an expert on people she hardly knew. Interestingly enough, the would-be detectives in this splinter group took her words as gospel and never questioned why this person or any of her family were not listed as friends on my social media.

That was a reoccurring theme. Without knowing the area, the people involved or even all the facts, it would be difficult to formulate an accurate representation about what occurred the evening of February 17. We transparently shared everything we knew but were not privy to everything the investigation entailed. While I could have admired this group's passion and evident engagement, the fact that they were uninterested in correcting false information made them reckless. This didn't just affect our family, but it spread to Ryan's friends, roommates and the partygoers. If they were critical of me, they were downright disgusting with them. Group members would message them directly on their social media pages with their theories that included their active participation in Ryan's disappearance. I will always regret that, even though I had no control over these fanatics. What a poor way to treat those who cared about Ryan.

There were so many theories. Scott and I woke up to a recurring nightmare every day and spent the day going over every possible scenario. We discussed, dismissed and rehashed each one. I don't know if we thought this would help move the search forward or if we just wanted to say the words out loud so we could be prepared for any eventuality. Speaking our fears out loud was like razor blades cutting our skin, and we were left to bleed with each pump of our broken hearts. It was not healing, but we couldn't help ourselves. We tortured our minds wondering what Ryan's final moments could have been like. There could never be peace in that.

Our journey was laid bare to anyone that knew us or joined our group. It wasn't by design that we were so transparent—it was because we didn't know better. To have strangers be critical might have been a good reminder of the negativity that can sometimes come about, but how do you reconcile it when it surfaces in people you know? My emotions ebbed and flowed from day to day—no two days were alike—but in February two years later, I awoke to a barrage of messages and texts about a young boy that had gone missing in Sun Peaks overnight. Despite the initial reports of him getting caught outside the no ski zone, Ryan's page was abuzz with theories about something sinister happening in the community. I spent the day fielding calls from members wanting information so they could assist in the search. We had people on the ground almost immediately in the morning and more bringing food to the volunteers. I prayed for a happy ending. Luckily, this resourceful young man made his way to a building, and although he couldn't get in, he was able to dig enough cover to keep him safe during the cold, wintery night. I cried a lot. I was overjoyed that this fourteen year old was safe and back with his family, but I also spilled grief-stricken tears about an ending for us that would never turn out this happily.

Sometimes when the emotions come, they feel like they sit on the surface of my skin, ready to erupt at the slightest touch. So, when I received a phone call to look at a post made on someone's Facebook page, my heart was not ready for what I was about to see. A co-worker, someone who lived in my hometown and was followed by many of my WestJet peers, decided to weigh in on me, and, more importantly, Ryan. Perhaps upset that her ex-husband was, after years of separation, in the beginning stages of a relationship with my friend, she felt it necessary to not only include me in her rant but to make me the focus. It was awful. I was shocked. I'd had no contact with this person in over two and half years outside of our professional relationship at work where I was her manager. Sure, my younger children were familiar with hers, but we had no other connection. I couldn't understand. Maybe on any other day I could have shaken it off, dismissed it for narcissistic venting by someone who projected herself as the ultimate victim and let it go. Except that it was on a public page for anyone—including all of our mutual friends and co-workers—to see. I felt humiliated and attacked, but what hurt the most were the comments about Ryan. My shoulders slumped in defeat as I sobbed in my bathtub.

"Don't let it bother you," people said. "I wouldn't listen to her, Heather."

In essence, I was told to rise above it. I suppose that sage advice is easier to say to someone who has been on the receiving end of judgement in a most spectacular way if they had never experienced it themselves. It wasn't as if their name were smeared. I was so disappointed in the response. But perhaps in that moment, they believed it was like every other message or comment that I had received: to be taken and not absorbed. A soul gets tired over time. Tired of carrying the burden and tired of doing it alone. I may be able to rise above the fray time and time again, but every once in a while, it would be nice to have someone else's wings to carry me there so that I may rest.

No one stood up for me except Max. That night was a low one, but a tiny ray of light shone into the darkness. Max saw the injustice and addressed it. Without my knowledge, he defended me on the post, which was deleted later that night. Normally our guideline is to not comment on negative posts because it detracts from Ryan and his legacy, but for this one moment, I looked to a young man who was unafraid to stand with his convictions. He loved me, he adored my daughter and showed honour to my son. With that knowledge, I dried my tears, threw on my mask of stoicism and rose again.

I'm not telling you this to elicit sympathy. Every action has a consequence, and we all bare the responsibilities of our actions. While we may not have chosen where we found ourselves in life, we will never regret the way we advocated for Ryan, even if that puts us in the crosshairs of unpleasantness. I recognize the circumstances surrounding my son's disappearance and the questions it raises, and we have never shied away from open discussions, especially the fact that Ryan drank that night, and, from all accounts, took recreational party drugs. But I refuse to acknowledge negativity. We were the parents of a missing child, and I thought that may be my moniker for the rest of my days. It is a title I can advocate for on Ryan's behalf and others' as well. If we are a sum of all parts, that detail about his consumption was only one facet of our son and not the totality. Scott and I did not condone nor condemn the actions of a young man.

I openly had discussions about drugs and alcohol with all my children.

"Who controls the food you eat?" I would ask.

The blank expression on their faces told me they were trying to figure where this conversation was leading.

"Umm, I do?"

"But who buys the food you eat, even if you don't like it?"

"Oh," they replied warming to the game. "You do."

"And who controls what you wear by buying the clothes in your closet?"

"You."

"And your friends? Where you go and what you do?"

"The answer stays the same. I do."

"So, right now, the only thing that you have any control over is your mind. Why would you want to give up the one thing in your possession that is so very precious to drugs and alcohol? Teenage years should be the beginning of self-discovery, but some things should wait until you are in control of everything before exploring."

Maybe it was a good conversation. We never had issues with our children, although with Julianna being only fifteen, perhaps I will hold my self-congratulations until a later date. No one broke their curfew, spiralled out of control or went on late night drunken escapades. I just wish it had held true for Ryan. I truly don't know what happened to my son that night, but it is inescapable that drugs and alcohol played a part. How significant of role remains undetermined.

It took time to process all the information that comes at us. We heard about the recreational drugs on day one, and I was surprised, quite frankly. I knew he had smoked weed, but doing MDMA was new to me. Should I be surprised that he was almost twenty-one and had tried things I wouldn't approve of? There was only so much I could have known. It was nothing dramatic or sensational but the usual growth from a child to an adult.

But, later on, the news settled on me like a weight. I was angry. I was angry at Ryan. Why on earth would he feel the need to experiment? Why would he ignore all reasoning and our conversations? Truthfully, although the anger was quite natural, it burned out equally as fast. Whatever choices Ryan made that evening, he paid the ultimate price, and it was not for me to proclaim judgement. Every action has a consequence, even if the end result was not our intention.

I loathe the word karma. I understand the meaning behind it but have difficulty understanding what I, or Ryan, could have done that was so wrong that his life was the sacrifice. Instead, I choose to believe that life has a way of balancing things out. Those who continue to create havoc or destruction will reap the same, but the majority of us rise to life's challenges with humanity. When we falter, we grow and we learn. With life comes a combination of amazing possibilities and terrible tragedies. No one is immune to the harshness in this world, but they are also shown the beauty. In people, in my community and in the world. Even if it is small, it is never insignificant.

September 26, 2018

This week Scott went back to work.

I don't know if it was time or if he was ready, however, sometimes we don't have a choice.

I know he feels guilty. I know he has hesitation. I wish I could alleviate that stress for Scott. But I'm no better. I don't have the answers to help him.

*Don't second-guess the mistakes you've made; others will do that for you. Make things as simple as possible but not simpler.*

\- Albert Einstein

Humans second guess themselves every day. What we wore, what we said, how we acted; we have tiny spheres of doubt that nag us throughout the day. Thankfully, they tend to be easily dismissed as we move on to the next questionable decision.

Until.

You make a decision where the outcome can have long-lasting consequences.

Grade 1: We had just moved to Beaumont from the city. I had researched and convinced Scott to place Ryan in French Immersion. Brand new town, new school and having to meet new friends was already a heavy burden on a six year old. I thought he could handle it. I wanted Ryan to have every opportunity available to him. As we walked into that classroom where the teachers and students were greeting each other in French, I had my first panicked moment. Leaving him sitting in his desk looking lost was the hardest thing I had ever done. I cried all the way home. I needn't have worried. It took little time for him to learn the language and even less time to make friends. Lifelong friends.

His driver's test: Ryan didn't start driving until the summer he was 18. No desire, threats or coercions could move him. Finally, he made the choice. He had only been driving 2 weeks and was understandably nervous going for the driver's test. We drove to Devon two hours early so he could practice the route. I insisted we stop at the registry to confirm all the details. Luckily or unluckily, the opportunity was given to take the test before his allotted time. Ryan started to shake his head, but my voice was the only thing that carried through. Off he went. I remember watching him looking afraid and nervous. Immediately, I was struck by the same lost look. I sat on my hands the entire time. But he walked through those doors with a paper and pride.

Ironically, I encouraged Ryan to follow his dream to move to Sun Peaks. I never second-guessed his decision. I saw the look in his eyes. It gave me such peace.

Guilt makes us second-guess everything. Perhaps it is because we have been inherently given a choice. Those choices we make will always put us at odds with another. We are not the same, but our capacity to judge our decisions harshly will always remain constant.

It all comes down to cost.

What will our decision bring us and what will it take away? Even indecision has a price.

But what is life without mistakes? How can we move forward if we are not prepared to challenge what we know or how far we can go?

I will never second-guess Ryan's move to the beautiful ski town of Sun Peaks. I only hurt at the cost.

I pray Scott will be as forgiving of himself.

October 2, 2018

*Often it is the deepest pain which empowers you to grow into your highest self.*

\- Karen Salmansohn

Monday, February 19th, will always be an awakening for me.

Petrified, paralyzed with doubt and fear, I walked into an empty command centre. In that moment, I knew that whatever I was before wasn't enough. The need to be focused, driven, determined and unrelenting permeated every fibre of my being.

It is the unravelling of everything you know and the becoming of something new. Something so foreign that at the end, you wonder how you survived the process.

Pieces of me remain, but these new descriptive words have become my mantra. *I can do this. I have to. There is no other way.*

Luckily, I have moments I can draw on. Brief, but their cellular imprint has impacted who I am trying to be today.

Like Patience.

Like the patience of a mother registering her son for high school. 2011.

Grade 9. The transition from elementary to high school. The transformation of child to teenager. I will hereby call it Hell Day.

We arrived on the appointed day. Oh, the thrill of seeing all your friends. The changes. Familiar faces. New faces. My how we have changed.

Unbeknownst to me, you can register for Grade 9 in two ways. The smart, efficient, latte-in-hand-as-you-lounge-on-your-couch way ... or the route I took.

Punctual, forms in hand, chequebook with my very own pen on my very own person, I had come prepared. Every little detail had been thought out and planned for. Register, get textbooks, student i.d., school pictures and a quick tour of the school.

I chose my outfit in the same way you would if you were preparing to greet royalty. A beautiful mix of stylish and cute. Not soccer mom but nothing embarrassing either.

Not that it mattered. As soon as we walked into the foyer, I saw waves of teenagers like an unending sea of hormones crashing against each other.

"Look, Ryan," (I think I might have yelled that), "we need to go stand in this line."

The kid, not my son, that suddenly appeared beside me gave me a pitying look.

"Mom, I'm going to find everyone," Ryan called over his shoulder. "You don't mind, do you?"

What? No, no. I'm a cool mom. Nope. Go on. I'll be fine. Just waiting in this long line.

And I stood. And I waited. And I listened to mindless chatter about the special effects of today's cinematic masterpieces. One by one, every special effect, every movie. I debated curling into the fetal position and covering my ears, but I thought that would make me noticeable.

Why is the line not getting shorter?

Oh, because only one teenager was standing in line and they would switch each other out. Until it was their turn. Then suddenly, 14 of them swarmed the registration table.

Ryan, bless his heart, came towards me every 20 minutes or so. Not close enough to be identifiable, but I was certain he was checking on me.

Finally, it was my turn! The teacher sitting at the table looked at my rumpled outfit, the tears of exhaustion and mascara running down my face and said kindly, "You must have the patience of a saint! Most parents just send their kids to register themselves."

I swallowed my sobs and wrote my cheque.

As we walked out of the school, Ryan wondrously exclaimed, "That didn't take long. I'm gonna walk home with my friends, okay?"

He walked away before briefly coming back to kiss me on the cheek.

"Thanks, Mom."

For him, I would stand forever.

I continue to grow every day. I only hope it's enough.

October 5, 2018

*Happiness cannot be travelled to, owned, earned, worn or consumed. Happiness is the spiritual experience of living every minute with love, grace and gratitude.*

\- Denis Waitley

Most people fear burdening me. They are hesitant to remind me that life indeed goes on. Messy, complicated, beautiful and serene.

When they try to shield me, that is when I am most afraid.

What kind of monster would I become if I couldn't participate in the lives of others? How hardened and callous I should be if I found myself unable to rejoice in your celebrations or to give comfort in the trying times? To be an inspiration to some and be inspired by so many.

Perhaps it would be easy to exist in my own world. No explanations, justifications or judgements but also no relief from the pain and sadness.

In this way, I find myself grateful that I am surrounded by an ever-growing community of everyday heroes. Not heroes because they perform extraordinary feats but because they persevere and endure despite the circumstances they find themselves in. They show me what it means to fully engage with what's left of the life I have before me.

This is the world I want to be part of.

These heroes are my inspiration to be more than I was before. They have taught me that life is not linear. The curves and the overgrown paths of your journey may lead you to places you never expected to go. Nor would you have ever wanted to. And yet that is precisely where you find your purpose.

Grace and gratitude.

October 7, 2018 (Thanksgiving Day)

*Life is a series of thousands of tiny miracles. Notice them.*

- Tamara Kulish

Today is not where I imagined I would be. I don't have all the people I love surrounding me. I don't feel complete. My heart is raw and open, wounded and sore.

And yet I am grateful.

I am the mother of 3 beautiful children. Each of them perfect in their own imperfect way. They have given my soul the ability to fly. They have defined my purpose. I am imbued with the strength of loving someone unconditionally, unselfishly and purely. They are mine own.

How can I be anything but thankful?

My miracle will always be their love. A thousand memories to hold me over until we are all together again.

Until then ...

\*     \*     \*

On October 8, 2018, I flew to Vancouver to meet with Wendy, one of the producers for the documentary *Peaks and Valleys*. She wanted to do a consultation and outline the progress that Past 11 Productions had been making since receiving the Storyhive grant. Jared, Russ and Allan had approached us back in May to do a story about Ryan. In these past couple of months, they had developed a vision and, luckily for Scott and me, they valued our input.

It had been almost a year since I walked through the doors at the airport for work. I was apprehensive, although I couldn't really pinpoint why. Maybe it was, in part, that so much had changed for me with Ryan's disappearance. Seeing their faces filled with such compassion only reminded me that I looked like a pitiable, broken woman. It felt fresh all over again. The tears flowed freely no matter my attempts to curb them. It was an unsettling and stark reminder of what I'd lost in the previous eight months. I remembered the excitement eight years earlier when I received an offer of employment with WestJet. I thought I had won the lottery.

I never knew what I wanted to be when I grew up. Sick days as a child involved me sitting at home "smoking" a pencil and dialling my rotary phone like a businesswoman might as I watched daytime soap operas. It was the 80s. Women could be anything as long as that meant a teacher, a nurse or a secretary. My loftier goals were reserved for evil twin sisters who were secretly part of a foreign spy agency and, in the end, were always redeemable until they met their untimely death. Don't mind me. I had chicken pox for two weeks. Lots of TV.

I graduated from high school in Ontario a year early. At the time, students destined for university needed grades 9 to 12 and then six Ontario Academic Credits to graduate. At the end of Grade 11, my father, a warrant officer in the Armed Forces received a transfer to Ottawa. We were to move for the last two years of high school. Ever dramatic, I begged, pleaded and ultimately refused to go. How that would have been received by a disciplined man such as my father only proved my immaturity. He was immoveable.

But there was a glimmer of hope.

A precedent had been set with the military whereby they would allow my father to move there, pay for short-term accommodations and allow us to stay where we were. I overhead my father telling my mother one night, so I desperately showcased my grades and promised to fast-track my studies. Surprisingly, he agreed. For years, I believed my argumentative skills rivalled those of Atticus Finch, so you can imagine my disappointment to learn that my mother didn't really want to move that quickly either.

We moved to Ottawa one year later after I graduated with honours. University as an English major didn't offer me any glimpse of my future life, and I was easily influenced by those around me.

"You should be this ..." and "You are so good at doing that ..."

I just could never get settled. When my father retired from the Armed Forces and took his last move to Alberta, I went with them in search of a fresh start. That's where I met Scott and started this journey of marriage and family. There can be no regret.

I attended McEwan University in Edmonton for early childhood education and soon found employment. I loved the theoretical knowledge about children and their education but didn't find a passion in the work. I then moved to an office where business people actually smoking pierced those fantasies of sophistication from my youth. Married and now with an infant, I decided to stay home. One baby, then two, but my love of learning always remained, and I looked for ways to stay connected. I took university courses in accounting and payroll management.

Fast forward twelve years. Life was a little less hectic and my desire to return to the work force a little more practical. I saw an advertisement for a customer service agent with WestJet. Nervously, I applied, and to my everlasting delight, received a callback, an interview and finally a position. I will always find it interesting that after years of school I found the most joy in working in customer service in the travel industry. I worked alongside eighteen year olds who had just graduated from high school but who possessed much more purpose than I did at the age. Going to work was a joy each day. I loved the people I worked with and the hustle and bustle of people off on great adventures. Travelling had always been a passion, but I suppose up until that moment, I hadn't discovered a way to combine that with a career.

My responsibilities within WestJet grew as the years passed. As a family, we adjusted to shift work. Early, early mornings found me in bed at 7:00 p.m. And then there were the late evenings and, of course, weekends. I quickly became a training liaison, and I took great pleasure in looking at the excited, fresh faces of those beginning their journey.

"This company is a twenty-four-hour-a-day operation, seven days a week, 365 days a year," I'd say. "You will be expected to work mornings, evenings, weekends, holidays, even soon after the birth of your first child. But if this is something you genuinely want, then you will find yourself enriched with possibilities."

I always knew the ones that fit well with WestJet's culture because the look in their eyes never diminished.

I was passionate about my job and proud to tell everyone where I worked, even if they didn't ask. I honestly never thought I would leave. As I took my last breath, they would wheel my one hundred-year-old body out of the airport.

As I transitioned to guest services manager, I learned to refine my conflict resolution skills and leaned heavily into empathy to navigate the many challenges of cancelled/delayed flights and crises such as the Fort McMurray fires that displaced so many people and created the need for rescue flights. There was also the general chaos that comes from flying in general. It was busy and hectic, but I loved it. I remember doing a YouTube blurb that asked me what I thought was an important takeaway from my job. My answer? "You will never know the reasons why someone travels. It is as important to a family that has saved for years for a trip to Walt Disney World as to a person flying into a work camp after suffering a layoff for many months as to a child visiting their aging parent for the last time. The trip itself is less important than the reasons behind it. Don't lose sight of that."

It was clear that my company and my co-workers took that lesson to heart. From the moment Ryan's disappearance made headlines, WestJet rallied behind us. There were fundraisers, and green ribbons that even now are pinned to uniforms. We had offers of buddy passes (reduced standby passes) so our family could be surrounded with whatever resources we needed. For the first couple of months, Sun Peaks hosted many WestJetters each weekend who scoured the hills searching with us. Our leadership team came to the Edmonton base often and would always mention our family and Ryan as they, too, wore green ribbons. I will forever be grateful for the care and attention they gave us.

Still, one year later as I walked the halls of the airport, it became painfully clear that Ryan was not the only thing of importance I had lost. I looked dully around me, and the busyness—the sheer noise—seemed too chaotic. Thinking outside the box had served me well in this environment, and I applied all my lessons at the command centre, but my passion for travelling had been replaced by the desperate need to find Ryan. The joyous reunions were bitter reminders. The angry faces and gestures given to my co-workers for issues outside their control were draining. How do you look in the eye of an irate traveller who blusters that his flight to Kelowna being delayed and him subsequently missing a tee time is the worst thing that has ever happened to him? I am so afraid that any empathy or compassion I once had would be hardened and embittered.

"Give it time," I was told.

I did try to find my way back. WestJet was such a part of my identity and such a joy for so long, but shift work demanded something of me that I couldn't imagine as the girls processed their grief and wanted me with them. Going to Sun Peaks each month to continue the search for Ryan was also problematic for my job, but I was immovable on that. He was paramount, so I stayed at home, unpaid. For all of WestJet's support, our healthcare provider was less so. Less than a month after Ryan's disappearance, I applied for short-term disability based on advice from WestJet leadership. Even with supporting documentation from a grief counsellor and my own doctor, I was denied. The response letter indicated that, "Although you are going through a difficult personal decision, it didn't appear to affect your ability to return to work."

How absurd. It was an incredible disappointment, but I had more important things to concern myself with. Except for friendly check ins from my immediate leadership team, I never heard from the healthcare provider or WestJet for another eighteen months. Only when I was able to reflect on my experience and make a difficult decision about how and when I was to return did I question their judgment. It took many more months for an appeal that resulted in the initial assessment being overturned, but even that was not a clear victory. The whole process was designed to make appealing difficult. There were lost emails, incomplete interviews and in the end, an admonishment that left me feeling like I was trying to milk the system I had happily paid into bi-weekly for years with no claims and few sick days. It left a bad taste in my mouth. It is shameful that people suffering tragedy are thwarted at every turn by the provider who is meant to protect them. I was fortunate for the support around me, but I often wondered what it is like for those less persistent whose tragedy hampers their ability to keep fighting.

My fight ended April 1, 2020, with COVID-19. So many of my friends and co-workers made tough decisions to leave the company with the unprecedented downturn in the travel industry. Some, like myself, were able to retire early. Others were not as lucky as they waited out a pandemic.

I salute you all.

October 11, 2018

*Each friend represents a world in us, a world possibly not born until they arrive, and it's only by this meeting that a new world is born.*

- Anais Nin

I could never have predicted what my life would be like nearly 8 months after the disappearance of my son, Ryan.

Perhaps, I would have been strong, determined and focused, but please understand that I am also aware that I could have been completely incapacitated. Stilled with grief and loss that filled my every thought, dogged my every step.

If I am who you see today, it is almost surely in part to the friends who surround me. The ones who came and never left. Those who treated me with a combination of kid gloves and quick wit. The friends that loved me with an absoluteness that has calmed the storm within my soul.

I am lucky.

Isn't that a terrible oxymoron?

But as much as I feel tragedy as it seeps into my bones, I know the blessings that I have found through the friendships of others.

Strong, beautiful and confident women show me the way. With backroad car trips and pajama days. Dinner dates and bike rides. I am full.

As I sit on a plane heading to Denver to attend a wellness conference, I know I will be surrounded by motivational women who seek to inspire me.

Some things you cannot change ... and in the end they will change you.

\*     \*     \*

It is hard to know what you need when you need it most. I still find it difficult to stay home for long. I feel restless and unsorted; like I'm destined to be in once place but needed in another. Neither allows me to be whole, but travelling is a reminder of who I used to be, and for a small period of time, I can still pretend. And I so desperately want to escape the pain, the guilt and the expectation that I can be so strong—that I alone will hold everyone together.

Sometimes, I felt like I was trapped behind a mirror. My reflection on the one side was calm and steadfast. That is the one the world chooses to see, the side that my children look to and rely on. On the other side, without imagery, I banged my fists against the glass begging for someone to see me—really see me—and set me free. Perhaps when the light shone just so, my fractured self was visible to those looking beyond the blurring lines.

It was Jen who held the key to unlock my prison, if only temporarily. Friends for ten years through our work, she came to

Sun Peaks early on and returned regularly. Her love language has always been acts of service and words of affirmation. Each morning, she would rise early and have coffee and breakfast ready for Scott and our crew. Throughout the day, she always found ways to show our appreciation to the searchers with her kind words. At night, Jen shielded us from the harshness of the world in our little cocoon, filling it with laughter and love. For someone whose very nature is to care for and nurture those around her, perhaps it was easy to see the double glaze and realize that the mirror lies.

"Come to Denver with me," she coaxed.

The old me would have already had the bags packed, waiting impatiently to leave. Instead, I smiled wistfully and said, "We will see."

"It is a conference that highlights self-love, forgiveness and transformation. It will be filled with amazing speakers who have inspirational messages," she murmured weeks later.

Before I would have been jumping up and down, screaming, "Yes! Let's go already!"

"Maybe next time," I suggested with no conviction.

"Love, I bought us the plane tickets. I think this would be so healing for you," she said. "I can cancel the trip if you really feel you can't go, but it will only be a couple of days. You can rest and be ready to go back to Sun Peaks to search again."

She said this in the presence of Scott and the girls, who encouraged me to go, and I confess I felt a yearning to go.

"OK. But if it gets closer to the date and I can't go, we can cancel?"

"Yes, of course," she said wisely.

I have discovered that having an escape route gives me comfort. I am always looking at every situation now for the exits. Doing this every day can feel heavy. Walking through even the grocery store is a necessity, but some days I feel lost and sad. I can do my everyday tasks on these days, but I cannot bear the pitying questions from acquaintances or the comforting embraces of good friends.

Navigating the world on these days feels like avoiding landmines. So, I take note of what is possible, what is passable and what is impossible. Adjust, accommodate and avoid. Perhaps these are my new tag lines.

As our October trip came closer, I changed my mind a hundred times. Our family vacation in July was one thing—it was a fulfillment of a commitment to our children, and Ryan was with us every step of the way—but this trip was none of those things, so I had a hard time reconciling the reason to go. Jen was patient, and she waited for me to process my fears and decide to go with her.

I don't know what it is like to be a parent grieving the loss of their child. I can only imagine the guilt they must feel as they try to move forward. Even after all these months and all the hours spent searching for Ryan, we are still unable to process what it truly means. Some days I feel my son's energy around me like the quiet whispering of the love that remains, and I feel like he is gone. But even to say such words aloud brought forth the recriminations. *You are his mother. You should continue to have hope. He can still come home.* Maybe that will be true. I fear that it is not. But even if Ryan were to walk through that front door, he would not be the same child I nurtured or raised. That child was lost to us already, and I couldn't even imagine the way forward after that.

As the mother of a missing child, I am intimate with guilt. It is like I am this broken, ancient tree in a clearing that watches fresh green shoots pop up from the ground as they spiral and reach towards the sky above while I, filled with rot and disease, neither grow nor die. Every day feels like Groundhog Day. We live the same moment over and over. Some days we have faith in the facts. Other days we are mired in our own questions and speculations. I may grieve Ryan's absence, but I haven't quite processed his loss.

This guilt prevented me from moving forward to notice simple joys—or even the banality of small disappointments—once again. I felt such guilt in doing anything frivolous—anything that was not search or Ryan related—because a voice in my head was constantly saying, *How can you possibly enjoy life while your son is still waiting for you to find him?*

Logic won out most days. The foundations that had been built around me to keep the enemy at bay felt sturdy and strong. The walls were high, and the moat was deep. I was protected and safe in my perch. But emotion was ever-present, lurking about and seeking cracks and pressure points that indicated a breach was possible. Even through my vigilance, emotion found ways to get inside. Brief bouts of intense fighting filled with casualties ensued before logic repaired the wall and life continued. As I write this now, the violent war has subsided with only mild skirmishes every now and then.

Logic often wins because of the steps I take each day. Every experience that was once defined as normal requires a commitment to try again with fresh eyes and an open heart. Nothing is the same, but having focused on the blessings for all this time, perhaps they can be considered new beginnings.

Our four-day trip to Denver was a seedling of hope and promise. Jen was absolutely right. The conference was filled with inspirational speakers that came with their truth, broken but with such light shining through that I could not help but feel braver having listened to their stories of redemption and transformation. For three days, Jen and I were surrounded with hundreds of women who were raw emotionally, which helped me understand that grief was not just my companion alone. It powerfully touched each of us in so many different ways. In between the sessions, we met some amazing women that I am lucky to include as friends. I learned how to introduce myself to people who were unaware of my story and how to have conversations with strangers that were equally give and take. I learned to smile, laugh and shed tears with others that included Ryan but also included the important people in their lives. It was so simple, and it allowed me to peek at my new future and see what possibilities might still exist.

Jen and I walked around downtown Denver, ate in eclectic restaurants, browsed in quaint boutiques and went to the most amazing champagne bar for happy hour cocktails. We hiked and dined with friends. My beautiful friend, so full of love, was right. I did feel the stirrings of life within me again. Perhaps the rot in the tree could come to life again. Maybe the saplings could still find enough nutrients to spring forth, hold me up and allow me to heal so that I, too, may reach for the skies above. Time will tell.

October 15, 2018

I didn't want to come to Denver.

I couldn't see past the tragedy that is my every day and decide to put it aside for one weekend.

"How," I asked Jen, who encouraged me at first and insisted as the time got nearer, "can I possibly learn anything from people whose stories are not my own?"

Until.

I looked around the room and saw the walking wounded, raw in their pain and strong in their determination to rise above the fears and the doubts to be more than what they were before. Each with a story to tell.

Ah, I have found my place.

That is why.

I would sit through the speakers and the performers with tears trickling down my face and feel wonder at how well they knew my song.

I gathered with the women we met and found kindred spirits in their diversity. Beautiful, strong women radiating with love. And they become my own. My tribe.

And I realize that the only way through my pain is to continue to gather strength from the tribe of women I have surrounding me. The ones who came in the beginning and never left, the ones who joined and became ones I couldn't live without and the ones who will continually seek me out so they may pass on their wisdom.

That is the purpose. That is why I was destined to come.

I owe my gratitude to all of the women for the courage they showed. It was nothing short of divine.

Perhaps today is the day I can begin the journey of loving myself as much as I love my son.

October 17, 2018

What if everyone decided to rise up?

To go beyond what they thought probable. To have possibility conversations filled with affirmations.

To leap.

To be more present.

To forgive the one person who deserves it the most ... yourself.

Would we be kinder? More emotionally intelligent? More cognizant of how our actions land and impact others?

I want desperately to believe we are capable of so much more.

You see, I have to.

I am still here. That has to mean something.

October 26, 2018

Some days I feel like I'm the emperor with new clothes.

I have been given two sets and I must choose the one that fits me best. Both feel heavy and unwieldy. One, so clearly what I used to wear before Ryan's disappearance, and a completely new outfit. Both undeniably foreign to me.

Do I stand before you in in the everyday? Just like you as you move through the events of your life? Structured and sturdy with momentary sparks of magnificence and beauty?

Or do I find myself with nothing on, bereft of comforting material and warmth? Raw and naked? Wary of my appearance, I look to others for advice. With an encouraging smile, they patiently say, "No, my dear, you look beautiful."

Sylvia Plath once said, "I felt very still and empty, the way the eye of a tornado must feel, moving dully along in the middle of the surrounding hullabaloo."

I can relate.

I don't know how to describe normal anymore.

"That's okay," you say. "You are entering into a new stage of what that looks like. Whatever you create is what will be."

And yet I struggle so.

Because there is a beginning.

But for now, there is no ending.

How can you create a sense of normalcy in the place we find ourselves in?

How can I participate and find pleasure in the everyday moments? To relish and love the people surrounding me yet remember and honour my son? A tenuous balancing act at best. One I am constantly working on.

So, I worry that each time I stand before the mirror looking at these clothes that sorrow and grief will win out.

But they haven't yet.

I suppose it won't come as a surprise that the image I see so clearly is two beautiful girls who urge me to wear what feels most comfortable for now.

And a handsome boy who looks on smiling with pride no matter my choice.

My new normal.

That will have to do.

October 31, 2018

*When witches go riding, and black cats are seen,*
*the moon laughs and whispers tis near Halloween.*
- Unknown

Let me explain the kind of mother I am at Halloween. I usually don't remember the decorations I have until the day before. I know I have lots of spooky ghosts and terrifying goblins,

I just never put them back in the same place. Each year, it is an exercise in patience to find the new storage place. Why I choose to scatter them as well, I will never know.

I buy candy the day of. Now this, I feel is genius. Chocolate is my downfall, so I try to delay the inevitable. No one can run that fast or long to burn those calories.

But I love to dress up. I enjoyed watching my kids dress up. I loved the artistry that only children can imagine and try to bring to life.

It is the ultimate decision of what to be that can take weeks. Back and forth. Consultations with friends.

It all comes down to the final reveal.

And that's just me!!

Ryan's brotherly advice to Julianna: "Be clever or be scary or don't be anything."

Hmmmm, I will say he must have discovered that after years of kitty cats and dinosaurs.

Last year, housebound, I sat and watched my parents hand out candy. After a while I heard the short screams of little ones outside my door. I lied. I don't really have scary ghosts or goblins. I am more of a scarecrow and gravestones kinda girl. Simplistic but totally in keeping with the theme. So, it came as a surprise that anyone under the age of 8 would find my house foreboding and scary.

Yet the screams continued.

I hobbled over to the door. Everything looked boring, serene and super basic. Except, in the driveway, I see a tall creature on stilts standing still. An unmoving fixture. On my doorstep, in the corner sits a werewolf. Motionless.

Until a costume clad child comes up to the door.

The stilted creature jolts, with reaching arms blocking the way and forcing the wary trick or treater forward. As they approach the door, my son growls menacingly as he slowly rises to his feet.

Thanks to Gage and Ryan, I was left with quite a bit of leftover candy.

I can't say I was mad. In fact, I was incredibly generous and shared the bounty.

It is these moments that I treasure.

Happy Halloween 🎃

November 2, 2018

*If human beings had genuine courage, they'd wear their costumes every day of the year, not just on Halloween.*

-Doug Coupland

Everyone wears masks.

We settle our faces into a mould of distant friendliness upon meeting new people. We align our looks to match the majority when doing business. We shift and structure and change so that we may fit in. We hide away parts of who we are lest someone see us truly and completely. What if we were to find ourselves unworthy?

I suppose I'm no different.

My masks are piled haphazardly and in arms reach. I juggle between so many at any given time, and I am surprised I can keep track of them all.

My parents left yesterday to head back to Florida. The mask I chose was of happiness and excitement for their trip home. They will be surrounded by such good friends that will help them through some of their darkest days. My parents want to be here. They need to be there. They want to give me comfort—and they do—but I'm afraid I can't lean on them. It is not my way.

I set upon my face a mask of parental patience as I watch my two daughters make plans to go out on Halloween. Two different experiences and two different directions. All I know is that one of my children is lost in his search for his own identity, his own path to adulthood. I see the girls stretching their wings and wanting to explore what is beyond our four walls. I can feel the worry and anxiety bubbling up inside, threatening to spill over, but the mask holds me in place. Their lives should not be altered by a disproportionate fear that I have as they walk out my front door.

On the way to Sun Peaks, I wear a mask that is gentle and serene. Like I am doing the everyday, which in a way, I suppose I am. I greet my dear friends with a mixture of gratitude and love. That mask feels light, almost sheer. That mask feels the closest to my own reflection. Perhaps because love is the most real emotion I possess. I love deep. I love with everything I have. I love soulfully. It is a souvenir that tells me life's purpose.

But it cracks and slips as I drive up the hill. Dotted along the drive to Sun Peaks are Ryan's billboards that

Scott has put up. They stand before me. His face like a beacon. So lifelike. I almost feel like I can reach out and touch him. Oh god, I want that so very much.

Nancy and I sit still with tears streaming down our faces. Perhaps it is the truest form of who I am now. No filters and no mask fits me when I feel this raw.

I am so sad.

I wake up with an ache in my heart each day.

I go to my bed with the same unending sadness each night.

Every moment in the in-between is clouded by my fear and my pain.

I am not strong enough or courageous enough to bare my true self.

So, I will reach for my masks aplenty. Perhaps as time goes on, they will become fewer and fewer until one day I can stand before the world as my best new self.

November 10, 2018

*When everything is moving and shifting, the only way to counteract chaos is stillness. When things feel extraordinary, strive for ordinary. When the surface is wavy, dive deeper for quieter waters.*
                                        - Kristin Armstrong

The snow falls and I cry.

The temperature steadily drops, and I can only shiver with it. Tiny goosebumps cover my skin, and I believe I will never feel warm again.

Each day I feel like I am descending into a controlled madness.

Every moment, I feel utterly alone. No one sees me in the same way I see myself. Broken and tired. I am so very tired.

Except Scott.

He sees through the many masks I wear. He knows the coming winter breaks my heart just a little more. He knows and feels all because even though I may believe I'm alone, I am not. He is right along beside me.

Still ... he takes on this caring of me. He holds all the jagged pieces firmly together unconcerned by the tearing of his own hands. He whispers hope and strength to me each morning when I wake and each night before I sleep.

He is sending Julianna and I to visit friends in Nuevo Vallarta. He prays that I will be able to wade through the chaos and dive deep into stiller waters. He hopes that I can quiet my fears, even for just a bit. He asks that I make memories with our daughter so that her life is not always about sadness and grief.

He tells me to love myself in the same way he does. The same way our children do.

I make no promises on the last one.

But if my life feels like chaos, Scott will forever be my calm.

November 15, 2018

A beautiful day on the water.

It is easy to see why so many people flock to Mexico. It has warmth. Not just the sun and the sand but within the hearts of the people who inhabit this country.

So many days are filled with sadness, grief and pain. Not just for me but for each and every one of us.

Wouldn't it be wonderful if we could bask in the joy and happiness of within and turn those outwards? Imagine what we could create.

This week I have thought of Ryan every day, but I do that no matter where I am. However, I was able to think and experience outside my grief.

That is a wondrous thing.

November 22, 2018

*Even when November's sun is low and Winter flaps his fleecy wings, Thy gold among his silvery snow a solace in the sadness brings.*

- James Rigg

November has always been my nemesis.

You see ... my husband is a hunter. So, this month has always been marked by weekends away and unexpected days off to spend—not by my side but in the uncomfortable coolness of a tree stand— and plans interrupted on the news of a tag filled.

In the early stages, I was mildly supportive. After all, I didn't understand the full ramifications of my acceptance. I thought it was a passing fancy that would wane as we grew and moved through our adult stages in life. I, of course, underestimated the draw of Scott's passion.

I admit that I was churlish after I gave birth to Ryan. Every weekend ... for a month????? I was like a puppy at the window waiting for Scott to get home in the afternoon. "Is it now? Is it now? Do you see Daddy?" Uncontainable excitement at the door. "Yay, you're home. Did you have a good day? Okay, here's Ryan. I'm going to go upstairs and perhaps brush my hair or go to the bathroom ... by myself!"

I was so envious that on top of going off to work each day, Scott had each weekend in November that was allotted for fun, free time.

But he loved it. As a child it was a passion he shared with his uncles, father and cousins. It was not a hunt based on trophies or the quest to prove to be the better opponent—they have such great respect for the gravity of life and the nourishment it brings—it is time spent in solitude and moments to reflect in nature.

Hunting and taking life is not something I wholly understand, but the need to be alone in the beauty that this world can create is enviable.

Time passed and I grew. I grew to see his passion. I grew to carve interests of my own. I grew to see him teaching Ryan the love of the wild. To value the quietness, to practice patience and to respect the scarcity of life.

And he did.

I can now see November for all its glory. The love passed through the generations, the sharing of knowledge and the time spent between a father and a son. I look at my husband's face that is just a tad more lined and his eyes just a bit sadder, and I think, *It is but one more thing that life has taken away from you.*

Until I see the excitement in my youngest's eyes. She is more like her father and brother than she knows. She has been waiting for this year and this moment to finally arrive so that she could join them on their expeditions.

Instead of Scott dwelling on what's lost, he sees his passion come alive again through Julianna's eyes.

George Elliott said, "Every limit is a beginning as well as an ending."

There is a lesson to be learned and a gift we can hold tight to if we find the courage to look.

November 30, 2018

*Tradition is not the worship of ashes, but the preservation of fire.*

- Gustav Mahler

Every year since Ryan was born, we have celebrated the beginning of the Christmas season by going to the Festival of Trees.

I love the beautifully decorated trees, the sugarplum fairies that dance upon the stage, the carolers who sing a melodic tune and the pure delight on the kids' faces as they wait impatiently to sit on Santa's knee.

It is our tradition. Wonderfully kept and preciously preserved.

I confess, I worry that such traditions have burned to ashes in the fire of grief we have felt.

Nothing is the same. It never will be again.

But traditions are not built on one person.

We feel the loss of Ryan, and yet somehow, we are meant to carry on. To remake a new life without him.

Most days I hate the thought.

Tonight, though, it was peaceful. The twinkling of the lights was reminiscent of brightly lit stars.

Ryan's friend Dany came to the Festival of Trees for the first time. I feel comforted that he wants to spend time with us. Like the connection to my son is just out of my reach but his friends provide a pathway. For that, I am grateful.

So, we preserve the tradition, not just for ourselves, but for the memories that they provide.

December 1, 2018

I'm sorry I made you cry, Ryan.

Today of all days, that is all I can think about. The moments I hurt your feelings, the times that my distracted indifference deflated your childish enthusiasm, the words that came from my mouth that were unnecessary and disheartening.

My mind punishes me.

You were given to me, entrusted in my care on the day you were born, so that I may care and protect you.

And I couldn't. I didn't.

You have given me so much.

You made me rethink all my notions of love from the very moment you were placed into my arms. Your eyes brightened when I came in the room, and your tiny hands grasped mine so tightly in fear that I might let go. At one time, I was your whole world.

But, baby, you have always been mine.

It's been a year since I last saw you. A year since I kissed your cheek and hugged you close to me. A year since I said goodbye.

Your voice comes and goes. The memories, once so vivid, are beginning to dull. I no longer smell you in your clothes or in your blankets.

I should be treasuring all that is left to me.

But right now, I can't.

I'm sorry I ever made you cry, my son.

December 2, 2018

*Joy multiplies when it is shared among friends, but grief diminishes with every division. That is life.*
- R. A. Salvatore

Yesterday marked a year since we last saw Ryan. The last day I hugged my son and looked upon his face. *A beginning and ending of sorts*, I thought. A new adventure for him and the last vestiges of his childhood for me. Looking back, it holds a much deeper meaning. Despite the difficultly of the day and perhaps the upcoming Christmas season, we are doing okay. There were definite moments when we cried. Seconds of manic frenzy where we tried to find distractions. But our friends, true to form, wrapped us in love. We read every message and every post. We got ourselves lost in the humanity that was gifted to us by collective strangers.

Grief is still visible, but if that is wholly what we concentrate on, then all is lost.

So today I took stock. I looked around at this community, my friends and family, and found a peaceful surrender.

Thank you to everyone for their kindness, their gifts, their love and their overwhelming support.

Given the opportunity, you sought to spread goodwill and Christmas cheer.

It reminds me why I love this season.

I want to continue what you all have started.

Let's shower others that find themselves lonely, grief-stricken and financially strapped during the holiday season with the gifts that we have so readily shared with each other.

In Ryan's name, I want love to be his lasting legacy.

December 5, 2018

*We are all tattooed in our cradles with the beliefs of our tribe; the record may seem superficial, but it is indelible.*

                       - Oliver Wendell Holmes Jr.

For centuries, we have been painting and adorning our bodies. Thousands of years of cultures that tell stories. Tales of who we are at our very primitive self and what is meaningful to us. Markings on our skin to capture the essence of our circumstances.

They are beauty personified if you care to see behind the ink to read the accounting of one's life.

I got my first tattoo at 36.

"Love Family Happiness"

So simplistic at its core, but it accurately reflects me. My family are my loves, and they will always be my source of happiness. Even in grief, I will always value the joy they bring me.

My second tattoo is there to remind me of my strength.

"She flies with her own wings"

Like indelible marks, they fuse together and bind my beliefs for all the world to see.

Scott adores my tattoos. He appreciates their beauty and loves their meanings.

But it has always been my thing.

Until last week.

My handsome unadorned husband has a story that will now be shared with anyone who cares to listen. A proclamation owning his new identity.

I think they are magnificent.

December 11, 2018

Twas the night before Christmas and all through the house ...

It is no secret that I love Christmas. The twinkly lights, the chorus of carolers singing heavenly hymns, freshly fallen snow and the feeling of togetherness that seems to permeate and crackle in the air around me.

It was a gift that my parents passed onto my brother and me.

Impoverished, my parents came to adulthood with fractured and painful pasts. But together, they were determined to take a different path with their children. Life is about learning, and although they struggled sometimes, they always seemed to create Christmas miracles.

I will forever remember the feeling of being so completely and wholly loved during this particular holiday season.

I wonder now how my parents managed to pull off such miracles year after year. They truly must have scrimped and saved in the months before to give my brother and me such spectacular Christmases.

It always began on the 24th of December.

Early morning marked the flurry of activity and preparation that would lead to the commencement of Christmas Eve. There was meat to be sliced, cheese to be placed on platters overflowing with pickles and grainy mustards. Month-long baking to be set out and last-minute shopping to be rushed and fussed about.

My brother and I waited impatiently for night to fall.

And then behold ... out came the culmination of December for just the four of us. Extravagant and once a year.

My dad would look upon us with a serious expression and formally ask what one drink we would like to try. Giddy with excitement, I would always choose the milkiest, creamiest concoction garnished with bright red cherries. And every year, I could barely choke down more than a few sips of the alcoholic beverage. My dad's face was smug as he turned his back, carrying my drink to the sink to drain the contents.

"Perhaps next year, you can try again. Luckily, I have some ginger ale here that I can put in a wine glass if you like?"

Grateful, I would nod.

Gorging ourselves, we laughed and teased each other about what the next day might bring.

When we were finally satiated, I snuggled into my father as we watched *A Christmas Carol*. Black and white, it was morose and miraculous all at the same time. Trying as hard as I might to keep my eyes open, I nonetheless always drifted off to sleep. My father would gently wake me and send me to my bed.

For Christmas morning and all its wonder could never come soon enough.

These are my fondest memories of childhood Christmas Eves, and I wanted so much to share them. Traditions are only stories that are told and acted upon generation by generation.

December is a month full of love and miracles, and I would love to hear some of yours. Your traditions, your memories ... let's see if we can fill the rest of the holiday season and this page with time-honoured customs.

December 13, 2018

Greed, generosity and forgiveness.

*A Christmas Carol* is a profound story of misery and redemption. Ignorance and morality.

Ebenezer Scrooge is a man of little warmth and is bitter because of life circumstances, and yet he continues to make choices that prolong his wretchedness. Visited by 3 ghosts that represent his past, present and future, he is able to step outside himself and see how others view him. The visions he is shown allow him to clearly see the path of the destructive life he has led and what will happen if he continues to ignore the call to humanity. The very macabre telling of this tale only serves to highlight the incredible transformation of this shallow man.

"Ghost of the Future!" he exclaimed, "I fear you more than any spectre I have seen. But as I know your purpose is to do me good, and as I how to live to be another man from what I was, I am prepared to bear you company and do it with a thankful heart. Will you not speak to me?"

Everyone has a moment when they take stock of the life they have led and decide whether their path is true or if they need to course correct. Some catalysts for change are not of our own making, however, the decision remains the same.

My life was good. I might have wished for things that I didn't have, been a little distant with the ones I loved most, insensitive and reluctant to change. I was impatient with my children at times and flittered time away waiting for them to need me less.

That doesn't make me a monster. It makes me normal.

But if there are lessons to be learned in order for me to forgive myself, it is to live in the moments; with the moments. To make memories and to love completely.

I want to believe that I will be a better person after all of this. One that has suffered a great tragedy but better, nonetheless.

I don't need ghostly apparitions to tell me that change is inevitable; I need to remember that the choice to change is mine.

December 17, 2018

"Ummm, Heather, I wanted to tell you that Carson has been using swear words lately. Could you talk to Ryan?" my sister-in-law asks gently.

Horrified, I nod. Inside my mind is racing. *Scott doesn't swear around the kids. Oh my god! It's me! Ryan is swearing because of me!*

I become determined to clean up my language. Children should hear loving words not those of a lifelong sailor ...

Later that night, Brenda goes home with her children, leaving Uncle Kyle behind to play NHL on Ryan's PlayStation. Scott, Ryan and Kyle have been doing this nightly for quite some time. Tonight, though, I am upstairs tidying when I hear the ruckus of the boys winning and losing at the hockey game. Ryan, the constant winner, is giggling while Scott and Kyle pepper him with the most ungodly words known to man. The more he wins, the saltier the language becomes.

I actually blushed.

Thankfully, the cordless phone was able to capture the moment in my call to Brenda. I'm not sure what she said to Kyle but the games were tamer after that.

Ryan was lucky to have you as his uncle. From the moment he was born, you showered him with love. And for that he looked up to you. You have always been a safe place to land.

And when he needs you most, I see your dogged determination to find him. There is nothing you wouldn't do, no one you won't talk to, no stone you will leave unturned. You are one of his biggest champions.

I suppose that shouldn't surprise me. All those years ago, when I came to visit with Ryan, we would go for hikes in Jasper. When I couldn't carry his weight anymore, you took him from me. You held him to your chest and watched over him.

There is no end to the earth that you wouldn't go for him then and most certainly not now.

Happy Birthday Kyle.

December 18, 2018

*We all, without exception, need relationships to achieve extraordinary things.*

\- Saidi Medal

This past Saturday, Scott and I hosted a Christmas party. The intention was to invite Ryan's friends to help us celebrate the holiday season. To do so with loving memory.

And so many came.

I looked in the faces of the friends Ryan has made over the years. I saw the brightest, the funniest and the kindest. I look at the potential in these faces, and all I can see is the great things they will accomplish.

In those moments, I see Ryan. And it makes me proud. Bittersweet, perhaps, but filled with such love that my son was always surrounded by the wonder of friendships. A circle that sought to inspire, to grow together and to exemplify the true meaning of loyalty.

Scott and I were honoured that Ryan impacted so many. It speaks volumes of his character and of those who surrounded him his whole life.

It was a night full of laughter, lots of hugs, too much food and maybe some tears.

It was imperfectly perfect.

Just as it should be.

December 21, 2018

*There is no teacher more discriminating or transforming than loss.*

\- Pat Conroy

"Heather, Ryan's here. He is crying. He sees you crying and it makes him so sad." Those words were uttered to me by an intuitive medium within the first week of Ryan's disappearance. They were spoken to connect me to my son, I suppose, but the words cut deep. For someone floundering with spirituality and faith, it is a tenuous connection to my son that I am desperate for. To believe wholeheartedly that there exists something beyond right now. That if I can just quiet my mind, my doubts, my reasoning, faith will follow.

But those words, given to me by the well-intentioned only taught me lessons.

In my journey of strength and endurance, this was my most important instruction in the beginning.

If Ryan could truly see me, and my tears only created unimaginable suffering to him, then I must steel myself to be stronger. Oh, I believe he would understand if I faltered from time to time. I also think that when closure finally comes, he will know that tears are the natural progression of grief.

But as his mother, I never want to cause unnecessary pain to my children. If it is in my power to spare this, I reserve the right to do so.

Still ... some things take my breath away.

Flipping through the photo album, my fingers open exactly to a page. There sits my son. This towhead little boy perched on our front step looking back at me. He is expecting someone to come up our driveway.

I can hear his voice, in my head, as real and true to life.

"Mom ... I'm waiting."

And the tears come. The grief feels like a tumultuous storm that threatens to rip me away from this shaky shore. Untethered and drifting. This I cannot do.

Yet.

It is not time.

Because the only other lesson that I have burned in me is that my son needs me.

I will endure.

Until there is nothing but dust and dirt, I will continue to search for Ryan.

December 25, 2018

*The rigid cause themselves to be broken; the pliable cause themselves to be bound.*

- Xunzi

Traditions, like everything else, are fluid.

You change with the times and with the circumstances.

As our children grow into adulthood, nothing seems to be the same as what we planned or wanted when they were young.

They adapt and so must we.

Of course, this year is different. Everything is different. I accept that things must change, but I wanted it to be because we chose it. Or they did. Our children grew. They had plans for their future. They struggled to claim their own identities. What would come would be the result.

But that is not what happened.

Ironic that I have no choice but to say, "If it be your will."

That has never been my way. I'm too stubborn and too opinionated to leave life up to chance.

I am learning.

My girls have minds of their own. Journeys they must travel. Paths only they can choose.

Traditions they may embrace or put aside.
I will learn to remember what has passed and accept what will be.
There is beauty in both if one is not so rigid.

December 27, 2018

*We are better throughout the year for having, in spirit, become a child again at Christmastime.*
- Laura Ingalls Wilder

"Psssst ... Heather, wake up. Santa was here!" came the urgent whisper of my brother.

I open my eyes to see Kevin pulling my stocking onto the bed. Our wonder was barely contained as we opened our gifts. We sat waiting for the moment that was deemed safe enough to wake up our parents.

My father, a merciless teaser, savoured Christmas morning as retribution for a year's worth of childish misbehaviour.

No presents could be opened until my dad was seated downstairs in his chair. No easy feat.

The General, who rose early every morning for 364 days of the year always seemed to have difficulty opening his eyes this particular day. Only the whisper of "Dad, we made you tea," seemed to rouse him. Oh, never has tea been drunk so slowly.

During this time, my father would contemplate his breakfast menu.

"Hmm, shall I have eggs Benedict? No no, I think maybe waffles with some delicious whipped cream. Or perhaps French toast topped with fresh berries. Oh, I don't know ..."

Our faces contorted and anxious, my mother would finally take pity on us and tell us to quickly help her make bacon and eggs.

As my father leisurely ate, we would show him our gifts so far. Hours seemed to pass until my father lumbered from his bed to the bathroom. We took his absence as a chance to quickly make his bed. A man with such a stern military background could never go back to a made bed!

Finally, the moment arrives!

Like a king benevolently perched on his throne, my father would finally grant permission to open our presents. Our eyes were wide as we looked under the tree. In our house, no gift was placed there until after we went to bed on Christmas Eve.

Scott and I have continued some of those traditions with our own children. Some were too miserable to have endured. But they are always remembered fondly.

This Christmas was the first we shared without knowing where Ryan was.

Difficult. Grievous. Agonizing.

Such is every moment before this day and every moment after.

But I want to share the love and the joy that we also experienced. From our friends and family that showered us with love, and more importantly, their time during this busy season, to the good wishes, kind thoughts and prayers from each and every one of you. Our family never felt alone.

We honoured our past traditions while creating new ones.

Our lives will forever be a blend of what was, what is and what will be.

But isn't that true for everybody?

December 31, 2018

*Chains of habit are too light to be felt until they are too heavy to be broken.*

- Warren Buffett

I'm not broken.

I am battered and oh so bruised. Some pieces of me seem to be hanging on precariously, like shards filled with grief, ready to shatter at any given moment.

But I am not broken.

There is still a light that yearns to shine through. To find a way to be enveloped in love and peace.

This year has been, without exaggeration, a trial. It has robbed me of so much. Relentless and unrecoverable. I hurt in ways I thought impossible.

And yet there has been mercy.

Beautiful, raw and open, my heart knows of joy and love only because I have been shown sorrow and loss.

This year draws to a close and I find myself different. I have traversed obstacles I never thought I'd have to overcome. I have discovered a courage and a strength within me that was forged of necessity. I have learned to give all that I have without reservation and that growth comes not from another's intention but my own. I have searched for my faith in a world that made me question all of my foundations and beliefs.

I have been shown love. In moments of my despair, I have felt the power of a community. Hearts beating in collective unison for Ryan. Compassion and kindness for each other, we are set to move humankind forward.

As the clock strikes midnight and a new year dawns upon us, I ask that 2019 bring with it a softer and gentler time.

I want the chance to change the words that were my mantra last year—grief, sadness, anger, exhaustion—and try to create a new language.

Life is sacred. Love is treasured. Kindness is valued.

Even if I were so fractured, broken can be beautiful.

And that, my dear ones, is the unique but wonderful difference.

Much love in the new year.

# Tu Me Manques

There are so many moving pieces when a missing person's case begins. Of course, there are the families and loved ones left behind. There are the missing persons themselves, and the backstories that may lend insight into the movements behind the disappearance. There are the volunteers and members of the support groups that help bring awareness to the cases. Search and rescue groups, whether they be official resources or civilian services, that are brought in to aid in the search. And, of course, there are the local police enforcement agencies that investigate a missing persons case in the hopes to bring them home safely or give families answers so that they move forward to achieve some form of closure.

Each piece plays an integral part that can overlap each other or work independently to get the answers each family deserves. That is the goal, anyways. However, as unique as the journeys are to the individuals experiencing them, so will be the way the cases are handled. Sadly, the horror inflicted on families will be a new experience. There seems to be no manual on how to comprehend, compartmentalize and then co-ordinate search efforts. Families are left to their own devices with little to no direction. If they are lucky (which seems like such an offensive phrase), they will have a large network of individuals that will bring time, logistics, analogical thinking and resources to the search efforts. But in a time of grief and terror, it is a task that seems insurmountable. So they rely heavily on resources such as police enforcement agencies that have been put in place to do this kind of work. They pray fervently that training combined with experience will do what they themselves cannot. How frightful must this be?

Our relationship with the RCMP can be best described as a marriage of sorts. There have been ups and downs, disappointments and recoveries, but we've experienced consistency and developed trust with them that gives us faith to see us through our nightmarish days. I have maintained, perhaps jokingly, that the rural detachment handling Ryan's case is the place where all superintendents come to retire. True or untrue, we have seen quite a few moves in the rural detachment throughout our years. I suppose that is to be expected. As with any business, there are lateral moves, promotions, transfers and retirements. It just seemed we experienced quite a few in just the first year alone. It hardly inspired confidence when we had to explain our case—and most particularly who our son is and was—to someone new almost quarterly. Most superintendents were conscientious and respectful with each new encounter.

We were introduced to our third detachment commander in the four months of living in Sun Peaks on the morning we were leaving the hill for the last time in June 2018. We had packed up our rental and knew that we would never be coming up to live like we had for the previous four months. From there on out, we would be there for a few days or weeks at a time. You cannot imagine the grief and sorrow I felt on that particular day. I believed I had failed my child in such a profound way and it broke open a chasm that will never heal. So, being introduced to a new superintendent who hadn't taken the time to fully read his file was more than a little disappointing. To add insult to injury, he outlined his responsibilities to us in the most egregious way.

"I will be the only contact going forward. All emails will be directed to me to maintain consistency. My hours are from 7 a.m. to 4 p.m., Monday through Friday. To maintain a work-life balance,

I will return calls or emails the following day or Monday following the weekend."

Shocked would be one adjective to describe our feelings, but a burning anger filled every fibre of my being and, I confess, I struggled to control it.

"Considering Ryan has been missing for four months, any conversations now can wait until business hours," I replied evenly. "If there is something critical and requires immediate attention, we will call 911."

I think that began our most tumultuous part in this "marriage." I won't say he wasn't efficient or dedicated, but he lacked a certain empathy that I found difficult to get past. My opinion was altered further on January 4, 2019. Up until this point, Scott would send monthly emails asking for any updates, and as per the direction, he sent all emails to the specified account. On this day, Scott received a bounce back automated response that said the superintendent had retired and any further communication would be handled in the interim by two other constables.

I'd be lying if I said I hadn't felt anger during this terrible time. I have run through the gamut of emotions that anyone experiences during traumatic circumstances, but I have sat in my feelings and tried hard to process them in order to move forward.

But this moment challenged me.

They say that anger is the manifestation of an underlying emotion. If you can address what lies at the root of your anger, you may be able to change your response. Yes, I was outraged. Why did the retiring superintendent extend no common courtesy to us? A simple email prior to his retirement letting us know what changes lie ahead is the bare necessity we should have received. I may have been able to process it better had we not been emphatically told to contact this man and no one else.

But beyond my anger, I was scared.

So afraid that coming upon a year anniversary of Ryan going missing, his case might get lost in the transition. That our son would be forgotten. I can raise awareness like this world has never seen. I can advocate for Ryan with a fierceness that is unparalleled. Scott and I can search this world until we are dust and dirt, leaving no stone unturned or ground uncovered. We can do all of that and more. But what we cannot do—and will never be able to do—is gain enough experience or the skill set that is needed to investigate our son's disappearance.

Oh, how I wanted to take to Ryan's Facebook site and lay out my fears and frustrations to illustrate the unfairness and anger I was feeling. Perhaps it could have been a rallying point, although to what end, I don't know. I might very well have, too, but I recalled another valuable piece of advice that I carry with me through my most challenging times.

Back in March, after I had written post after daily post, my local MP, a person with whom I shared several mutual friends with but had never actually met, reached out to me. Our acquaintances had shared Ryan's story, and the MP had read several of my posts. He messaged me to see if there was anything he was able to do on his end. This initial contact led to several conversations and finally to him coming up to Sun Peaks to help search. He went to meetings with Kamloops Search and Rescue as well as the rural detachment and the superintendent of the entire Kamloops area to discuss Ryan, find out what could be done to aid us in the ongoing search and understand what we could expect moving forward. He put politics aside and never advertised his presence in Sun Peaks because he genuinely wanted to help a family in need. Even in the months after, he continued to check with us to see how we were doing.

He contacted me shortly after we found out the news about the superintendent, and my anger fuelled the conversation as he listened silently. I won't say that the RCMP hadn't done their jobs well to this point—our liaisons, previous superintendents and constables had done an incredible job providing updates, engaging us in conversations and holding themselves accountable. Deep down I knew that. Scott knew that. Our MP knew that. So when I outlined my ideas on a post, he suggested something that resonated with me.

"Why don't you wait a bit before you follow through with that? Take a day, two days, a week or even two weeks. Sit with it. If you still feel compelled to write what you feel, I guarantee you it will still have the same impact on your audience as if you had posted it today."

Simple, perhaps, but quite powerful. I took his advice, let my anger run its course and discovered that fear of Ryan becoming a cold case was motivating my rage. I was also able to gain perspective into what had been accomplished in Ryan's case and the relationships we had forged with the majority of our contacts.

I didn't write that post.

But I did express my fears to our interim contacts along with the southeast district missing persons co-ordinator in a meeting later in January. I also articulated my disappointment in how the retirement was handled. The response was an acknowledgement with the caveat that, like in every business, there are always movements and changes. My rebuttal was that, unlike other businesses, I did not have the opportunity to dismiss them if I felt their services were not adequately provided.

The way we reconciled this setback set us up for more manageable expectations, and the saving grace was that the same constable has attended almost every meeting since. He was the first person Scott spoke to on the phone February 17. His care and concern, as well as the respect given to us as Ryan's parents, was consistent from day one. The way he heard our concerns and addressed them reminded us that this empathy was not unique to him. The entire task force held themselves to the same standards.

And so, with every marriage or partnership, you grow, you learn and you adapt. You understand and you forgive. If Ryan is to be found, it will require all of us dedicated and invested to the cause. My son deserves nothing less.

January 18, 2019

*The two most powerful warriors are patience and time.*

- Leo Tolstoy

Every day a battle rages on. An internal struggle that would rival any Hollywood adventure movie. Epic and heroic.

It is always between reason and emotion.

Logic presents its case.

I would give everything I owned, achieved or accumulated, as would Scott, to trade places with our son. To have him back where he belonged amongst the people that loved him the most and with the ability to live any life he chose. Without a second thought, without a doubt, I would give myself.

Maybe that is so easy to promise. A commitment of good intention with no reasonable expectation of follow through.

After all, 2 months down the line ... it is not as if someone will take us aside and say, "Hey, have I got a deal for you!"

But when I look in my husband's eyes and they mirror mine, I know it to be true.

Furthermore, reason asks me to look to Ryan. If my son, taking his experiences thus far, were given the opportunity to regain his life as he knew it, would he be changed? Breathe in the sweet air just a little deeper? Cherish the moments and love more openly? Choose to be more than he thought he could ever be because he was incredibly aware of the fragility of life?

So, each day, I recognize that which I desire and cannot offer and what Ryan would have wanted and cannot have. And I have to make a choice. When I stand before my son, I never want him to say, "Mom, you had this life and you squandered it on grief alone. You didn't find purpose. You didn't serve others. You didn't move yourself or humankind forward."

However, emotion is a temptress, fickle and relentless, gentle and generous. Some days she wraps those fingers around my heart and with every beat, squeezes them so a tightness settles in my chest. My breath is ragged and memories flood in. On those days, she feels more powerful than anything I have ever known before.

"You have no right to be happy. How can you take joy in this life ... and why would you want to?"

Other days, most days, she is kind. She soothes me with remembrances and allows me to appreciate all the love I have been given. She reminds me that I still have so much to do.

I have come to realize that there is no devil or angel that sits on either shoulder whispering their rhetoric in my ears. No good or evil that forces me to choose a side. Just a thousand battles and a thousand decisions that determine who is victorious.

And yet some days they are together in harmony. One day, I hope there will be more of these ... continuous and uplifting.

Until then I will choose to be brave.

January 28, 2019

*There is nothing new in the world except the history you do not know.*

\- Harry S. Truman

The Killing Fields.

Just a few miles outside the capital city of Phnom Penh lies a small section of land. A popular tourist attraction, it is but one of the sites that serves to remember Cambodia's tragic past.

A country that was decimated by US bombings during the Vietnam War, constant and destructive, found themselves in political upheaval. Hundreds of thousands of Cambodians fleeing the countryside head to the cities for safety and respite. April 17th, 1975, these same people, tired and beleaguered, cheer as the Khmer Rouge march into their cities. In less than 3 hours, this triumph would turn to fear. A terror that would last 3 years, 8 months and 20 days.

The Khmer Rouge, intent on creating a classless society, ordered everyone out of the city and into the countryside. Families separated, taking only what they could carry, began a mass exodus. People ill-equipped to live or work in harsh agricultural conditions were the first casualties. Thousands died.

When the Khmer Rouge's ideology faltered against impossible expectations, the torture and killing of their own people began. Men, women and children; no one was exempt. In the end, not even the Khmer Rouge compadres were spared.

It is not known how many Cambodians suffered and died at the hands of the Khmer Rouge, but some estimate as many as 3 million.

The Killing Fields is their final resting place.

You might ask how someone could possibly go to visit such a horrific and tragic place.

Because they deserve to be remembered. To be honoured. For someone to hold space and know that, despite the ending, they mattered.

When creating a wedding invite list, one never goes through a selection process and thinks, *I couldn't invite them, their happiness will overshadow ours!* We know that people are capable of suspending their own emotions and life situations to partake in the occasions of others. Good or bad. Momentous or tragic.

I walked through the Genocide Museum and the Killing Fields, horrified by the actions of man but awed by the courageous will to survive. I learned of a time in history so recently passed.

The people of Cambodia remember and now so shall I. Before entering the Stupa, I knelt, placing a flower and lighting incense. I said a prayer for those that lie within its walls, and for my son, Ryan.

There is something poetic in that.

January 28, 2019

*Humanity should be our race. Love should be our religion.*

- Unknown

As dawn breaks, the sky lights up to reveal the beauty of Angkor Wat. Cloaked in the darkness of the night, it sits quietly, waiting patiently for the sun to crest the trees. Known as one of the largest religious monuments in the world, it covers almost 162.6 hectares. Despite the crowds that have come to witness it's unveiling, there is an uncanny silence.

I've come here to pray.

As I kneel before a Buddhist monk, dressed in his traditional orange robe and receive my blessing, my mind wanders. I recall conversations of religion with my son. Ryan was inquisitive and curious. Too practical growing up, he often questioned what he read in the Bible or heard in a sermon. He grew up in a household that was a mix of Anglicanism and Catholicism. But religious we were not. We absolutely subscribed to the belief of love, kindness, caring for others and responsibility to uphold the laws laid out before us. We had faith in a oneness that connects us all together but did not often attend a formal service.

But I have always prayed.

Walking in nature, seeing the rugged landscapes, vast and wild, that lay before me, I marvel at their creation. Travelling lands that are far from home and surveying the beauty this world holds, I am in awe. Looking into faces that hold reverence and love, I know that I am not and have never been alone.

I also have this unyielding faith that we are borne to create, to serve, to fulfill a purpose, even if it is not always known to us. Perhaps in this way, we can move ourselves and humankind forward.

As the holy water splashes upon my face, it feel like the tears of my ancestors come to share my grief. Centuries of loved ones gently holding me up so that I might rest for a moment. Space to breathe.

I bring my hands to a prayer position and whisper thank you.

As I stand in the warm sunlight and look around these ancient ruins, I feel my son's approval.

Ryan may never have found a place in one religion or another, but he saw, felt and understood unconditional love.

January 29, 2019

*i carry your heart with me (i carry it in my heart)*
*i am never without it*

— E. E. Cummings

I got a third tattoo in Cambodia. It reads "Tu me manques." In French, they don't say "I miss you" but rather "You are missing from me."

I love that.

For no matter where my children go … they remain in my heart for always.

Ryan, you are missing from me.
Continuing to move mountains.

January 30, 2019

*Travel makes one modest. You see what a tiny place you occupy in the world.*
- Gustav Flaubert

In some ways, the trip to Cambodia pushed my limits.

Working for an airline, of course, I have travelled. For business. For pleasure. I am intimately familiar with the process of check-in and airport standards.

But I have never been that far east. I have never navigated through border controls and done 20-hour flights. Alone.

Content can't possibly describe my feelings about the country of Cambodia. Inspiring. Peaceful. Courageous. Adventurous.

Thankful.

I watched the women who wake up at 4:30 a.m., travel 5 hours to arrive at the market and sell their wares for 2 hours before returning home. Each day, every day. I met students who attend school each morning at 7:00 and then work 9 hours in the hopes of paying for the privilege of attending university. They are hardworking and tireless.

They are beautiful. Their smiles light up no matter the circumstances they find themselves in. Proud with an incredible sense of culture and tradition.

I was awestruck in the presence of 12th century structures. I was moved by a terrible and tragic past.

And then it struck me. Why I had to come to this country. What had moved me to venture outside my comfort zone.

They had a lesson to teach me.

Cambodia and its people lived their life, some kindly, some prosperous, some quietly; oblivious to the catastrophe that would soon be upon them.

In a moment, everything changed. What they knew. How they would see themselves and others. Gone was their normality. Ushered in was their greatest tragedy.

And when it was over, they had a choice.

Stay in a painful past or honour, to remember, and then choose to forge a new way. A way that has more steps forward than steps back. A way that allows them to not just survive but to thrive. Whatever the challenges.

They are my kindred spirits.

Travel far and wide not so you change the world but so that the world may change you.

Feb 3, 2019

You may notice a bit of change on how the page will look in the next little while.

When this Facebook site was created, it was to inform people on the search efforts thus far. As the days wore on, it become cathartic for me to write, to update and to share memories of Ryan.

So many people asked to be part of this community, and the awareness for our son grew. You prayed, joined the search efforts, shared his story and donated.

And we were and are so grateful.

It quickly became apparent that some people found us through other missing persons sites and others discovered that they could add value to these groups as well.

We saw a need and gladly wanted to contribute in any way possible.

We will continue to do that. We are just adjusting the format.

We will provide links for anyone missing. Please take a moment to read their story and follow the link to their groups where the focus is deservedly on them.

Once the link is provided and in the albums section of this page, it will remain there but you will not see it in Ryan's main page. This will help streamline the site as well as provide an avenue for all missing people.

Whether someone walks away willing, unwilling or unknowingly, there is always someone left behind that loves them.

Everyone matters.

Feb 7, 2019

My husband doesn't post much, but when he does it breaks my heart just a little bit more.

Scott's post on Instagram:

Let me tell you story about a boy and his dog!

Ryan has always loved animals...

Oscar has always been his dog and he has been waiting every day for his Ryan to come blasting through our door and give him the biggest hugs!

Wherever you are, my son, I know you are waiting for Oscar and I know he will give you the biggest hugs and licks!

He misses you more than we all can imagine, and I can honestly tell that by the sad look on his face every day you are not home!

You are always on our minds and forever in our hearts!

Even Oscar's!

\*   \*   \*

Our plans to go to Sun Peaks to mark the one-year anniversary of Ryan's disappearance included lots of discussion about how that would look and what it would represent. This would be the first time the girls would be returning since June of 2018. It was an anniversary of such tragic proportions and unrelenting heartache that still was not resolved. We knew we needed to mark the occasion. We knew we wanted to honour Ryan. We also knew that we didn't just want our time there to be overwhelmingly sad.

Our plans included renting two houses. Coco, Shelley, Jeff and Terri, our dearest friends and constant companions in those first months of searching, were able to make the trip. Nancy, her three children, Maddie, Cohen and Laycie (along with her boyfriend Freddy) came. Shelley's son Parker, Kenan, Brady, Ryan, Dany and

Derek all travelled as well. It was important that these friends of Ryan's were included on the trip. The invitation was open to all of our son's friends, but the timing with university midterms and work commitments made it difficult for everyone to come. Scott, Jordyn, Julianna, Max and I rounded out the group. I won't lie. It was a chaotic group of people. The houses were filled to the brim but overflowing with such love for Ryan, which made our time there bearable.

Adding to our chaos was a jam-packed four days that included a press conference with the RCMP to mark the one-year anniversary, interviews and shooting with the producers/filmmakers for the documentary, an interview with a journalist from Whistler's *Pique* magazine, several phone and television interviews for media outlets, the Run for Ryan (taking the last ski run down the hill in honour of our son) and a candlelight vigil. It was an exhausting schedule, and I never really considered the emotional toll it would take. I felt separated from the girls and Scott. Of course, that reflection on my state of mind would only come in hindsight. When you are in the thick of it, it is hard to see any way but forward despite the toll.

Early Friday morning, we were invited to do a press conference in conjunction with the Kamloops RCMP. It was such a hard statement to write. I spent the night before writing down what I wanted to say, but how do you make the world care for that which they do not know, could never quite comprehend and most likely will never experience? It fell heavily on my shoulders to make this moment impactful. I stood in front of that podium, the notes before me that would remain unread, and spoke the words that I longed for the world to hear from my grieving heart. All I could do as I stood in front of the media was tell my truth.

> So, February 17th, 2018, we received probably what would have been the text of every parent's worst nightmare.

"Heather, Ryan didn't show up to work today and he didn't come home last night."

At that time, we thought that talking to the RCMP and hearing our son was missing was the worst thing any parent would have to hear. In the 12 months since, we have learned that there's far worse things we will have to hear.

"We haven't found your son; we're not sure where he is."

For Scott and I are not sure if or when this journey will ever end for us. And I remember on the drive up—nine and a half hours we drove up from Beaumont, Alberta, to Sun Peaks—and I remember sitting in that car and begging and pleading and making bargains.

"Please, whatever happens, whatever this is, if you could at least spare our son."

And when we came up to Sun Peaks, we looked around and saw the vast amounts of snow, we saw the vast terrain that we had to search in sub-zero temperatures, and I think we quickly came to the realization that finding Ryan out in those elements alive would have been miraculous at best. And so, then I bargained again.

"Please, if we can find him, let's find him so that I can do what a mother should be able to do: to look at my son one last time before I let him go and say to him, 'I love you. I'm so very proud of you and you've had this amazing impact on me, your father, your two sisters and so many other people around us.'"

And even that is lost to us now.

I could tell you so many things about Ryan. I could tell you that he was smart, and he was

funny, super handsome—I have to say that so that
he knows that—super handsome, bright, athletic,
loyal. But those are really words anyone can say if
they're describing someone. He was all of that and
so much more.

Every morning I think about Ryan as soon as I
wake up and he's the very last thing I think about
before I go to bed at night, but it's the in between
time that is the worst. It is the remembering that
brings me the greatest torment and the most
heartbreak. Because I remember this beautiful baby
boy. I remember this curious child who talked non-
stop about Bionicles and Yu-Gi-Oh! and dinosaurs.
I remember the somewhat surly teenager who teased
his sisters relentlessly and then would feel bad and
surprise them with slushies. And I remember the
promising young man who came here to Sun Peaks
to live out this dream he had.

And as we come to this one-year anniversary,
all I need everyone to know is how much we miss
our son and how much he matters and how much
we love him.

And we just want to know what happened
to him.

That night, an event planned by one of Ryan's most ardent
supporters, Theresa Edstrom, was being held at a local Kamloops
bar. Filled with our friends and the community, we were able to
meet so many people that were part of our story from the beginning.
Looking at the faces of strangers that cared so deeply for Ryan was
incredibly humbling, but in a strange way also soothing. Our son
had not been forgotten. He continued to impact not only us but also
people unknown to him. It was a beautiful night.

It was a good weekend. Despite our uncertainty of what honouring or remembering the one year would mean to us, being with our daughters, Ryan's friends and our loved ones made February 17 more passable and gentle on our hearts.

Someone, perhaps a reporter, asked how the one year made me feel. I am not sure I described it accurately or coherently enough, but this is my thought.

The saddest day for me is February 16, 2018, because I know what the next day brings. We have been living every day like it is Groundhog Day since the very first notification. We relive the horror each and every day. Except everything is different, nothing is the same. There is no forgetting. Because our son is missing. There can be no lapsing into a dreamless fugue or escaping the reality on the days after. But February 16 was the last day that any of us felt normal and whole. Ryan was enjoying his life in Sun Peaks, snowboarding, working and hanging with friends. Little did he know the events that were to transpire later that night. We were at home going about our busy lives and imagining that tragedy was the ill fortune of others, safe in a make-believe world where we were a family of five. As this day approaches me, it is a stark reminder that nothing will ever be whole for us again.

Feb 20, 2019

Life is tragically beautiful.

A year has gone by in a blink of an eye, and yet so much has happened in the 365 days that have crept by.

A year of contrast. The stark polarity of devastation and grace. A year where growth was painful yet expectedly necessary.

Ryan, if you could stand beside us today, these are the things I think you would know.

You would have been mortified by all the attention placed on the dinosaur. After all, it was something you loved as a child. Not even a T-Rex or velociraptor but rather a pleasant, gentle, plant-eating long-necked dinosaur. Not exactly a young man's ideal representation. But I think it is fitting. Dinosaurs lived a million years ago and yet we still remember them. That, too, will be your legacy, Ryan.

Ryan, you never loved the spotlight unless it was scoring a goal, a touchdown or a try. Those are concrete accomplishments. But I like to believe that wherever you are now, the ego has gone and you can appreciate what this year has brought.

I think you would be amazed by the coming together of so many communities. The caring of a collective group of people that have embraced kindness because you inspire them. Thousands of people have heard your story, Ryan, and they have volunteered, shared and paid it forward. Random acts of kindness are no longer random but deliberate because of you.

Our son would have been surprised yet honoured by how many people have been impacted by his life. So many of us find ourselves different— better—because of this tragedy. How such a quiet and, at most times, introspective young man could create such a noise. A noise that has travelled the world to the most unlikely places. A noise that has helped others as they navigate through their own tragedies.

Ryan, you would have felt such grief to look upon the faces of your friends, your sisters and your loved ones and see their suffering. To know that you have altered the compass by which they have charted their lives. But you would also be so proud of all of them. They are brave, they are strong and they will continue to do amazing things.

But there is also joy.

Standing before us, I see the faces of those, once strangers, who have now become cherished loved ones.

Life is a balance of joy and sorrow. It is in the embracing of both, however messy, however beautiful, that makes up the human experience.

Ryan, wherever you are on this night almost a year later, I want you to know how so very much you are loved, how much you matter and how you will never, ever be forgotten.

# From Grief to Grace:
## Healing Our Hearts with Purpose

These posts encapsulate one year. A year of loss but also of love. A year of rediscovery. I know I can't always live in grief, but for the last year it has been my constant companion. Who am I without it?

Our journey is not over. It may never be over. It is how we move forward that will take more strength than I'm sure I possess. The greatest battle in an endless war of grief and harmony.

There are always two sides to every coin.

I could never lie and say that along with the grief we have managed that there isn't anger. Anger at the circumstances surrounding Ryan's disappearance, cameras that weren't working, the recollections of people who had contact with our son that night, the lateness of reporting him missing, frustration at no progress in the investigation and finally anger at Ryan who played a part, perhaps unwittingly, on the evening of February 17.

"You don't express it," I am told. "You need to stop being so nice."

There are a lot of adjectives I would use to describe myself. I am not sure "nice" would have topped my list. If you had asked me a year ago and counting, I would have told you first that I could never have believed that Scott and I could have accomplished so much or advocated so hard on Ryan's behalf. Of course, we would want to, but I would have believed us so incapacitated with grief that lying curled in the fetal position would have been our only action. Conversely, I could never imagine how we would seek to find blessings in such an unimaginable tragedy. I honestly believed that anger would flow through my veins.

But here is the thing; I can be angry tomorrow and it can last the rest of my lifetime. It can burn with such righteousness until the world erupts in fiery, soul-cleansing flames that scorch the very ground on which those who are responsible stand on. I just choose not to do it today. It has no place to go, no direction that it can cast its fierce gaze upon with any certainty. But it has the ability to infect my family, friends and, in the end, me. It is too high a price to pay. I cannot automatically judge those who may very well be undeserving of it. There can be no grace in our lives if we cannot extend it to those without cause.

I will hold space and judgement for now. I will show grace and kindness until such time as I learn differently. I will ask for accountability but reserve condemnation. But rest assured, if I were to discover that my son's disappearance was through inaction or malicious intent, then my anger will burn as bright and righteous as the day Ryan went missing. Our continued perseverance will drive us to dog their every step for a lifetime. There will be no peace. We will not stop because Ryan matters and deserves nothing less.

Having said this, it certainly doesn't mean Scott and I don't ebb and flow with our emotions about that night. We may differ with our reasoning and our thoughts. I strongly believe they balance and prepare us for any eventuality. We talk, we confront, we comfort and we move forward together. It may not satisfy the masses. It will also not suit most people's justification for our decisions, but for our journey alone, it is the right course of action. With every step on any journey, there are stops along the way, forks in the road that require vigilance and careful consideration and usually an end destination. I cannot fathom nor foresee what our future holds, so I am trying to embrace the rest stops that allow me to view the world in a reflective way. It allows me the knowledge to face those forks with more confidence. I may not understand the purpose of our journey, but it is important for me to be impactful. To use our circumstances to provide comfort, insight and assistance has become this new mantra for not only Scott and myself but for others we have been blessed to meet along the way.

In the early days, we received so many offers of help, typically from families that had experienced or were experiencing similar circumstances. They would often give suggestions or pass along resources that perhaps could aid us in our search for Ryan. Two extraordinary women that were knee deep in their own search took the time to message us words of support and encouragement. On November 25, 2017, Dominic Neron and Ashley Bourgeault went missing in a presumed airplane crash on their way from Penticton, BC, to Edmonton. For nine days, military, RCMP and search and rescue scoured the Revelstoke area of BC for any signs of the plane or wreckage. Determining the probability of a successful rescue to be low, the search was called off.

Dominic's sister Tammy Neron and sister-in-law Kate Sinclair began their own journey, much like ours, to bring Dominic and Ashley home. Their search lasted ten months with concentrated efforts on aerial and rugged ground searches before the wreckage was spotted by an air ambulance making a routine run. It was through their push for awareness that the coordinates and plane information were forefront in the minds of the pilots flying in the area. The families of Dominic and Ashley were finally able to have closure.

It was through their shared experience in dealing with the unknown and with limited resources that Tammy and Kate initially began The Free Bird Project. They felt strongly that families have the support, organization and resources available in the event the unthinkable should happen. In the midst of their searching, they heard about Ryan and reached out to us. There is a certain amount of comfort that comes from knowing you are not quite alone. Each person's journey through grief is unique to them, but those first feelings of disbelief, terror, anger, despair are universal, I believe. Their calmness gave me hope that I could eventually find a way forward.

Sitting in the command centre in the early days and trying to make sense of the world that was now ours, I contemplated how we would function as a family with one whole part missing. All the paths Ryan could have taken, the ways in which he would contribute to his community, the lives impacted by his presence were now completely unknown. Unfinished. I felt such sorrow in that, and it became important to me to continue a legacy in my son's name. Perhaps it is nothing as great as the accomplishments he may have created himself, but it is still something that tells the world that he was here, that he mattered and that he left his indelible mark on so many people.

Messaging Tammy and Kate gave me the first sense of how I could do that. Their experience in extensive aerial searches and our extensive experience in ground searches became the collaboration between our two families. Joined by Coco, we became a partnership of four. Through our combined loss, our goal is to help other families going through similar circumstances and navigate the unknowable. In this way, I believe we honour Dominic, Ashley and Ryan. In this way, I believe we have created a legacy on their behalf that is far reaching and impactful.

Life is not linear. There will still be curves and dead ends. We will need to retrace our steps and lament the paths we should have avoided. But perhaps one day we can find enjoyment in our travels. Our journey is not one of moving on but moving forward. Who knows where the final destination will lead us, but I hope that we make Ryan proud.

The twins

Searching through the seasons

Paul Dennis out searching

Jesse and Barrie

Jordyn and Max graduation

Cherie, Indigo and Jodell

Gerry searching

Searching

First year anniversary

Candlelight vigil

PEAKS &

THE SEARCH FOR RYAN SHTUBKA

VALLEYS

.

Manufactured by Amazon.ca
Bolton, ON

30727091R00232